Social Safety Nets
Issues and Recent Experiences

Social Safety Nets
Issues and Recent Experiences

Editors

Ke-young Chu and
Sanjeev Gupta

International Monetary Fund
Washington • 1998

Cover design, charts, and composition:
In-Ok Yoon, Choon Lee, and IMF Graphics Section

Cataloging-in-Publication Data

Social safety nets: : issues and recent experiences / editors Ke-young Chu
and Sanjeev Gupta — Washington : International Monetary Fund 1998.
    p.   cm.
Includes bibliographical references.
ISBN 1-55775-680-5

1. Structural adjustment (Economic policy) — Developing countries.
2. Poor — Developing countries.   3. Human services — Developing
countries — Finance.   4. Social security — Developing countries.
5. International Monetary Fund —Developing countries.
I. Chu, Ke-young, 1941– .   II. Gupta, Sanjeev.
HG59.7. S63 1998

Price: $22.50

Please send orders to:
International Monetary Fund, Publication Services
700 19th Street, N.W., Washington, D.C. 20431, U.S.A.
Tel.: (202) 623-7430   Telefax: (202) 623-7201
E-mail: publications@imf.org
Internet: http://www.imf.org

recycled paper

Foreword

In the early 1980s, as a consequence of the debt crisis, the IMF's activities in developing member countries intensified. A large number of countries approached the IMF to obtain financial support to help them carry out the policy changes necessary to stabilize and adjust their economies and thus make growth possible. In the 1990s, about 30 countries entered the process of transition from central planning toward a market economy. These countries were also in need of IMF support.

The intensity of the problems faced by all of these economies was very severe. It became obvious that these countries needed major, not just routine, structural adjustment. Some had to devalue by substantial amounts and eliminate the use of multiple exchange rates. Some had to reduce the large subsidies they were providing to particular sectors or groups. Most had to reduce large fiscal deficits by cutting spending or raising the level of taxation. These policies, negotiated in IMF-supported programs, had large and often disproportionate impacts on some groups, some of which were the society's most vulnerable. These effects became a concern for the IMF.

In the late 1980s, IMF staff started to pay close attention to these effects. At the beginning, they did so by analyzing carefully the design of Fund-supported programs to determine whether some less damaging, but still feasible, policy options could replace the more damaging ones. If so, the programs could incorporate the more socially attractive options. Unfortunately, in many countries, because of institutional constraints, the freedom to choose policy instruments was very limited. In such cases, the only realistic alternative was to proceed with the necessary adjustment policies but complement them with the adoption of social safety nets, that is, mitigating policies aimed at supporting the income—or better, the consumption—of the most vulnerable groups.

The design of these safety nets was limited by the strict budgetary limits imposed by the need to reduce fiscal deficits. In some countries, the work on safety nets was centered on efforts to reduce social expenditure while making it more targeted and efficient. This was particularly the case in economies in transition, which, especially in the earlier years, were spending an unsustainably large share of their budget on poorly targeted social spending.

The 14 papers that comprise this book provide a comprehensive review of the IMF's work on social safety nets. The book is made up of three parts. Part I provides a broad overview of the social concerns in structural policy and the basic work related to social safety nets. Part II deals with the design of social safety nets. Part III provides case studies on nine countries from different parts of the world. The reader will find these studies particularly informative and, I hope, will appreciate the scope of the IMF's work in this area. At the time these studies were written, all the writers except one were IMF staff members. The exception, Ravi Kanbur, was with the World Bank.

The coeditors of this book, Ke-young Chu and Sanjeev Gupta, have contributed much to the development of this work, as heads of several missions that dealt with these aspects, as consecutive chiefs of the division in the Fiscal Affairs Department where much of the work on safety nets was done, and as authors of some of the papers.

VITO TANZI
Director
Fiscal Affairs Department
International Monetary Fund

Acknowledgments

Many IMF staff members have contributed to the preparation of this volume, but the staff of the Fiscal Affairs Department's Expenditure Policy Division undertook the principal responsibility for selecting, editing, and revising papers. In this connection, the role of Benedict Clements was pivotal; he worked closely with the editors during different stages of the preparation of the manuscript. Hamid Davoodi provided the much-needed final push to the project. Valuable assistance and advice were also extended by other members of the division, including Željko Bogetić, Elliott Harris, Alexandros Mourmouras, Edgardo Ruggiero, and Gerd Schwartz.

Theresa Garrison edited the manuscript, and Larry Hartwig meticulously coordinated the manuscript preparation and took the lead in converting the various papers into an acceptable format. They were ably supported by Leda Montero and Amy Deigh. Juanita Roushdy, of the External Affairs Department, gave the manuscript a final edit and coordinated publication.

The papers were prepared and published at various times over a 10-year period. Some papers, reprinted in this volume with minimal changes, assess the social implications of IMF-supported programs ongoing at the time of writing.

Contents

The following symbols have been used throughout this book:

. . .   to indicate that data are not available;

—   to indicate that the figure is zero or less than half the final digit shown, or that the item does not exist;

–   between years or months (for example, 1995–96 or January–June) to indicate the years or months covered, including the beginning and ending years or months;

/   between years or months (for example, 1995/96) to indicate a crop or fiscal (financial) year.

"Billion" means a thousand million; "trillion" means a thousand billion.

"Basis points" refer to hundredths of 1 percentage point (for example, 25 basis points are equivalent to ¼ of 1 percentage point).

Minor discrepancies between constituent figures and totals are due to rounding.

The term "country," as used in this book, does not in all cases refer to a territorial entity that is a state as understood by international law and practice; the term also covers some territorial entities that are not states, but for which statistical data are maintained and provided internationally on a separate and independent basis.

1
Overview

Social Dimensions
of the IMF's Policy Dialogue

IMF Involvement in Social Issues

The IMF's involvement in social issues has to be seen in the context of its mandate. The mandate, as laid down in its Articles of Agreement, is clear: (1) to promote international monetary cooperation; (2) to facilitate the expansion and balanced growth of international trade, and to contribute thereby to the promotion and maintenance of high levels of employment and real income; (3) to promote exchange stability and to maintain orderly exchange arrangements among members; (4) to assist in the establishment of a multilateral payments system; and (5) to give confidence to members by providing temporary financial resources to help them correct balance of payments disequilibria. Given this essentially macroeconomic mandate, the IMF's contribution to social development is mainly indirect, and its role in social policy advice is necessarily limited. Nevertheless, the IMF's involvement in social issues has evolved over time, drawing not only from its own experience but also from that of member countries and of other agencies.

During the 1950s and 1960s, when the IMF provided financial assistance mainly to industrial countries, its policy advice focused primarily on macroeconomic policies. With the shift to lending to developing countries since the 1970s and to economies in transition since the late 1980s, much greater attention has been given to the complementarity of macroeconomic policies and structural reforms and to the formula-

Note: Reprinted, in part, from *Social Dimensions of the IMF's Policy Dialogue,* IMF Pamphlet Series, No. 47 (Washington: IMF, 1995), pp. 3–8, which was prepared by the staff of the Expenditure Policy Division of the Fiscal Affairs Department and the Policy Development Review Department of the IMF.

tion of policies in a medium-term context.[1] With this broadened focus, the interrelationships between economic and social issues have also increasingly been recognized. Experience has shown the need for protecting vulnerable groups during the adjustment period by constructing well-targeted social safety nets and by safeguarding access of these groups to basic public services, such as primary health and education. These measures would also serve to enhance the political sustainability of economic reforms.

The broader context for the IMF's policy advice has called for much closer collaboration than in the past among international agencies, with a delineation of responsibilities according to each agency's mandate and expertise. Much of the analysis and policy and technical advice on social issues is undertaken by international agencies other than the IMF, such as the World Bank, regional development banks, the Food and Agriculture Organization (FAO), the International Labour Organization (ILO), the United Nations Development Programme (UNDP), and the United Nations Children's Fund (UNICEF), as well as by bilateral donors and nongovernmental organizations. The issues are complex, and analysis and action are often hindered by weak data and administrative structures. Given these difficulties, it has been important that the various parties build not only on their own experience but also on that of members and other agencies.

The increasing involvement of the IMF in social matters has been discussed by its Executive Board on several occasions. In 1988, for example, the Board stressed the need to assist member countries in evaluating the implications of IMF-supported adjustment programs for income distribution and poverty, to strengthen the staff's understanding of the channels through which adjustment policies affect the poor, and to draw more extensively on the expertise of the World Bank and UN institutions. At the same time, it reaffirmed its decision not to establish conditions on the use of IMF resources related to income distribution. The joint World Bank–IMF Development Committee, which also has discussed social issues, has encouraged both the World Bank and the IMF to further intensify their efforts, working closely together, in helping design and implement well-targeted measures to mitigate the costs of adjustment.

---

[1]The IMF created new facilities that emphasized structural reforms set in a medium-term context: the Extended Fund Facility (EFF) in 1974, and two concessional lending facilities—the Structural Adjustment Facility (SAF) in 1986, and the Enhanced Structural Adjustment Facility (ESAF) in 1987—for the benefit of low-income countries. The latter facility was extended and enlarged in 1993.

Sustained Economic and Social Development: The IMF's Perspective

While economic policies of individual countries can have diverse objectives, as experience has shown, three key points have particular relevance for social development.

Economic growth is required for sustainable social development. In the last few years, a broader concept of high-quality growth has emerged, namely, economic growth that brings lasting employment gains and poverty reduction, provides greater equality of income through greater equality of opportunity, including for women, respects human freedom, and protects the environment.

Controlling inflation can prevent or mitigate real-income losses, against which the poor are least protected because their income is often fixed in nominal terms and they tend to hold much of their assets in the form of currency.

By *promoting the agriculture sector,* which employs most of the poor, many developing countries can achieve a lasting reduction in poverty.

The main pillars of economic policy that would lead to progress in these three areas include sound macroeconomic and structural policies, with a strong social policy component, and good governance and participatory development.

Macroeconomic policy: sound macroeconomic policies—fiscal, monetary and credit, and exchange rate policies—are needed to secure financial stability and external viability with low inflation. In the absence of these conditions, it is difficult for a country to encourage productive investment or to promote the efficient use of scarce resources, both of which are essential for durable growth.

Structural policy: structural reforms are often vital in promoting a market-based environment with an outward orientation. These include liberal and open systems of prices, exchange, trade, and investment; a fiscal system that emphasizes efficient resource allocation and minimizes adverse effects on incentives; agricultural marketing arrangements that promote competition; a financial system that is free of direct credit allocation and effectively channels financial savings to productive investment; and policies that take into account their impact on the environment.

Social policy: social and supplementary structural policies are also needed to strengthen the social dimensions of economic development. These include labor market policies aimed at ensuring high employment through competitive and flexible wages and at removing other rigidities while adhering to ILO principles; public expenditure programs aimed at protecting and, when possible, increasing cost-effective programs for human development and reducing poverty (such as generally accessible health, education, and social security programs); a tax system that ensures a fair distribution of the tax burden; and well-targeted social safety nets to mitigate negative effects of economic reform on vulnerable groups.

Good governance and participatory development: effective governance involves such diverse elements as publicly accountable institutions for formulating and executing the budget, efficient tax administration and public expenditure management, prudent banking supervision, a transparent foreign trade and exchange regime, and a fair and transparent legal and regulatory framework. Transparency and checks and balances, at both the political and administrative levels, can help limit the influence of special vested interests.

There is a broad consensus among governments and in the international community on the importance of most of these elements. But translating them into concrete policies and priorities involves difficult choices concerning income distribution, as well as present and future consumption and investment. Consensus building often involves disseminating information, explaining policies to the general public, and, where appropriate, decentralizing the decision-making and implementation process. It is critical that key players—especially people at the grassroots level—have a stake in economic policymaking, and that the social policies are compatible with administrative capacity.

2

Social Safety Nets in Economic Reform

Social safety nets can be broadly defined as those instruments aimed at mitigating possible adverse effects of reform measures on the poor. These instruments include temporary arrangements, as well as existing social protection measures reformed and adapted for this purpose, such as limited food subsidies, social security arrangements for dealing with various life cycle and other contingencies (e.g., old age, disability, unemployment, sickness, and drought), and targeted public works.[1]

The chapter discusses major issues concerning social safety nets and reviews the IMF's recent experience in this regard.[2] It provides a rationale for social safety nets as an element of economic reform programs

---

Note: An earlier version of this paper was discussed by the IMF Executive Board on June 2, 1993. The paper represents a collective effort by the staff of the Expenditure Policy Division of the IMF's Fiscal Affairs Department. Ehtisham Ahmad prepared the initial draft.

[1]In many countries, formal public social protection schemes, including consumer subsidies and social security arrangements, coexist with traditional or informal private or community-based schemes. Social security arrangements in this chapter refer to social insurance and social assistance programs. The former (e.g., pensions and unemployment insurance) may not necessarily be targeted to the poor, while the latter generally are targeted to the poor. Note that the term social security is defined broadly in this chapter, although in countries such as the United States, it is often synonymous with state pensions. Social security arrangements provide cover against the loss of income resulting from various life cycle, natural, and other contingencies, even in the absence of economic reform; social safety nets as discussed in this chapter refer primarily to measures that protect vulnerable groups from the impact of reform, while, subject to resource constraints, also providing for other contingencies. See Atkinson (1992) for an alternative definition of social safety nets.

[2]It does not address the issue of the design of the macroeconomic and structural reform package, including the implications of its scope and speed for demands on social safety nets, but assesses appropriate social safety nets that would underpin the required adjustment.

and assesses the main options in designing the social safety nets. It then summarizes the IMF's efforts to integrate social safety nets in programs it has supported and the role of technical assistance in this regard.

Economic Reform and Social Safety Nets

Role of Social Safety Nets in Economic Reform

Economic reform measures are essential in establishing conditions for long-term sustained growth and poverty reduction and may benefit some of the poor directly. They are also essential in protecting the poor, who often suffer the most from open or repressed inflation during disorderly adjustment. Some of these measures, however, may precipitate an excessive decline in the living standards of certain poor or vulnerable groups of the population in the short run, although they may benefit some other poor groups. For example, although increasing prices toward remunerable levels benefits producers (e.g., small farmers), thereby immediately reducing poverty, net purchasers (e.g., of food) may suffer real income losses. If official consumer prices are not adjusted, however, raising producer prices will increase subsidy expenditures. Similarly, the reforms of inefficient state enterprises may generate unemployment, thus increasing poverty.

Reform programs should, where possible, be designed to minimize unnecessary adverse effects on poor or vulnerable groups. To this end, it is important that the mix and sequencing of reform measures be designed appropriately. Simple, broad-based, and equitable taxes with low rates, efficient public expenditure programs, and policies aimed at promoting appropriate relative prices constitute the major elements. In achieving a given fiscal deficit reduction target, it is important to explore alternative tax and expenditure policy mixes and to assess their implications for poverty as well as efficiency. The appropriate mix and sequencing of reform measures, however, cannot ensure that the adverse effects will be removed entirely, since the reform itself requires changes in relative income positions of various groups. Therefore, social safety nets are needed to mitigate possible short-run adverse effects on the poor.

Options for Cost-Effective Social Safety Nets During Reform

In designing social safety nets for a country, one has to consider a number of factors, including the composition of poor groups, potential effects of reform policy measures, financial and administrative constraints, and existing social protection arrangements. Different circumstances will require different mixes of instruments. Many reforming countries have various *private and public social security arrangements*. Many of them have *extended families and community-based arrangements*. Some have *ad hoc or permanent arrangements* (such as targeted small-scale self-employment enterprises and public works programs) set up in cooperation with donor organizations. Most reforming countries have costly budgetary and implicit *subsidies,* which are inefficient and badly targeted. In addition, some countries, particularly middle-income developing and transition countries, have *formal social security arrangements,* including social insurance (such as public pension plans and unemployment benefits), family allowances, and assistance instruments. Whereas coverage of these arrangements in middle-income developing countries is limited to some formal sector workers, most economies in transition have close to universal coverage.

As they are, these arrangements may not be appropriate as social safety nets. Despite limitations, however, they may be reformed, or adapted, to provide a basis for cost-effective social safety nets. Newly designed social safety nets should complement, rather than replace, existing cost-effective institutions.[3]

The challenge is to design these instruments in a *targeted and cost-effective fashion*. Targeting, however, is difficult for two reasons: (1) defining and identifying the poor is difficult, and (2) the "middle-class capture" of the existing benefits that need to be reformed makes targeting a politically sensitive issue.[4] Moreover, the requirement that the target groups include all the poor, not merely exclude the nonpoor, creates further administrative difficulties.

In principle, the *poor* could be defined as those whose consumption falls below a certain poverty line, based on a minimum consumption basket, and benefits could be provided as means-tested transfers, based on an income and asset threshold for the family or household unit. With a low poverty line, the financial resources required for

---

[3]The appendix to this chapter provides a brief discussion of major social protection institutions existing in various countries, focusing on consumer subsidies, social security arrangements, and certain targeted public works that proxy social assistance. Eventually, some of these measures (e.g., consumer subsidies) should be phased out, as more effective transfer mechanisms are established. See Cox and Jiménez (1992) for a discussion of the possibility that public transfers could crowd out private transfers.

[4]See LeGrand and Winter (1987).

the provision of benefits would be limited. In practice, however, defining the poor on this basis for the purpose of social safety nets would have demanding requirements in terms of criteria that remain controversial and detailed data on household incomes and expenditures.[5] In many reforming countries, a marked concentration of per capita income is often noted at relatively low-income thresholds. If a slight change in the minimum threshold led to a substantial change in the share of the officially designated poor, it would be controversial and difficult to determine a minimum threshold, and, in many cases, the administrative costs of verification for means testing would be substantial.[6] Moreover, marginal tax rates would be high at the point of withdrawal of a means-tested benefit based on an income and asset threshold for the family or household unit, and would generate major disincentives at low income levels (i.e., the "poverty trap").

It is possible, however, to take a pragmatic approach and restrict benefits to those who are vulnerable to policy shocks, through regional targeting (e.g., to urban areas) or categorical targeting (e.g., to infants, schoolchildren, nursing mothers, and the elderly), or a mix of the two.[7] The extent of protection provided on a categorical basis should be determined with reference to the actual consumption of the poorest deciles. The target groups should be determined on the basis of country-specific circumstances, including demographic characteristics, administrative capabilities, and the effects of reform policy measures.

There is a direct link between adequate and administratively feasible provisions for the vulnerable and the establishment of a simple tax system. If a system of social security or other measures are provided effectively for the vulnerable, then there would be less need to introduce complicated and differentiated tax structures for distributional objec-

---

[5]The World Bank has been helping countries enhance their capacity to compile household income and expenditure surveys and to define minimum consumption baskets. Eventually, this work will be helpful to the IMF's work.

[6]See, for example, Atkinson (1992b) for a discussion of administrative difficulties of means testing in industrial countries.

[7]The presumption is that rural residents generally benefit from the increases in procurement prices. This leaves the problem of identifying and providing benefits to net purchasers in rural areas. With a very substantial output response in agriculture, real food prices in China have fallen consistently in recent years, which together with the increase in the price of subsidized rations has led to a situation where the ration is being withdrawn without much of an impact on urban households. See Ahmad and Wang (1991).

tives. And, as with the tax system, there would be a need to establish administratively simple expenditure mechanisms—without excessive differentiation or complexity in design. The net effects on equity would thus involve a joint consideration of tax and social protection measures.[8]

Limited Transitory Consumer Subsidies

The issues in designing limited subsidies during the period of reform include the choice of commodities and delivery instruments. Reformed subsidies could lead to substantial budgetary savings over general subsidies, even if the beneficiaries included the entire population, while providing the government with an opportunity to liberalize prices. If quantities subsidized were restricted to quantities consumed by the poorest income groups, which are often a fraction of the average consumption, it would protect the poor from the effects of price adjustments. Since household groups would receive the same benefits, this would be more progressive in incidence than a generalized subsidy, which generally provides greater benefits to the rich.

Choice of commodities. Ideally, commodities to be subsidized should be consumed only by the poor. In general, however, it would be difficult to identify items consumed only by the poor.[9] Coarse grains and unrefined sugar are attractive in this respect, but many inferior commodities are not widely marketed.[10] The alternative would be to distinguish marketable commodities that are important in the consumption baskets of all the poor, even if these were also consumed by the nonpoor; examples include the major staples such as wheat, maize, and rice.

---

[8]New Zealand is an example of a country that introduced a flat-rate value-added (VAT) on all transactions but transferred all social security expenditures to the budget.

If a comprehensive income tax system could be established, it would be possible to "claw back" the provisions to middle-class and wealthy beneficiaries through taxation. In many developing and transition economies, however, it might be unrealistic to expect such a system to be established in the near future.

[9]This criterion also indicates that commodities not generally consumed by the poor should not be subsidized. While consumption patterns vary among countries, subsidies on frozen meats and macaroni in Egypt, and on sardines, chicken, and salted fish in Jamaica, are inappropriate, as such commodities are not generally consumed by the poor.

[10]Coarse grains and unrefined sugar are known as "gur" in India and Pakistan.

Delivery instruments. To avoid a general subsidy, various instruments could be used. In the case of adjustments where there is little impact on consumer prices of items consumed by the poor, there would be scant justification for the introduction of the instruments discussed below.[11] All of the instruments would require the maintenance of effective prices that deviate by varying degrees from market-clearing prices, and require special administrative arrangements (e.g., coupons and monitoring procedures); therefore, the potential for abuse (e.g., counterfeiting of coupons) and corruption would increase. These costs should be contained as much as possible but should be assessed against the potential benefits of the instruments. In many cases, a realistic comparison of budgetary costs of subsidies for the transition might not be between limited transitory subsidies and no subsidies, but between the former and existing generalized subsidies.

The various instruments discussed below resemble, but are not necessarily identical to, in-kind or cash provision. The choice between the two contrasting forms of transfer—limited *cash provision* compensating the removal of subsidies and *in-kind* provision—would depend on the nature of the risk facing consumers and the administrative capabilities of the country in question. Provided that adverse effects on production were avoided by assuring producers remunerative prices for their output, the welfare effect of cash and in-kind provision would be equivalent if prices were known with certainty and resale were permissible and costless. Cash compensation generally provides a greater choice to the consumer, hence the possibility of increasing welfare gains, and also might mean lower administrative and transaction costs than the alternatives. If the price adjustments were uncertain, then cash provision would lead to higher risk for the consumer than in-kind provision. The ability of the government to import subsidized goods would place an upper limit on budgetary outlays, and could also influence the variation in market prices faced by consumers. Thus, the risks facing the government would likely be much lower than those confronting an individual in an imperfect and unstable local market. Moreover, in periods of rapid and large price changes, the administrative costs of monitoring the price changes and ensuring the adequate payments to consumers could be substantial.

---

[11]This was the case in many "adjusting" countries in South Asia in the late 1980s. For example, during this period in Bangladesh, a special ration provided benefits to civil servants and the military, and formed part of a real wage package but could not be conceived of as a social safety net.

Rations with public distribution systems, where dual prices exist at the retail level, could pose administrative difficulties.[12] This could encourage arbitrage and queues, and might not provide an adequate safety net for the vulnerable, as was the case in the Baltic States, Russia, and other former Soviet Union countries (BRO). Moreover, setting up a public distribution system from scratch might be expensive, time consuming, and inappropriate as a transitory mechanism that should be established rapidly. This system, however, could be effective in providing milk and preventive health care through schools or health clinics. An alternative, a system of *quantity food stamps,* using private distribution channels, could be categorically or regionally targeted and might be attractive on both administrative and distributional grounds. Beneficiaries could purchase these from local outlets (e.g., banks and post offices) at subsidized prices. The stamps could then be exchanged for given quantities of the specified items. The trader could be reimbursed in-kind (plus a handling charge), or in cash by the state. This arrangement would permit a single price to operate in the market, without the need for an expensive administrative machinery to oversee compliance. Resale of the quantity food stamps should be legal as there would be less danger of windfalls accruing to traders, or of corruption, compared with standard ration systems.[13] This system would combine the administrative advantages with more adequate consumer protection than feasible with a pure cash transfer.

It would be possible to provide *limited cash compensation* directly or through *coupons,* the latter for purchasing a specified set of commodities. Such provision could be means-tested, categorically targeted, or universal, where extensive private retail outlets would be present to satisfy demand. The provision of *cash-based food stamps* has involved an element of means testing in some countries. For example, initially introduced in the United States because there was political support for in-kind transfers rather than cash transfers, such a food stamp scheme has evolved into a major income transfer program. Despite the administrative capabilities of the United States, the stigma attached to income testing has restricted take-up rates to around 40 percent of the eligible population. Sri Lanka and Jamaica are the only two developing countries that have tried to establish such food stamps on a nationwide scale. In Sri Lanka, lack of political support

---

[12]This has been used in market economies at times of stress or disruptions of supplies, such as in the United Kingdom and its colonies during World War II.

[13]Jordan has successfully introduced this system.

led to the erosion of benefits, and means testing was not very effective, although the community-based screening programs improved targeting. In Jamaica, half of the aid-financed food stamps were allocated on a categorical basis to mothers and children, the rest to the needy on the basis of a self-declared certification. While in Sri Lanka the nonpoor did not hesitate to declare incomes below the cut-off point, in Jamaica, the procedure requiring certification led to stigma, largely excluding the nonpoor, but excluding also many of the poor.

Social Security Arrangements

Existing permanent social security arrangements, as in the BRO countries, can be a useful basis for designing social safety nets.[14] A major strand among social security systems is *social insurance*. This entails the financing of benefits by compulsory contributions or payroll taxes. It differs from private insurance in that contributions need not fully cover benefits for either certain groups[15] or the total population covered. Including the poor and bad-risk individuals implies an element of redistribution inherent in social insurance within each generation as well as over succeeding generations.

In addition, there are *targeted expenditures*, which may be either means-tested, as with many local social assistance programs, or related to particular indicators of need (such as disability, female gender, and old or young age), which also meet the criterion of protecting the vulnerable.[16]

The social security systems of most countries combine the above-described measures in various ways. Interactions between measures

---

[14]The earliest objectives of formal social security included maintaining—without stigma—minimum living standards, and replacing income in times of adversity. However, social security also entails a smoothing of consumption or a spreading of income over the life cycle, and reducing risk. Often there is a redistribution of income between groups with differing needs. Moreover, the different configurations of political and interest groups influence the directions that social provision has taken in different countries. This variety of objectives (in conjunction with political realities) has led to the different manifestations of social security.

[15]For example, old people that are already privately uninsurable but are strong candidates for social insurance.

[16]While means-tested social assistance, often provided at the local level, is an important element in the social security systems in many industrial countries, the development of social insurance and other categorical transfers, such as universal child benefits, are the result of "[t]he strength of popular objection to any kind of means test." See Beveridge (1942).

help determine whether the basic objective of "protecting" the vulnerable has been achieved. Focusing on one program, such as the public provision of retirement pensions, is therefore likely to be misleading. The fiscal evaluation of groups of related schemes and their alternatives is difficult but important, given the precarious budgetary positions of many countries and the escalating nature and extent of benefits and costs of provision.[17]

Public policy to ensure social security should take into account what individuals and households do to "protect" themselves. This involves an examination of (1) savings behavior and possibilities; (2) restrictions on the ability to smooth consumption over time, with limited access to credit markets; and (3) transfers and support mechanisms at the extended family or community levels. The scope for households or local communities to smooth consumption through accumulation and asset liquidation is limited, however, particularly in the case of major and repeated shocks.

Two issues that should be addressed in designing each instrument, depending on the administrative and demographic characteristics of each country, concern eligibility and structure of benefits.

Design options. An increase in the coverage of "formal" instruments in developing countries would take time. In transition economies, universal coverage might be reduced as private enterprises, particularly those in the informal sector, expand their activities.

Eligibility and the *level and duration of benefits* would determine the costs and adequacy of provision. Eligibility would need to be tightly defined. Whether benefits are flat or earnings-related would affect both administration and equity. In many countries, the dual objectives of the financial sustainability of social security funds and protection of minimum benefits imply that earnings-related benefits might have to be determined within a fairly narrow band, and thus resemble a flat benefit. Flat pension benefits would reduce the administrative complexity and costs of provisions, but might not be actuarially fair. Severely limited unemployment benefits might create a political bottleneck for enterprise reform or public sector retrenchment. A long duration of payments would necessitate high payroll contributions or large budgetary transfers, and would provide a disincentive to job search.

---

[17]This happens, for example, as increases continue in the proportion of old people, as in many Eastern European and Asian countries, or in the proportion of children under age five, as in Africa.

In many BRO countries, numerous and overlapping allowances and benefits, also largely financed by payroll contributions, have the effect of obscuring the net benefits conferred while adding to the complexity of administration and cost.

Policy tools. Overlapping policy tools would include a range of policies that could be grouped under (1) social insurance to provide cover for old age, disability, and health care; (2) minimum or basic benefits, categorically targeted, say, to the needy elderly through social pensions or to mothers with small children through family allowances; (3) unemployment benefits through severance pay and unemployment insurance; and (4) means-tested family support, which—in view of information costs and incentive effects—might well be feasible only at the local level with some community participation.

There would be a trade-off between average benefit levels and the overall costs, which would mean either higher payroll contribution rates or additional calls on budgetary resources. In a period of declining employment, real wages, and payroll contributions, it might not be feasible to index benefits fully to prices. Nonetheless, pensioners at subsistence levels would need to be assured access to minimum consumption requirements. In Eastern Europe, China, and BRO countries, the retirement age is a key factor in determining the cost of providing pensions for the elderly. There has already been a decline in the replacement rate (i.e., the value of average old-age pensions as a proportion of average wages) and the standard of living of pensioners in many countries.[18] At the same time, these pension expenditures require relatively high contribution rates, in part, as a result of relatively low statutory retirement ages and generous eligibility criteria. Major reforms are needed to ensure the viability of pension funds simultaneously with effective provision for the elderly.

In both developing countries and transition economies, public sector restructuring may not be feasible unless provision is made for the unemployed. In the transition period, when the restructuring is likely to lead to widespread unemployment (10 percent unemployment or more is not uncommon, as seen in Eastern Europe), a normally defined *unemployment insurance scheme* (together with severance pay) might not be appropriate. If payroll contributions were constrained, fairly tight eligibility criteria and limits on both the level and duration of benefits would be needed. Despite these measures, there might be substantial start-up costs, which would require support from the budget.

---

[18]For example, in BRO countries, the replacement rate for pensions fell from 60 percent in the late 1950s to around 30 percent by the late 1980s.

This would leave the problem of assisting fresh entrants to the workforce and the longer-term unemployed whose insurance benefits have expired. Such persons could be provided with training or minimum benefits in a manner that would not create a disincentive to job search. Appropriately designed public works at low wages (see below) might provide a cost-effective screening or assistance mechanism.

Family allowances, in general, are well targeted to families with children.[19] Such households tend to have low incomes relative to need and young children at an early stage of life cycle earnings; the arrival of additional children restricts opportunities for second-earner income. Provisions made directly to mothers would address the issue of intra-household distribution of incomes. Of course, universal benefits would also accrue to the well-to-do, and benefit levels should be related to available resources. However, it is unlikely that the level of family allowances could be expanded in line with inflation in the face of falling real revenue.[20] A low level of family allowances, however, might increase the need for social assistance for certain groups, such as the unemployed with children.

Targeted Public Works

Targeted public works would represent a screening mechanism that provides assistance to the truly needy. The dual aspects of low wages and the tying-up of the workday are crucial in effective targeting. An assistance scheme would be subject to open-ended abuse if recipients were permitted to draw cash support while working in the informal sector. Also, the wage rate should be low to encourage the longer-term unemployed to participate actively in the labor market, or opt for retraining, and to make the public works more self-targeted, thus reducing administrative costs.[21] High-wage public works would create opportunities for rent-seeking, which might be difficult to remove.

It is important to distinguish between public works as a safety net and public works designed for particular infrastructure needs. For the latter, skilled work at the appropriate market wage would be required; for the former, the creation of positive output should be considered an added bonus, although it should be sought where possible. For exam-

---

[19]They are, in general, "pro-poor." See Milanovic (1992).

[20]In some countries, such as in Central Asia or North Africa, high levels of family allowances might be quite inappropriate given demographic realities and fiscal constraints. See Ahmad (1992).

[21]See Grosh (1995) for a comparison of administrative costs for various targeting mechanisms in Latin American countries

ple, targeted public works programs, by improving feeder roads and other infrastructure, could reinforce the positive effects of pricing reform on supply. Safeguards would be needed to avoid transfers to phantom workers, discrimination in hiring, and other problems. For the most part, "safety net" public works could concentrate on low-skill employment. It would be advisable to prepare a list of "productive" projects that could be used for the safety net type of public works before a sharp increase in unemployment occurs.

Financing Social Safety Nets

The prospects for major increases in tax revenues in developing and transition economies are fairly limited in the short run. These prospects underscore the importance of improving the efficiency of public expenditure programs and restructuring them as a means of financing social safety net expenditures. In some countries, reforming generalized subsidies would generate enough resources to finance both targeted subsidies and some other productive government expenditures, or an improvement in the fiscal position.[22] However, in some low-income countries, given the magnitude of the need, the gap between average consumption and the consumption of the poorest groups might be quite small, limiting the potential savings under a quantity food stamp scheme and requiring foreign assistance to cushion major policy or other shocks.

The cost of providing even minimum benefits associated with the formal social security instruments (pensions, allowances, and unemployment insurance) could be fairly substantial in a range of countries. As mentioned above, payroll taxes are a major source of financing for such expenditures in many countries. However, excessively high payroll taxes could discourage enterprise activities and introduce labor market distortions (e.g., the use of informal sector or contract workers for whom no contribution is paid).[23] The use of general revenue to

---

[22]Under generalized food subsidies, the share of the benefits received by families that belong to the poorest quintile could be as low as 8 percent; for the wealthiest quintile, it could be as high as 36 percent (see Grosh, 1995). In Jordan, the replacement of generalized subsidies with a system of quantity food stamps led to a reduction in consumer subsidies from 3.2 percent of GDP in 1990/91 to 1.4 percent of GDP in 1991/92. Calculations for Russia and Algeria suggest that similar schemes could generate a 50–60 percent reduction in outlays on subsidies without adversely affecting the food consumption of the poorer groups of the population. See Ahmad and Chu (1993) for calculations for Russia.

[23]For example, payroll tax rates for pension funds in a 30–40 percent range are not uncommon in BRO countries.

finance all or part of such expenditures is an issue faced in transition economies, particularly with regard to expenditures on account of unemployment. In all such cases, budgetary trade-offs among expenditure choices are quite stark, leading to a need to minimize social security outlays.

Social Safety Nets in the IMF's Policy Advice

IMF-Supported Programs

The IMF has advised the authorities, at varying levels of detail, on the integration of social safety nets in designing reform programs. Programs have paid increasing attention to social policies, in general, and to measures to mitigate the short-run adverse effects of economic reform measures on the poor, in particular. Many programs contain specific social safety net measures, which are sometimes based on detailed assessments that resulted from prior IMF technical assistance.[24]

The reform of consumer subsidies has figured prominently in both Stand-By Arrangements and Structural Adjustment Facility (SAF) and Enhanced Structural Adjustment (ESAF) programs in a number of developing countries (e.g., Algeria, Ethiopia, Ghana, Guyana, Jordan, Tanzania, and Uganda), as well as for Eastern European countries. In other countries, the restructuring of the public sector has been important in discussions with country authorities. Provisions for civil service reform have been featured in the programs for countries such as Barbados, Benin, The Gambia, and Sri Lanka. The restructuring of public sector enterprises has been important in many former centrally planned economies. Some IMF-supported programs have explicitly included measures for those who might become unemployed, and similar measures would also be needed in the formerly centrally planned economies in Africa, such as Angola, Ethiopia, and Mozambique. Such measures may also be required for other countries, such as India.

In SAF and ESAF countries, financial and administrative constraints tend to be more severe than in middle-income developing or transition countries. The SAF and ESAF programs have tended to adopt a broad approach to poverty and the social impact of adjustment, emphasizing—in policy framework papers (PFPs)—the need to increase expenditure on items such as education and health, and to include other specific social sector policy measures (e.g., policies addressing population,

---

[24]See also Chapters 6 through 14 of this volume for experiences in integrating social safety nets in a range of countries with IMF-supported countries.

labor market, and women's issues) as well as those to improve food security. Many PFPs have attempted to assess the social impact of adjustment and specify social safety net measures—often designed by donor agencies with the IMF's cooperation.[25] The donor-supported social investment funds that provide quick-disbursing soft loans, inter alia, to small-scale businesses may not actually reach either the poorest or those primarily affected by adjustment. Without an emphasis on cost-effectiveness, recent social funds (e.g., those in Egypt and a number of countries in Latin America) could weaken budgetary discipline.

Social safety nets are mentioned prominently in IMF staff reports on the former centrally planned economies, in connection with the need to control costs and to improve the effectiveness of formal social security measures. For example, in Hungary—which has a high level of information technology and administrative sophistication—the IMF has stressed the need to make the social security fund actuarially sound and to target assistance. Despite reforms to the pension and unemployment insurance systems, however, some problems remain. The principal problem concerns the implementation of social assistance mechanisms and means testing. The targeting of the provision of benefits for the long-term unemployed remains an issue in a number of Eastern European countries, and indexation procedures threaten financial stability in several cases. The IMF is increasingly cognizant of the need to incorporate reforms of institutions in programs, as indicated by the examples of Poland and other Eastern European economies.

The choice of social safety net instruments has varied with the circumstances of the country and the effects of the program. The Jordanian experience points to the importance of well-designed, limited, consumer subsidies as a key element of a social safety net in the face of large changes in relative prices. The Bangladeshi experience stresses the importance of foreign-assisted public works in circumstances of widespread poverty and no large changes in relative prices. The Polish experience suggests the importance of the cost-effective design of unemployment compensation in addressing the substantial unemployment in reforming transition economies.

Technical Assistance

Major issues addressed by the IMF's technical assistance have ranged from reforming consumer subsidies to adapting permanent social security institutions to function as a social safety net. Most of the techni-

---

[25]See also Nashashibi and others (1992) and Gupta and Nashashibi (1990).

cal assistance work has highlighted the interactions between measures to mitigate the adverse effects of adjustment and formal social security instruments.

Reforming Consumer Subsidies

The IMF's advice with respect to subsidies has been more or less unanimous: eliminate generalized subsidies as soon as possible to allow a reduction in production distortions without a major cost to the budget. Recommendations have depended on administrative capability as well as the extent and type of price adjustment envisaged. Some technical assistance reports have recommended the consideration of limited quantity food stamps, which may be targeted by region (e.g., urban households) or category (e.g., the unemployed, households with children), with additional purchases made at market prices. This would permit a rapid freeing of prices without adverse impact on the poor. A frequently proposed alternative has been to provide the cash equivalent transfer of the quantity food stamps following the removal of subsidies, provided that adjustments could be made to payments in time, and that there are no difficulties in effecting the payments. Some reports have supported the authorities' intentions to introduce means-tested cash compensation while stressing caveats with respect to administrative capability and knowledge about incomes and cutoff points.

Many reports have recommended categorical transfers in-kind (e.g., milk) to young children and nursing mothers. Such provisions would tend to be better targeted than cash-based family allowances and would be more appropriate in countries with a relatively high birth rate because of lower budgetary outlays than with family allowances.[26]

Improving Social Security Arrangements as a Social Safety Net

Recommendations with respect to reform of the formal social security instruments have primarily concerned the adequacy of overall coverage and the financial implications of alternative measures. For pensions in BRO countries, recommendations have been that pension funds concentrate only on the financing and administration of pensions, and not allowances, to improve their overall financial viability. Most reports have commented on the need for pension funds to raise retirement ages and to limit early retirement provisions. Technical assistance reports, however, have been less unanimous with respect to

---

[26]It is also noteworthy that family allowances in many of these countries are pronatalist.

indexation of benefits: some have argued for full indexing of *minimum* pensions with respect to price change and less than full indexation of the rest, to assure the stability of funds with a declining real revenue base. The difficulty arises when most pensioners are at minimum subsistence levels. In this case, with less than full indexation of wages (i.e., the revenue base for pension funds), full indexation of minimum pensions would generate a worsening of the financial position of the funds in the short term, which would be exacerbated by population aging in the longer term. However, a dilemma, particularly with high inflation and indexation procedures applied quarterly, is that less than full indexation will erode the real value of pensions rather quickly, leading to a further deterioration of the living standards of pensioners. Some reports have argued for ad hoc adjustments in benefits to ensure that the growth in expenditures does not exceed the resources of the pension funds. The safety net for pensioners in this case may have to be provided by other schemes, such as quantity food stamps or their cash equivalent.

Recommendations concerning family allowances have varied. Some reports have argued for means testing, treating family allowances as social assistance. Others have taken the view that universal allowances have a role to play in reducing "need" and that means-tested assistance should be seen as a "local supplement" to the family allowances and other cash benefits. Under these circumstances, reports have recommended that the allowances be simplified—for example, a single allowance at a flat rate per child provided at a relatively low level commensurate with resources. With falling real revenues, however, full indexation of allowances would not be feasible. Some reports have cautioned against the use of such allowances in countries with high birth rates. Local social assistance requires institution building, and the scope for World Bank assistance in this context has been recognized.

Some countries are facing difficulty with the administration of earnings-related unemployment benefits, and some reports have supported the adoption of flat-rate benefits, set around the minimum wage; others have argued for a two-tier system, with low benefits (below the minimum wage) provided for fresh entrants to the labor force and the long-term unemployed. One problem, however, is that to ensure the political acceptability of unemployment, the flat-rate benefit for those laid off might have to exceed the minimum wage. To control costs and encourage job search, the duration of such higher-tier benefits would need to be limited to, say, six months. For the longer-term unemployed and fresh entrants, some reports argued for the adoption of targeted public works and the option to retrain if training objectives were made clear. The IMF's technical assistance has recognized the importance of institutional developments, and has supported the efforts of the World Bank, the European Economic Council (EEC), and other agencies to help establish employment agencies.

The IMF's technical assistance has taken into account the countries' varying conditions, administrative capabilities, macroeconomic constraints, and aggregate resource potential. These considerations have been helpful in evaluating policy options for the short run, incorporating both temporary social safety nets and some longer-term goals. Increasingly, such information is being used in the design of IMF-supported programs.

Concluding Observations

Recent experience suggests that it is possible to integrate a minimum set of social safety nets in economic reform programs. While detailed household income and expenditure data would be helpful, it is often possible even without such data to identify appropriate target groups and instruments, assess potential costs, and design social safety nets.

The mix of social safety net instruments should be determined by a number of factors: reform measures and their effects, the composition of vulnerable groups, and administrative and financial constraints. For example, with a large increase in food prices in real terms, it would be critical to introduce measures to provide the vulnerable with the means of obtaining basic foodstuffs; with a major public sector retrenchment program, it would be important to introduce unemployment benefits, but with due attention paid to promoting fast employment of the unemployed. Social safety nets should be aimed at mitigating the adverse effects of reform measures on the poor. Thus, a large increase in the consumer and producer prices of foodstuffs implies the need to target social safety nets to the vulnerable in urban areas. A high child dependency ratio implies the need to assist families with children; a high old-age dependency ratio implies the need to target the elderly. Limited subsidies are helpful, partly because governments often already have the necessary administrative arrangements in place. They need to be streamlined for the administration of transitory subsidies. As the reform proceeds longer-term approaches to social protection should be explored.

Recent experience has provided a number of lessons that are summarized here:

Targeting

Whereas targeting is important for cost-effectiveness, experience suggests that targeting by categories defined by household income and assets is administratively complex and might not be feasible in many cases. Alternatives are available, such as categorical targeting of limited subsidies on key commodities (e.g., through quantity food stamps) or cash transfers to certain groups (e.g., urban households, the elderly, women with children, and the unemployed); these alternatives could be effective in protecting the poorest, although some of the nonpoor might also benefit.

Over the longer term, governments should be encouraged to enhance the administrative capacity for targeting and for providing effective social assistance. In many cases, targeted public works programs could fulfill the assistance role with relatively low overhead but might need to be augmented by categorical transfers to those unable to participate (e.g., orphans or the disabled). The interactions among instruments is important and should be considered on a case-by-case basis.

Social Safety Net Instruments

There are a variety of informal and formal social security arrangements, including community-based arrangements, formal social security institutions, and those arrangements set up by bilateral and multilateral governmental and nongovernmental agencies. Where possible, social safety nets should be built on existing arrangements, with inefficient programs reformed or adapted to address the concerns for the poor.

Limited Transitory Consumer Subsidies

Whether transfers are made in-kind or through cash should be determined pragmatically, with administrative costs and other factors, such as efficiency and equity (including intrahousehold equity), taken into account. Cash transfers provide consumers with a greater choice but could force the beneficiaries to bear the risk of unexpected price changes and might not be equitable for some family members, such as female children. Generalized consumer subsidies would be expensive and could generate considerable production disincentives.

Major budgetary savings could be achieved by a shift to more targeted provisions, either through limited cash compensation following a removal of subsidies, in-kind transfers (e.g., milk provision targeted to schoolchildren or lactating mothers, through primary health clinics), or quantity food stamps (which would limit the extent of the transfer an individual could receive and could be targeted regionally). In this manner, a rapid transition to free market pricing would be feasible. At the same time, cushions against price shocks would reduce the need for indexed adjustments in pensions, allowances, and unemployment compensation.

Formal Social Security Institutions

Adapting or reforming formal social security institutions as an element of social safety nets is important. However, due attention should be paid to the coverage of the formal social security institutions. In terms of coverage, formal social security institutions might not benefit a large number of the vulnerable in the formal and informal sectors. However, an expansion of coverage of formal social security arrangements should take into account the existing informal and traditional social security arrangements.

In reforming formal social security benefits, *short-term and long-term aims* might diverge. While nominal benefits would have to be adjusted for higher prices in the long run, the indexation of benefits would exacerbate financing difficulties in a transition. For pensions, in the longer term, the role of the public and private sectors should be identified. For example, the public sector might be able to provide only a limited flat-rate universal pension, with additional earnings-related benefits as an option. In the short run, there would be little scope for private pensions, and earnings-related benefits might be administratively complex. A flat-rate pension on its own, however, would reduce the fairness of the system.

An important element in reducing pension fund imbalances in many transition economies would be to increase gradually the statutory retirement age. However, this solution might aggravate unemployment problems. This stresses the importance of efficiently functioning labor markets.

Unemployment benefits might be provided in combinations of lump-sum severance payments and benefits over time. There would be less unfairness in flat-rate benefits for unemployment than for pensions, but eligibility should be defined tightly, as should the duration of the benefits. Fresh entrants to the workforce or the long-term unemployed could be assisted through other targeted measures, such as public works programs, and financed from general revenue rather than from the unemployment insurance fund.

Implementation

Considerably more work is needed to identify effective administrative arrangements for social protection. It is important not only to integrate social safety nets in reform programs but also to review implementation experience.

Role of Member Governments

Experience shows that governments should play an active role in designing and integrating social safety nets in reform programs. Given the increasing body of international experience, it is important for member countries to seek assistance, for example, from international agencies, including the IMF, and bilateral donors.

Appendix

Potential Role of Existing Instruments as Social Safety Nets

Consumer Subsidies

Many countries use consumer subsidies as a means of social protection. The aim is often to ensure that vulnerable groups have access to low-priced basic necessities, such as foodstuffs, energy products, and transportation services. To achieve this goal, many countries rely on administrative controls on consumer prices set well below market-clearing levels. While such general subsidies can ensure wide coverage, the associated provision costs can place unsustainable burdens on the budget or the balance of payments. A general subsidy may also undermine the establishment of appropriate prices for farmers, given arbitrage possibilities. In some cases, compensatory input subsidies are provided to farmers, causing further production distortions and budgetary cost and creating a barrier to the effective operation of market signals. The administration of consumer subsidies through generalized price controls creates conditions for the wasteful consumption of subsidized commodities.

When unrealistically low consumer prices coexist with realistic producer prices, explicit consumer subsidies imply a substantial budgetary burden. In many cases, subsidies are *implicit* and not transparent, as governments finance them by either keeping domestic producer prices at low levels or applying an overvalued exchange rate to the imports of the subsidized products—thus creating allocative distortions, domestic shortages of subsidized products, and parallel markets where subsidized commodities are traded at much higher prices. Quite often, unrealistically low domestic prices result in the wasteful feeding of wheat to livestock and the smuggling of food and energy products.[27]

Generalized consumer subsidies on essential commodities (e.g., basic foodstuffs), although distortionary, do help the poor. These subsidies tend to provide wealthier groups with larger absolute benefits, but the benefits for poor groups account for a large share of their expenditure. It is important to phase out subsidies for items consumed primarily by the rich and to replace consumer subsidies with more targeted measures.

Social Security Arrangements

Existing institutions include informal arrangements in traditional societies and formal sector social security, with or without budgetary support.

Informal Social Security Arrangements in Traditional Societies

The extended family remains the principal source of support for the elderly in societies as diverse as rural China,[28] Indonesia, India, sub-Saharan Africa, and some BRO countries. This typically reinforces the desire and need for male children, limiting prospects for a reduction in the birth rate. Problems arise when there are no male offspring or when there is a breakdown in family relationships—often connected with an inability to provide support. In Africa, the term for being poor is often synonymous with the absence of family or friends.[29]

Support for the needy that have no sources of family support tends to be based on community-level food security arrangements. For example, in The Gambia, deliveries of staple food for the needy are based on the precept of *zakat* (a religious tax earmarked for the needy). The *zakat* is formalized in some Muslim countries and based entirely on personal responsibility for others. Also, informal arrangements of mutual labor transfers may provide up to half of the total labor input at the community level. For example, when able-bodied persons are sick, or if there is a local landslide, neighbors provide labor assistance (see von

---

[27]In some BRO countries, low producer prices have induced farmers to feed subsidized bread to their livestock or to sell wheat to neighboring countries rather than to the central procurement agency, forcing the governments to allocate scarce foreign exchange reserves to the importation of foreign wheat.

[28]See Ahmad and Hussain (1991).

[29]See Iliffe (1987).

Braun, 1991). In rural China, a community-based system of *wu bao* (five guarantees) provides social assistance to the needy who have no sources of family support. This system, however, suffers from stigma and take-up is low. Nevertheless, in the Islamic Republic of Iran, there is almost full take-up of community-based local support for categories of widows, orphans, and the elderly.

Coping mechanisms that work relatively well in normal times may fail in times of severe stress. For example, communities with marginal capacity to deal with normal shocks can be hard pressed to protect themselves in the face of consecutive shocks. With the evolution of urban, nuclear households, some family and ethnic ties have dissolved, weakening community support systems in many countries.

While such community-based social security provisions are often based on fairly sophisticated redistributive and insurance aspects, these provisions do not exist in all countries. Even where they do exist, traditional social security mechanisms based on the family encourage population growth and may lead to pressures on community resources.

While the local provision system can be effective in identifying the needy, without wider public support, it tends to break down if local shocks are widespread. Thus, formal mechanisms are needed to protect the vulnerable on a consistent basis, and particularly to ensure that the financing needs are met.

Formal Social Security Arrangements in Developing Countries

Although a number of countries have some formal social security arrangements (pensions, unemployment insurance, family allowances, and social assistance), the coverage is often limited to a part of the formal sector or the public sector. As such, they cannot protect broad groups of the population from the effects of economic shocks that may arise as a result of stabilization or structural adjustment in a country.

There is scope for formal instruments in low-income countries, keeping in mind overall fiscal constraints. In India, for example, formal sector employment, although a small part of the total labor force, accounts for 27 million persons. As in many other developing countries, the restructuring of the public sector is handicapped by the absence of unemployment insurance mechanisms, which in the past were considered inappropriate for low-income countries. Fairly rapid urbanization and the spread of wage-based activities in rural areas in India have increased the prospects for contribution-based social security systems, which, given demographic patterns, should generate surpluses for pensions in the immediate future. Noncontributory assistance schemes are also growing in importance, and the rural widows' pension programs in several states attest to the importance given to this vulnerable group.[30]

Many francophone countries in Africa have family allowance systems that provide cash transfers to children of covered individuals. As with pensions in Latin America, the crucial issues are limited coverage and cost. A system—financed through general revenue—under which only formal sector wage earners and their offspring are eligible would be badly targeted. Moreover, a pronatalist instrument may be an inappropriate transplant in countries where birth rates are already high.[31]

Many Latin American countries have programs with relatively extensive coverage and aging populations. Most began with full funding of social security through trust funds.[32] However, their financial positions have been weakened through the forced holdings of government paper at below-market interest rates, rising payroll tax rates (which have encouraged tax evasion), inappropriate investments, and the proliferation of benefits. A typical practice has been for governments to use pension fund surpluses to cross-subsidize burgeoning health care expenditures. The schemes have now become mainly pay-as-you-go (PAYG) and face financial crises—notably Argentina, Brazil, Mexico, and Uruguay, and also in Bolivia, Costa Rica, and Peru. Indexed benefits, in an inflationary context, together with declining contributions[33] have increased the pressure on general revenue to meet the deficits. There has been, however, an inability to raise resources to meet the current obligations and projected costs[34] because of the high rates of indirect, income, and payroll taxes.

---

[30]Widows without grown sons tend to face difficulties and, thus, are among the most vulnerable, even if their extended families are relatively prosperous (see Drèze, 1990). The Indian state of Kerala, which has performed exceptionally well in terms of social indicators, has maintained an old-age pension scheme for the unorganized sector since 1961, but destitution has not been a criterion for eligibility (see Guhan, 1988). Most other Indian states have been less successful in terms of coverage, as stringent means tests have restricted eligibility and have been administratively cumbersome.

[31]Children in large families are often quite vulnerable. However, the provision of family allowances with universal coverage may not be administratively feasible in some poor countries.

[32]Mesa-Lago (1991).

[33]This is due to collection lags (Tanzi effect) and increasing noncompliance in many cases, as well as to the shrinking formal resource base.

[34]An aging population can put additional pressure on the schemes. The relevant consideration, even with such demographic profiles, is to bring younger groups of workers into the system and to increase retirement ages. In countries with younger demographic profiles, there are likely to be surpluses in the initial stages. However, even in such countries, the viability of the social security system depends on the liabilities to be incurred relative to the contribution base of the *covered* workforce, and a young overall demographic structure does not guarantee surpluses.

The high payroll tax rates—in excess of 30 percent of the wage bill in many Latin American countries—have led to evasion, reducing the base for contributions and increasing the incentive to hire uninsured workers from the informal sector or use independent contractors. Thus, the potential for providing for the elderly has not always been realized, given the limitations of coverage to the formal, mainly urban, sector. However, relatively extensive coverage has been a major element in improving equity in Chile and Costa Rica,[35] where the labor force is relatively well organized in both the urban and rural sectors.[36] A number of countries in Latin America are making efforts to reform their social security systems.

Social Security Arrangements in Transition Economies

Formal social security arrangements in transition economies provide only partial social protection. In many former centrally planned economies, social security objectives have been met essentially through a system of employment guarantees, the provision of basic consumer goods at artificially low relative prices, and access to fairly costly social security programs, including various allowances administered by state-owned enterprises. However, such systems have not succeeded either in preventing poverty or in ensuring the availability of consumer items. The provision by state-owned enterprises of social functions such as housing, medical attention, and care for the elderly has contributed, in part, to a "soft" budget constraint,[37] impeding their speedy transformation. Reform issues thus include a reevaluation of the existing social security arrangements, adequate benefits to remove the responsibility of provision from enterprises beyond employers' contributions, and coverage of newly recognized contingencies (e.g., unemployment). These requirements have to be juxtaposed against the cost of provision and the disincentives created by excessively high rates of payroll contributions.

During the transition, a fall in the real level of revenues has often been observed, whereas expenditure commitments have continued unabated.[38] There are, therefore, severe budgetary constraints in meet-

---

[35]Mesa-Lago (1991).

[36]Evaluations of the distributional consequences of social security provisions would entail the examination of the entire system of benefits, funding, and taxes, and of the implications for the population as a whole.

[37]Because of the social services provided, additional subsidies or tax reductions were required to keep the enterprises functioning.

[38]See Tanzi (1992).

ing new expenditures on social protection. Moreover, it might not be possible to continue to increase payroll taxes, which are, in some cases, already as high as 50 percent or more of the wage bill.

To achieve cost-effective social protection for vulnerable groups in transition economies, it is evident that temporary measures (e.g., targeted food subsidies) might need to be considered, together with a reform of formal social security arrangements.

Targeted Public Works

Targeted public works could provide continued subsistence transfers where unemployment insurance is not available or is too costly. Such schemes could provide needed assistance rapidly at low cost, and could be effectively self-targeted if employment were provided at subsistence wages. Nonetheless, permanent employment guarantees, through wage subsidies and support to industries and sectors that are uncompetitive in an open trading environment, are unlikely to be sustainable in budgetary terms and have stifling effects on incentives and initiative. Furthermore, more efficient activities are penalized for the benefit of the inefficient.

Public works employment at subsistence wages and distribution of relief are also important for famine prevention,[39] as seen with the Maharashtra Employment Guarantee Scheme in India in 1972–73 and again in the early 1980s. The Maharashtra drought was of greater severity than those in sub-Saharan Africa, which resulted in several severe famines. Use of public works in Maharashtra and other similar projects prevented famine and appeared to be fairly well targeted. Similarly, in Bangladesh, the rural works program proved to be an effective safety net in preventing a repeat famine in 1988, under conditions similar to those which led to famine in 1974. Public works employment for famine prevention was also strikingly successful under very difficult conditions in the African context in the 1980s, such as in Botswana and Cape Verde (see Drèze and Sen, 1989).

Chile, which has one of the oldest and most advanced social insurance systems in Latin America, used self-targeted employment programs during two major crisis periods, 1974–77 and 1982–84, to compensate for severe unemployment and a decline in the real wage. The Programas de Empleo (EEP) employed at low wages, largely in the form of basic food products, around 6 percent of the labor force by 1976. At that stage, open unemployment was 16 percent of the labor force.

---

[39]See British India (1880).

During the second shock, a third of the labor force became unemployed, but only half sought protection from the EEP; others sought assistance elsewhere. Because of the self-selecting nature of the EEP, the total budgetary cost was 1.4 percent of GNP at the height of the crisis in 1983. The EEP was gradually run down with a tightening of the labor market, and was withdrawn completely in 1988 as open employment returned to around 6 percent, or close to 1970 levels (see World Bank, 1990).

References

Ahmad, Ehtisham, 1992, "Poverty, Demographic Characteristics and Public Policy in CIS Countries," paper presented at the 48th Congress of the International Institute of Public Finance, Seoul.

———, and Athar Hussain, 1991, "Social Security in China: A Historical Perspective," in *Social Security in Developing Countries*, ed. by Ehtisham Ahmad and others (Oxford, England: Clarendon Press).

Ahmad, Ehtisham, and Yan Wang, 1991, "Inequality and Poverty in China: Institutional Change and Public Policy, 1978 to 1988," *World Bank Economic Review (International)*, Vol. 5 (May), pp. 231–57.

Ahmad, Ehtisham, and Ke-young Chu, 1993, "Russian Federation: Economic Reform and Policy Options for Social Protection," in *Transition to Market: Studies in Fiscal Reform*, ed. by Vito Tanzi (Washington: International Monetary Fund), pp. 135–54.

Atkinson, A.B., 1992, "The Western Experience with Social Safety Nets," Welfare State Programme Discussion Paper No. 80 (London: Suntory-Toyota International Centre for Economics and Related Disciplines, London School of Economics).

———, 1993, "On Targeting Social Security: Theory and Western Experiences with Family Benefits," Welfare State Programme Discussion Paper No. 99 (London: Suntory-Toyota International Centre for Economic and Related Disciplines, London School of Economics).

Beveridge, Baron William Henry, 1942, *Social Insurance and Allied Services*, Cmnd. 6404 (London: HMSO).

British India, *Famine Commission Report* (British India, 1880).

Cox, D.R., and Emmanuel Jiménez, 1992, "Private Transfers and the Effectiveness of Public Income Redistribution in the Philippines" (unpublished; Washington: World Bank).

Drèze, Jean, 1990, "Widows in Rural India," Development Economics Research Program, Discussion Paper No. 26 (London: London School of Economics and Political Science).

———, and Amartya Sen, 1989, *Hunger and Public Action* (Oxford, England: Clarendon Press).

Grosh, Margaret E., 1995, "Toward Quantifying the Trade-Off: Administrative Costs and Incidence in Targeted Programs in Latin America," in *Public Spending and the Poor: Theory and Evidence*, ed. by Dominique van de Walle and Kimberly Nead (Baltimore: Johns Hopkins University Press for the World Bank).

Guhan, S., 1988, "Social Security in India," in *Poverty in India: Research and Policy*, ed. by B. Harriss, S. Guhan, and R. Cassen (New Delhi: Oxford University Press).

Gupta, Sanjeev, and Karim Nashashibi, 1990, "Poverty Concerns in Fund-Supported Programs," *Finance & Development*, Vol. 27 (September), pp. 12–14.

Iliffe, John, 1987, *The African Poor: A History* (New York; Cambridge: Cambridge University Press).

LeGrand, Julian, and David Winter, 1987, "The Middle Classes and the Defence of the British Welfare State," in *Not Only the Poor: The Middle Classes and the Welfare State*, ed. by Robert E. Goodin and Julian LeGrand, with John Dryzek and others (London; Boston: Allen & Unwin).

Mesa-Lago, C., 1991, "Social Security in Latin America and the Caribbean: A Comparative Assessment," in *Social Security in Developing Countries*, ed. by Ehtisham Ahmad and others (Oxford, England: Clarendon Press).

Milanovic, Branko, 1992, "Distributional Impact of Cash and In-Kind Transfers in Eastern Europe and Russia," Research Paper Series No. 9 (Washington: World Bank).

Nashashibi, Karim, Sanjeev Gupta, Claire Liuksila, Henri Lorie, and Walter Mahler, 1992, *The Fiscal Dimensions of Adjustment in Low-Income Countries*, IMF Occasional Paper No. 95 (Washington: International Monetary Fund).

Tanzi, Vito, ed., 1992, *Fiscal Policies in Economies in Transition* (Washington: International Monetary Fund).

von Braun, Joachim, 1991, "Social Security in Sub-Saharan Africa: Reflections on Policy Challenges," in *Social Security in Developing Countries*, ed. by Ehtisham Ahmad and others (Oxford, England: Clarendon Press).

World Bank, 1990, *World Development Report: Poverty* (Washington: World Bank).

II
Issues in the Design of
Social Safety Nets

3

The Implications of Adjustment Programs for Poverty: Conceptual Issues and Analytical Framework

Ravi Kanbur

During the past decade, many developing countries have faced severe macroeconomic imbalances that they have tried to correct through a series of programs. Many of the programs have been supported by the IMF. Over the years, concern has been expressed by international agencies and by the countries themselves that the adjustment programs have had an adverse effect on some poverty groups, and the issue of finding ways to minimize this effect, while still achieving the goal of macroeconomic balance, is now on the agenda. A prerequisite for such an exercise is a conceptual and analytical framework for discussion of poverty and the transmission mechanisms between measures in programs and their impact on the poor. The object of this chapter is to review the literature and to evaluate the frameworks currently available, the focus being on identifying methodologies that are or can be made operationally feasible.

Conceptual and Analytical Issues in Measuring Poverty

Standard of Living

Our concern in this study is with the impact of IMF-supported programs on the poor. This requires us to specify what we mean by the

Note: Originally prepared for presentation at an International Monetary Fund seminar on "The Implications of Adjustment Programs for Poverty," November 1988.

poor and by poverty. To do this, we must answer two questions: (1) What is the "standard of living" concept on which our discussions are to be based? and (2) Given this concept, how are we to delineate the poor from the nonpoor?

The definition of what constitutes the standard of living is not an easy task and the academic literature has often taken a philosophical turn on this issue (Sen and others, 1987). Even eschewing abstract discussions of what it means to have a certain standard of living, making the concept operational is difficult because of its multidimensional nature. A straightforward economic approach would focus on the consumption of goods and services. For market items, the many dimensions of the standard of living can be reduced to a single numeraire by using prices to convert quantities into expenditure. For items such as home-produced consumption, prices can be imputed and used in the same way. The same can be done for education and health, but the use of the market framework becomes more tenuous for these publicly supplied services and others, such as access to clean water and public transportation. In principle, of course, all these could be reduced to the same unit of account if we could find appropriate shadow prices. However, this is bound to be a controversial exercise. For this reason, from the operational point of view, it seems appropriate to separate private consumption from "basic needs" indicators such as health or education.

Monetary Measures

For operational purposes, then, it is useful to have a unidimensional monetary measure of the standard of living. But what should this be? Should it be income, expenditure, or something else? An important issue here is the time horizon. Conceptually, the ideal would be permanent income or expenditure. But what we have in most cases is a snapshot household survey with measured income and expenditure for a year (or an even shorter period). If one is interested in current consumption then expenditure is a better indicator to use. In fact, given the difficulties of measuring income in rural areas of developing countries, it can be argued that total expenditure is probably a better track of "permanent income" than is measured income. Some have argued that a narrower category—food expenditure—would be even better (Anand and Harris, 1985). If we focus on expenditure, then we need to allow, of course, for price differences within a country and over time. The extent to which this can be done depends entirely on data availability.

Given the focus on real expenditure, there is still the question of *whose* real expenditure we are interested in—the individual, the family, the household, or the extended household, and so forth. From the normative point of view, it can be argued that we should ultimately be interested in the welfare of individuals and that larger groupings are relevant only insofar as there is income sharing. In fact, data availability largely forces upon us the use of household expenditure—the only question being how this is to be corrected for household size and composition. While there is a large literature on the use of adult equivalent scales to adjust for household composition, this literature is controversial (Deaton and Muellbauer, 1986). In any case, equivalent scales will have to be country specific and their calculation is a major research effort.

An additional issue, which has generated much literature in recent years, is that of intrahousehold inequality. The use of adult equivalent scales corrects for different needs of adults and children (or men and women), but their use in a normative context implies the assumption that consumption is distributed according to these needs. There is some evidence that there may be discrimination against female children in some parts of the world (Kynch and Sen, 1983), while other attempts to identify such discrimination have concluded that the evidence does not support this (Deaton, 1987). At the theoretical level, much work is now under way in modeling intrahousehold allocation decisions in the framework of noncooperative game theory. However, we must conclude that the literature as it currently stands does not provide clear guidelines on how intrahousehold inequality is to be incorporated into poverty measurement, particularly if, as is almost always the case, the only data available are income or expenditure at the household level.

Thus, while there are clearly a number of important issues unresolved in the literature, and the analyst should be aware of these, our recommendation is that for operational purposes real household expenditure (or income) per capita be used as the measure of individual welfare.

Inequality Versus Poverty, and the Poverty Line

Given that what we are interested in is the distribution of individuals by household expenditure per capita, the next question is, What features of this distribution are we most interested in? In the literature on income distribution, a distinction is made between a concern with inequality, which has to do with the distribution as a whole, and a concern with poverty, where the focus is on the lower end of the distribution. Here is not the place to get embroiled in the debate on which of these is the more important, or the conditions under which these two concerns are consistent with each other (in general they are not, but see Atkinson, 1987). Rather, we base our argument on the current policy concerns with *poverty* groups. In addition, it may be easier to arrive at a consensus on poverty alleviation as an objective as opposed to inequality reduction—the latter might involve, for example, weighing the relative incomes of the rich and the super rich.

Accepting a poverty focus, this still leaves open the question of *where* a poverty line should be drawn. This is related to the question of whether a poverty line (along the *real* expenditure per capita dimension) should differ from country to country, and whether it should change over time. This is in turn related to the absolute versus relative poverty debate.

Clearly, the nature and meaning of poverty are country and culture specific, so that there is an undeniable relativistic element to it. It is neither inconsistent nor incoherent to say of two individuals, one in the United States and one in Côte d'Ivoire, that both are in poverty even though the *real* income of the former (after making all relevant price corrections) is far greater than the real income of the latter. Moreover, as the income and structure of a country change, what constitutes poverty also changes, although this change may occur over a long period—too long to be of relevance to an adjustment program of, say, three years.

Ideally, what one would like is a specification of a basket of goods and services that an individual should be able to purchase to be considered not to be in poverty. This would include not only basic food and nutrition but also clothing and housing. It is in the specification of these and other items that differences may arise between countries. However, one would like an operational shortcut to arrive at the poverty line that would be reasonably applicable in a range of situations.

If an established poverty line already exists in a country (as it does, for example, in India and Sri Lanka, where it is based on nutritional standards), the analyst would do best to adopt this line but do a sensitivity analysis for variations in this line. The development of such lines, however, is not an easy task and controversies may take a long time to resolve (in the case of India, a high-level Committee of the Planning Commission arrived at the line). In the absence of any other widely accepted line, we would recommend the following operational procedure: Given a distribution of individuals by real household expenditure per capita, choose a poverty line that cuts off the bottom 10 percent of individuals in some base period. These become the poverty lines with which to evaluate changes in poverty over time and differences across regions at a point in time. It should be emphasized that the procedure is meant as an operational device, and one which may address some problems regarding differences across cultures in what is meant by poverty. However, once chosen, these lines are to remain fixed in real terms, so that the poverty figures capture changes in absolute poverty over time. This device was used, for example, in Kanbur (1990).

Poverty Index and Poverty Profile

Given the distribution of real per capita expenditure and the poverty line, we still have the problem of how to represent the information on poor incomes in an operationally convenient and normatively significant way. There is now a large literature on axiomatic approaches to poverty measurement (Sen, 1976; Donaldson and Weymark, 1986). However, for operational purposes the chosen measure must be able to capture a range of value judgments on the significance of the extent and depth of poverty but be easy to handle and interpret. One measure that has been found to be useful in this context is that put forward by Foster, Greer, and Thorbecke (1984). If real expenditures or incomes are ranked as follows:

$$Y_1 \leq Y_2 \leq \ldots \leq Y_q < z < Y_{q+1} \leq -- \leq Y_n$$

where z is the poverty line, n is the total population, and q is the number of poor, then the Foster, Greer, and Thorbecke measure is

$$P_\alpha = \frac{1}{n} \sum_{i=1}^{q} \left(\frac{z - y_i}{z} \right)^\alpha ; \alpha \geq 0. \tag{1}$$

What the measure does is take the proportional shortfall of income for each poor person, $(z - y_i/z)$, raise it to a power α (≥ 0) to reflect concern about the depth of poverty, take the sum of these over all poor units, and normalize by the population size.

As α varies, P_α takes on a number of interesting features. When $\alpha = 0$, so that there is no concern for depth of poverty,

$$P_0 = \frac{q}{n} = H. \tag{2}$$

This is simply the "head-count ratio"—the fraction of poor units in the population. This has been criticized (Sen, 1976) for focusing on the number of the poor and ignoring how poor they are. However, with $\alpha = 1$,

$$P_1 = HI = H \left(\frac{z - \bar{y}^p}{z} \right), \tag{3}$$

where $\bar{y}^p$ is the mean income of the poor and I ($= z - \bar{y}^p/z$) is known as the "income gap ratio"—the average shortfall of income from the poverty line. As can be seen, $P_0 = H$ focuses on the number of the poor but not on the extent of their poverty, while I focuses on the average extent of poverty but not on the number of the poor. P_1 combines these two and is perhaps a benchmark poverty index that should be the focus of interest in policy-oriented analyses. It should also be noted that nzP_1 is, quite simply, the total amount of resources required to eliminate poverty (1) if there were no incentive efforts in transferring money, and (2) if targeting was preferred. As such, it gives a lower bound on the financial commitment required to eliminate poverty.

Although the P_1 measure should become, in our view, a standard measure of poverty, it is insensitive to redistribution among the poor (since it depends only upon their mean income). However, with $\alpha = 2$, this sensitivity can be ensured. Whereas with $\alpha = 1$, a dollar gained by the very poor would have the same effect on poverty as a dollar gained by the moderately poor; with $\alpha = 2$, those two would be differentiated in the increases, and more weight is given to the poorest of the poor.

Another important feature of the P_α measure is that it is subgroup decomposable. By this is meant that if we divide the population into mutually exclusive and exhaustive groups indexed by j, and if $P_{\alpha,j}$ is the poverty in the j th group, then

$$P_\alpha = \sum_{j=l}^{m} x_j P_{\alpha,j}, \tag{4}$$

where x_j is the proportion of total population in group j. The above expression is useful, since we can assign the "contribution" of poverty in group j to national poverty as

$$C_j = \frac{x_j P_{\alpha,j}}{P_\alpha}. \tag{5}$$

Such a decomposition of national poverty into regional, occupational, crop production, or other sectoral groups can help in developing a poverty profile for the country in question. An example of a regional profile for Côte d'Ivoire is given in Table 3.1. The poverty line is defined as that point on the distribution of individuals by real household expenditure per capita that cuts off the bottom 30 percent of the population. The data are for 1985 and described in Kanbur (1990). The regional division adopted is a fairly standard one in Côte d'Ivoire and points out the extreme poverty in the northern Savannah region. The incidence of poverty is 61.3 percent in that region, more than double the 30.0 percent incidence for all of Côte d'Ivoire. Moreover, it is not only the incidence but the *depth* of poverty in the Savannah region that is a problem. This is shown by the fact that as α

Table 3.1. Côte d'Ivoire: Decomposition of the P_α Class of Poverty Measures by Region

	P_0 Value	Contribution to National Poverty	P_1 Value	Contribution to National Poverty	P_2 Value	Contribution to National Poverty
		(In percent)		*(In percent)*		*(In percent)*
Abidjan	0.052	3.3	0.010	1.9	0.003	1.2
Other urban	0.129	9.7	0.029	6.4	0.011	5.1
West Forest	0.211	10.6	0.059	8.7	0.024	7.3
East Forest	0.456	37.5	0.151	36.6	0.070	35.3
Savannah	0.613	38.9	0.251	46.4	0.131	51.1
All	0.300	100.0	0.102	100.0	0.049	100.0

Source: Kanbur (1990).

increases from 0 through 1 to 2, the contribution of the Savannah region to national poverty increases significantly.

Nonmonetary Measures

As argued earlier, although in principle all aspects of the standard of living might be reducible to a single monetary measure, there are some dimensions in which it is difficult to so reduce. Access to education, literacy, quality of education, health care and its quality, drinking water, and basic housing amenities, and so forth, are all dimensions that seem to fall into the category. The term "basic needs" is sometimes used to capture the distinction between them and more conventional income-expenditure measures. However, it is to be expected that income-expenditure may well be correlated with achievements along the other dimensions. If the achievement, or lack of it, compounds a low income-expenditure measure, then this is significant from the policy point of view. What is also significant for policy is that the bulk of these basic needs is usually supplied by the government. Cuts in government expenditure in these areas—unless managed and targeted in particular ways—may well end up worsening basic needs achievements of the poor.

Table 3.2 summarizes some information on nonmonetary indicators for the poor and nonpoor in Côte d'Ivoire. Perhaps not surprisingly, the poor have very much lower literacy and school attendance rates than the nonpoor. The primary school age attendance rates, for example, are 36.5 percent for the hard core poor and 63.6 percent for all Ivoiriens. Similarly, the poor consult health personnel less frequently than the nonpoor, and they have lower rates of preventive consultation.

Table 3.2. Côte d'Ivoire: Some Nonmonetary Indicators

	Hard-Core Poor	Poor	All
Literacy (reading) rate (in percent)	16.2	20.7	36.0
Literacy (writing) rate (in percent)	12.6	16.2	31.3
School attendance rate, age 7–12 (in percent)	36.5	46.8	63.6
Percentage of ill individuals who consulted health personnel	39.3	42.5	51.5
Percentage of ill individuals who consulted health personnel in a hospital	19.2	23.6	34.6
Percentage having preventive consultation	14.9	16.2	22.7

Source: Kanbur (1990).

Of course, much more detailed analysis is required before the reasons for these achievements in health and education can be precisely identified. However, as an adjunct to the income-expenditure measures of poverty, figures such as those in Table 3.2 are useful in serving to remind us of other dimensions of poverty.

The Nature of IMF-Supported Programs, Their Macroeconomic Rationale, and Criteria for Judging Their Success

IMF-supported adjustment programs have many dimensions. IMF, Fiscal Affairs Department (1986) classifies the policy instruments in 117 Stand-By Arrangements and 23 Extended Fund Facilities, from January 1980 to December 1984, into 7 major categories (monetary and financial policies, public sector policies, external debt policies, exchange and trade policies, wages and prices, other structural adjustment measures, and others). Each in turn has several subcategories. For example, in public sector policies various measures to restrain central government current expenditures are included, such as freezing or reducing numbers of government employees and their wage increases, capping or reducing food and fuel subsidies, or improving expenditure control mechanisms. With more recent developments of the Structural Adjustment Facility and the Enhanced Structural Adjustment Facility, greater emphasis on structural adjustment measures, such as a shift of activities from the public sector to the private sector, or removal of relative price distortions, is to be expected.

However, despite the plethora of measures often listed in IMF-supported programs, it should be clear that some measures are more important than others, and that the measures have a rationale in terms of a particular view of the nature of macroeconomic imbalances and their cure. To cut through the complications that would inevitably arise in assessing the poverty impact of each of a detailed set of measures specified or to be specified in a program, the approach adopted here is twofold—first, to analyze the impact of what are held to be the most important measures, and second, to do so in light of how they are judged to improve macroeconomic imbalances.

The central macroeconomic imbalance that attracts attention in IMF-supported programs is, of course, the balance of payments. Typically, it is an unsustainable deficit in the external balance that prompts a country's approaching the IMF. The macroeconomic framework that is used to analyze the problem is focused on the balance of payments (IMF, 1987), and the success of a program is judged by the restoration of external balance within a limited period of time while not sacrificing other macroeconomic objectives.

The macroeconomic framework underlying IMF-supported adjustment programs is too well known to require detailed rehearsal. It is nevertheless useful to have a brief statement of the overall framework as a backdrop to our subsequent discussion on poverty and adjustment. The nature of the macroeconomic problem that initiates a country's approaching the IMF might be summarized as an excess of aggregate demand over aggregate supply. The manifestations of this are inflationary pressure in the economy and a balance of payments deficit. The balance of payments deficit is only problematic insofar as it is unsustainable. Many countries have historically run large deficits as they imported capital to aid their development—in other words, the deficits were part of a rational intertemporal allocation plan, which was sustainable because of the perceived productivity of the ongoing investment. However, it is believed that in many or most cases the deficits being run by developing countries are not at their sustainable levels. They therefore have to be cut—if they are not cut in a planned way, then a "hard landing" is likely, with unpredictable and possibly hazardous consequences.

The deficit can clearly be cut in one of two ways—reducing aggregate demand and increasing aggregate supply. The latter is clearly preferable of the two, but it is also the slower of the two routes. If the nature of the macroeconomic problem is to reduce the deficit within a short horizon, greater reliance will necessarily have to be placed on quick-acting measures—in practice, this means measures that curtail aggregate demand. However, a given change in aggregate demand is consistent with many different compositions of the change, and the same is true for aggregate supply. Thus, a reduction in demand can come about through a reduction in the absorption of the public sector or the private sector, of consumption or of investment. A major focus in IMF programs is the reduction of public sector absorption through increasing revenues and reducing expenditure. Here again, any given total reduction in expenditure is consistent with a number of different patterns of reduction. Sometimes, for example, IMF-supported programs seek to cap expenditure on food and fuel subsidies.

On aggregate supply, there are similarly many ways of achieving a given increase in supply. One might attempt to eliminate inefficiencies in production directly, for example, by reforming the parastatal sector. Thus, the focus on structural reforms helps a country improve the efficiency with which it uses its scarce resources. Or one might attempt to improve allocative efficiency through relative price measures, for example, by reducing the wedge between consumer and producer prices for particular commodities (such as rice in West Africa). One important relative price is that between tradable and nontradable goods. As IMF (1987, p. 6) notes: "The dichotomy between "nontradable" and "tradable" goods has become a principal analytical tool for analyzing devaluation and other expenditure-switching policies." Expenditure switching policies become important if there is a rigidity in the relative price between tradable and nontradable goods—perhaps because of a rigidity in wages. However, like all relative price measures their success depends on elasticities of supply response, the short-run values of which may be low.

To summarize, the following seem to be the most important aspects of IMF-supported programs:
(1) Reducing absorption through monetary restraint;
(2) Reducing absorption through government expenditure restraint;
(3) Increasing the production of tradables by increasing their price relative to nontradables;
(4) Increasing the production of tradables and nontradables by eliminating price distortions and production inefficiencies within these sectors; and
(5) Mobilizing domestic and foreign savings to promote growth.

Analytical Framework for Assessing Poverty and Adjustment

What Are the Questions?

Before specifying a framework for linking macro adjustment to micro poverty, we must specify the questions to which the framework is meant to provide an answer.[1] Here are some questions which might be of interest to the IMF:

(1) What has happened to the extent and nature of poverty over the life of an IMF-supported program? This purely factual question could be answered directly if, for example, there was an annual household income and expenditure survey in the country. Such data simply do not exist in many developing countries, although a major effort is now under way in the World Bank to create the institutional capacity for collecting such data in sub-Saharan Africa. In the absence of household-level data, we may use more aggregated data on sectoral incomes to get a feel for what has been happening. It should be noted, of course, that what happens to the extent and nature of poverty over the life of a program is a product not only of program policies, but also of exogenous events (e.g., external terms of trade developments, natural phenomena) and preprogram policies.

(2) What would have happened to the extent and nature of poverty in the absence of an IMF-supported program? This question immediately raises further questions, since an answer to it requires not only a model of the economy but also a counterfactual on what would have happened to policy instruments without an IMF-supported program. Notice, however, that these issues arise not only for poverty but for *any* economic variable. Even for a basic macroeconomic variable such as the balance of payments, a counterfactual assessment of what would have happened without an IMF-supported program requires a model and a view on what would have happened to key policy instruments. The problem of the counterfactual is not peculiar to the poverty question.

(3) What would have happened to the extent and nature of poverty if the IMF-supported program had been different? It is important to specify the sense in which the IMF-supported program could have been different. Clearly, if more resources had been available, then the expenditure reduction would have needed to be less drastic, and poverty would have been less adversely affected. The appropriate comparison is clearly with an alternative program that achieves the same adjustment with the same resources over the same period. If this is accepted then the focus is on alternative *compositions* of expenditure reduction or supply enhancement that lead to the same deficit reduction over the same period. Could some alternatives be better than others from the poverty point of view?

(4) What might happen in the future, in the absence of an IMF-supported program? There are several routes that a country might take.

---

[1]An annex describing the derivation of several of the key mathematical expressions presented in this section is available from the author on request.

One of them is to, in fact, enact the measures that would have been in an IMF-supported program anyway. But without the injection of resources that an arrangement with the IMF makes possible, such a "go it alone" strategy may cause more hardship. Or the country might try a different combination of instruments, accepting that it would not have access to IMF resources. It might, for example, impose or intensify quantitative controls to deal with the external deficit. The consequences of this for poverty should also be worked out, since it is an alternative to the IMF package.

(5) What should be the nature of a future IMF-supported program that has the least adverse effects on poverty? This question is closely related to the last one, and in many ways is the central question for policy. It requires a stipulation of the adjustment strategy, a macro model of the economy that links instruments to outcomes, and a menu of instrument combinations, all of which give rise to the same adjustment in the balance of payments deficit but (it is to be hoped) different poverty consequences. It should be clear, therefore, that if one is analyzing the impact of an instrument one should focus not only on its impact on poverty but also on its impact on the deficit—it is the poverty impact "per unit of deficit reduction" that is important. Throughout our discussion, this aspect will be stressed.

The Basic Approach

The basic approach adopted here is that of viewing the macroeconomic instruments in IMF-supported programs as affecting household real incomes either directly or indirectly through their effect on the production structure of the economy. We view households as drawing their incomes from different production activities, supplying factors of production to different sectors. As the composition and level of national output and income change, so will the distribution of household income. It is important, therefore, to have a characterization of how households in general, and poor households in particular, tie in with the production structure of the economy. This is where a poverty profile comes in, providing a policy-relevant guide to how sectoral changes in income might feed through to household incomes.

It should be emphasized that the level of production disaggregation required in an operational setting will depend upon the instrument in question and the policy being considered. Thus, if the instrument is the nominal exchange rate and the policy is devaluation so as to increase the output and income of the tradable goods sector *as a whole,* it would seem appropriate to use the tradable/nontradable disaggregation. However, if the policy instrument is tariff reform, then the disaggregation should be importables, exportables, and nontradables. Since the macroeconomic analysis *must* have made (implicitly or explicitly) the relevant disaggregation in order to arrive at forecasts of the impact on the balance of payments, it must also give some indication of the outputs and incomes of the different sectors after the reform. It is these outputs that can be used to generate implications for the household distribution of incomes and for poverty, provided certain assumptions are made.

Another basic question that arises in analyzing the micro impact of macro changes is the extent to which feedbacks should be taken into account. Our approach is driven by the need to translate IMF-supported measures, which are primarily directed toward improving the balance of payments, into impacts on poverty. Our approach is thus to take feedbacks into account only insofar as the macroeconomic analysis does so. Presumably, the forecasts of balance of payments based on the implementation of an IMF-supported program take feedbacks into account to the extent they are considered relevant, and to the extent it is feasible to do so. We take the output of the macroeconomic analysis as given—our task is to convert it into implications for poverty.

Poverty Decomposition and Some Impacts on Income Poverty

Aggregative Impact of Absorption Reduction

Absorption reduction measures reduce total domestic expenditure. They act quickly and for this reason are important in adjustment programs. A very simple and highly aggregative approach to assessing the impact of this on poverty is to assume that all household incomes are reduced in the same proportion as the absorption reduction. If we have the current distribution of individual real income per capita, we can shift this accordingly, and for a fixed poverty line, we can calculate the new numbers in poverty and the extent of poverty. This is bound to be higher relative to the current position—somebody has to lose during an austerity program, and all we are doing is developing a benchmark by assuming that everybody loses proportionately to their income. Of course, it is the absorption reduction that gets you the balance of payments deficit reduction—it is the trade-off that is important.

One way of quantifying this trade-off is to use the P_α measure and to see how that changes with absorption reduction under the assumptions made. If all incomes fall by a factor θ, then for small θ it can be shown that

$$\frac{dP_\alpha}{d\theta} = \alpha(P_{\alpha-1} - P_\alpha). \tag{6}$$

Notice that this result does not depend on the specific functional form of the income distribution, only on the form of the poverty index and on the assumption that the reduction in total income does not change the relative distribution of income among income groups. For $\alpha = 1$, we get an approximation

$$\frac{dP_1}{P_1} = \left(\frac{1-I}{I}\right)d\theta \tag{7}$$

where I is the income gap ratio defined previously. Thus if $I = \frac{1}{3}$, which is close to the figure for Côte d'Ivoire from Kanbur (1990), it follows that a 100 θ percent fall in absorption will lead to a 200 θ percent increase in the P_1 measure (as a first order of approximation). Notice that the impact is inversely proportional to I, but upon reflection, this is not at all paradoxical—if the extent of poverty is already great, then a given decrease in incomes will have a proportionately smaller impact.

The above assumes that the reduction is proportionate to current household income. To get an idea of how a more unequal sharing of the burden could affect matters, consider the case where the θ percent reduction in total consumption is divided equally between households—so that the poor bear a disproportionate share of the burden. It can be shown that, for small θ,

$$\frac{1}{P_\alpha}\left(\frac{dP_\alpha}{d\theta}\right) = \alpha\left(\frac{P_\alpha - 1}{P_\alpha}\right)\left(\frac{M}{z}\right), \tag{8}$$

where z is the poverty line and M is mean income. For $\alpha = 1$, we get as an approximation

$$\frac{dP_1}{P_1} = \frac{1}{I}\left(\frac{M}{z}\right)d\theta. \tag{9}$$

Thus, if $z = (\frac{1}{2}) M$ and $I = \frac{1}{3}$ (approximately the Côte d'Ivoire's figures again),

$$\frac{dP_1}{P_1} = 6d\theta \tag{10}$$

so that the proportionate increase in poverty is *six* times the proportionate decrease in income.

Unemployment Effects of Absorption Reduction at the National Level

The foregoing analysis assumed that expenditure reduction affected all incomes uniformly, whether additive or multiplicative. However, if there is wage rigidity then a contraction in aggregate demand will be accompanied by an increase in unemployment. The extent of this increase is, of course, a matter for country-specific analysis, and one of the outputs of the modeling underlying the macroeconomic analysis of an IMF-supported program should be the impact on unemployment.

Let $P_{\alpha,E}$ be poverty among the employed and $P_{\alpha,U}$ the poverty among the unemployed. Assuming these to be mutually exclusive and exhaustive categories, if x_U is the unemployment rate and x_E is the employment rate, $(x_U + x_E = 1)$, then national poverty is

$$P_\alpha = x_U P_{\alpha,U} + x_E P_{\alpha,E}. \tag{11}$$

The impact on poverty of an increase in the unemployment rate following from a change in policy instruments is given by

$$\frac{dP_\alpha}{d\pi} = (P_{\alpha,U} - P_{\alpha,E}) \frac{dx_U}{d\pi}, \tag{12}$$

where π is the policy instrument, and we assume that the newly unemployed take on the poverty characteristics of the existing unemployed.

The differential in poverty between the unemployed and employed is thus a key parameter that should be borne in mind in assessing IMF-supported programs. If we take P_0 as the measure, then, on the basis of 1981–82 data for Sri Lanka, the differential incidence of poverty among individuals living in households where the head was employed or unemployed was 11.2 percentage points. Thus, under the assumptions made, every percentage point increase in the unemployment rate would lead to an increase in the national incidence of poverty of 0.112 percentage points.

Income Effects of Absorption Reduction at the Sectoral Level

The analysis has so far assumed a certain uniformity in the pattern of absorption reduction across the different sectors of the economy. In fact, in most IMF-supported programs there is an attempt to control the government's absorption, and this has certain specific effects. First, there is an attempt to reduce the number of government workers and to restrain their wages. To discover the possible impact of this on poverty, we need to identify the extent of poverty in this sector. Table 3.3 presents poverty figures for individuals living in households headed by government sector employees in Côte d'Ivoire in 1985. The incidence of poverty among these individuals is 3.1 percent, compared with 30.1 percent for all Ivoiriens. Now, a 1 percent cut in the incomes of these individuals would, using the formula in equation (7), lead to a 5.6 percent increase in the P_1 measure in this sector, but since this sector only contributes 0.8 percent to national poverty, the impact on

Table 3.3. Côte d'Ivoire: Decomposition of the P_α Class of Poverty Measures by Socioeconomic Group

	P_0 Value	Contribution	P_1 Value	Contribution	P_2 Value	Contribution
		(In percent)		*(In percent)*		*(In percent)*
Export crop farmers	0.365	22.3	0.114	20.4	0.050	18.8
Food crop farmers	0.495	59.0	0.184	64.1	0.090	65.9
Government workers	0.031	1.3	0.002	0.2	0.002	0.1
Formal private sector	0.061	1.9	0.009	0.8	0.003	0.6
Informal sector	0.193	15.5	0.062	14.5	0.030	14.6
All	0.301	100.0	0.103	100.0	0.049	100.0

Source: Kanbur (1990).

the national P_1 would be only 0.04 percent. Of course, these figures are only approximately true, but they should not be surprising given the pattern in Table 3.3. While there may be some poor government workers badly affected for whom special compensatory measures might be instituted, the overall effect on poverty at the national level is likely to be small.

Absorption Reduction: Food and Fuel Subsidies

Capping or reducing food and fuel subsidies is another major component of some IMF-supported programs. This method of absorption reduction has very particular effects depending on the commodity involved and the nature of the subsidy. However, the question still remains—what is the poverty impact of different schemes per unit of expenditure saved? Besley and Kanbur (1988a) provide a general theoretical analysis of this question. Here, we provide an operationally oriented application of those results.

If the subsidy is given in the form of a general ration, which is subsidized below market prices, and if there are no obstacles to the resale of the ration, then the scheme is equivalent to an income transfer equal to the ration multiplied by the subsidy relative to the free market price. This closely approximates the system in Sri Lanka before 1977. Since the ration and the subsidy would be the same for all in a universal scheme, the government would effectively be engaging in an equal income transfer to everyone with ration cards. A cutback in either the quantity of the ration or the subsidy would be equivalent to a cutback in the income transfer. Thus, the formula in equations (8) and (9) would be relevant in gauging the percentage poverty impact per 1 percent cutback in expenditure.

On the other hand, if the subsidy was given in the form of an import subsidy, then upon its removal consumers lose in proportion to their current consumption, while producers gain in proportion to their current production. For small changes, the overall cut in subsidy to consumers is the cut in subsidy per unit multiplied by total consumption, and the overall improvement for producers is the increase in price multiplied by their net marketed surplus. In evaluating the poverty impact, therefore, we need to know the poverty configuration among producers and consumers of this commodity, as shown in Table 3.4, which gives the net consumption of a subsidized commodity by various groups. It is assumed that poor net producers supply an amount Q_{11} of the commodity, while nonpoor net producers supply Q_{12}. Poor net consumers consume Q_{21}, while nonpoor net consumers consume Q_{22}. To a first order of approximation, a one-unit reduction in the price subsidy saves the government $(Q_{21} + Q_{22}) - (Q_{11} + Q_{12})$, but it costs the poor $Q_{21} - Q_{11}$. If consumption by the poor dominates production by the poor, then removing the subsidy has net poverty costs that have to be set against the deficit reduction.

Clearly, the answers to the question of the poverty cost per unit of reduction in expenditure depends very much on the commodity in question. The above schema can also be applied if producer price and consumer price are different. The poverty cost per unit of expenditure reduction on producers is then given approximately by $Q_{11}/(Q_{11} + Q_{12})$, and the corresponding expression for consumers is $Q_{21}/(Q_{21} + Q_{22})$. An illustration of the use of these expressions using household-level data on rice production and consumption in Côte d'Ivoire is to be found in Kanbur (1990).

Of course, the analysis up to now assumes no behavioral responses. This may be valid in the short run, but not so in the long run, where net producers may become net consumers, and quantities produced and consumed may change. The degree of complication introduced depends on how widely we wish to model the complete effects. If we focus purely on own-price effects, then the entries in the matrix in Table 3.4 can be simply adjusted for own-price elasticities of supply and demand. If we wish to take into account the full demand system, then the techniques developed in Ravallion and van de Walle (1988), which rely on an estimation of the equivalent income function, may be used. Substitution in production can also be introduced, using the "multimarket" methodology of Braverman and Hammer (1988). We would suggest, however, that as a first cut it would be useful to produce Table 3.4 for all commodities being considered for policy reform.

In fact, the ratios calculated from Table 3.4 can be helpful in comparing the poverty impact of price changes of alternative commodities.

Table 3.4. Net Consumption of a Subsidized Commodity, by Net Producer/Net Consumer and Poor/Nonpoor

	Poor	Nonpoor	All
Net producer	$-Q_{11}$	$-Q_{12}$	$-(Q_{11} + Q_{12})$
Net consumer	$+Q_{21}$	$+Q_{22}$	$+(Q_{21} + Q_{22})$
All	$Q_{21} - Q_{11}$	$Q_{22} - Q_{12}$	$(Q_{21} + Q_{22}) - (Q_{11} + Q_{12})$

Source: Kanbur (1990).

For simplicity, let production be zero. Then, Table 3.4 suggests that an approximate indicator of poverty impact per unit of deficit reduction is simply $Q_{11}/(Q_{11} + Q_{12})$. This can be calculated from household income expenditure surveys. Notice, however, that the critical ratio is not the fraction of their total expenditure that poor households spend on this commodity, but the fraction of the total expenditure in the economy on this commodity that is accounted for by poor households. The latter is what is needed. Yet, one often finds the former purporting to play a similar role in many poverty profiles that have been produced.

Expenditure Switching: Effect of a Change in Relative Price of Tradables and Nontradables

The central reallocation attempted in IMF-supported programs is that between tradables and nontradables through a change in their relative price, and this in turn is attempted through a nominal devaluation. Much of the literature discusses various nominal feedbacks through wages and other variables. Whether or not a nominal devaluation will actually succeed in raising the price of tradables relative to nontradables is an empirical issue, and is as much a matter of political economy as macromodeling. However, for our purposes, it will suffice to assume that a given change in the relative price has indeed taken place, and then to inquire as to its effects on poverty.

Since we are interested in expenditure switching, let us assume that total expenditure is kept constant. Then, a shift in the relative price, if successful, will alter the composition of national output in favor of the tradable sector. The impact on poverty depends on how exactly this alteration affects factor incomes and therefore household incomes. Over the very long term, we know that under assumptions of competition in product and factor markets, those factors used intensively in the tradable sector will benefit in terms of an increase in their incomes.

Thus, if the tradable sector is relatively labor intensive, then the returns to labor will rise. To some extent, the computable general equilibrium models are capable of quantifying this result, since they in effect solve for the new price and quantity equilibrium following a policy change (Bourguignon, Branson, and de Melo, 1989). This change in wages can then be applied to an assumed distribution of the total wage bill to derive poverty impacts.

At the other extreme, in the very short run, the change in relative price will simply affect entrepreneurs' incomes in the two sectors. Tradable sector entrepreneurs' incomes will rise, so that if a large number of these are poor, there will be a positive impact on poverty. But nontradable sector entrepreneurs' returns will fall. As they adjust by lowering output, there will initially be an increase in unemployment if wages are rigid downward. This will cause hardship temporarily, for which compensatory measures may be required. In any case, those who receive incomes from nontradable sector activities will be made *worse off* in the short to medium term. To get a quantitative expression for the poverty impact, first we need to get a forecast for the value of each sector's output in the short to medium term following the policy shift. This output can then be distributed across household income groups according to patterns revealed in a base-year household income and expenditure survey.

For simplicity, suppose that household participation in the two sectors is mutually exclusive and exhaustive. Then, if output changes translate into income changes in fixed proportion, it can be shown that pure expenditure switching that increases the share of the tradable sector, π_T, leads to a poverty impact of approximately

$$\frac{dP_\alpha}{d\pi_T} = -\alpha M \left[\frac{1}{M_T} (P_{\alpha-1,T} - P_{\alpha,T}) - \frac{1}{M_N} (P_{\alpha-1,N} - P_{\alpha,N}) \right] \tag{13}$$

where M is mean income, and subscripts N and T refer to sectors. This expression, which was introduced in Kanbur (1987) and can be derived, can be recognized to be the development of equation (6) in the two-sector case. If output changes in a sector translate into income changes in additive fashion, that is, all incomes in that sector gain or lose equally, then

$$\frac{dP_\alpha}{d\pi_T} = -\alpha \frac{M}{z} (P_{\alpha-1,T} - P_{\alpha-1,N}). \tag{14}$$

These expressions are, in principle, calculable from household income and expenditure surveys. What they highlight is the need to be able to develop poverty profiles along the tradable-nontradable dimension. This could be attempted using information on occupation of the head of household, for example, or information on the main crop grown. An attempt to develop a production-sector-oriented poverty profile is illustrated in Table 3.3. Export crop farmers, food crop farmers, and formal private sector workers might be grouped together into the tradable sector, while government workers and the informal sector (largely urban) could be classified as nontradable. Using the information in Table 3.3, the expressions in equations (13) and (14) can be calculated.

From equation (14), it can be seen that if $\alpha = 1$, then expenditure switching reduces poverty if the incidence of poverty in the tradable sector exceeds that in the nontradable sector. It seems to us that attempts to establish whether this is actually so in specific cases will have a high payoff. However, a number of objections can be raised against the foregoing analysis. First, it takes an overly simple view of how greater or lesser profitability in a sector translates into factor incomes. If the tradable sector is dominated by smallholders, then an increase in the price of tradables translates directly into their incomes. However, if there is a large landless class, then the extent to which they benefit may be circumscribed by the workings of the local labor market. Thus, if there is essentially surplus labor in this sector, then all the gain will be appropriated by landlords, and the impact on poverty will be minimal. Similarly, if there are wage rigidities in the labor market serving the nontradable sector, then unemployment may result, so that there will be an unequal distribution of the income loss. We might attempt to model these directly, but a shortcut might be to assume that income loss is additive and income gain is multiplicative, that is, the distribution of gains and of losses is not equalizing. Then we get a hybrid expression

$$\frac{dP_\alpha}{d\pi_T} = -\alpha \frac{M}{z} \left[\frac{z}{M_T} (P_{\alpha-1,T} - P_{\alpha,T}) - P_{\alpha-1,N} \right]. \tag{15}$$

which could, in principle, be estimated from data.

Finally, we have focused on sources of income and not on uses of income. A change in the relative price of tradables and nontradables will also affect households as consumers. But the effects of these on poverty can be analyzed in similar fashion to the price changes accompanying food subsidy removals, provided of course that a link can be made between available data on commodity demands on the tradable-nontradable divide.

Another objection is that some households may have sources of income both in the T and in the N sectors. In classifying households as definitely belonging to one sector or another, one may be making a major miscalculation of the impact of expenditure switching, since poor households may well be "diversified" with respect to incomes from these two sectors. We do not have good information on this, and it is an important item on the research agenda.

Other Relative Price Reforms

Most other types of relative price reform in IMF-supported programs can be analyzed using one or the other of the techniques mentioned above. For example, a tariff reduction would alter the relative price between exportables and importables, as well as between nontradables and importables. Any forecast of the effects of these on the balance of payments must contain an account of how the output levels in these three sectors change. Once we have these, then, making assumptions on factor markets, the price changes can be translated into income distribution effects.

Imposition of Tariffs and Quantitative Controls

One route that is often taken by governments when faced with an unsustainable balance of payments deficit is to impose quantitative controls on foreign exchange and on imports. This is, in fact, an alternative to an IMF-supported program that some countries have followed. What is the poverty impact per unit of deficit reduction of such a strategy?

Let us, first of all, take the case where a tariff is imposed on an imported luxury item largely consumed by the rich. On the consumption side, this is a good way of reducing the deficit without a significant poverty impact. In addition to reducing the deficit, the government raises revenue. However, domestic producers of close substitutes for this product benefit as their prices increase. The empirical question in this case is the distribution of income from production of substitutes for luxury imports. Motor cars, for example, are capital intensive. However, for smaller personal items the substitutes could well be labor intensive.

The use of a quota rather than its tariff equivalent has a similar economic effect, except that the income that previously accrued to the government as tariff revenue accrues to those who have the quota as rent. There can be little doubt that these rents do not go to the poor (except perhaps through the demands of the recipients of these rents for services), although it would be difficult to establish this on the basis of household income-expenditure surveys. However, it might perhaps be stated as a reasonable generalization that the replacement of quotas by their tariff equivalents, which is the first stage in many liberalization sequences, is by and large not regressive in its distributional implications.

Once one moves away from luxury imports to commodities consumed further down the income distribution, then tariffs on these to protect the balance of payments begin to have greater impact on consumer poverty, an effect that can be quantified to a first order by the ratio of poor consumption to total consumption. However, one needs to know how the production of import substitutes, which is made more profitable relative to exports, is linked to poor incomes. But data on production structure are rarely available in such detail that we can separate importables from exportables—this is a problem for quantification.

Some Further Considerations

The foregoing analysis has focused on the parts of an IMF-supported program instrument by instrument, as it were. What of the total package? In principle, the different effects can be combined into a coherent whole. Thus, if there is expenditure reduction that leads to a reduction of all incomes and an increase in the share of the tradable sector by $d\pi_T$, the net effect on poverty will, to a first order of approximation, be given by a combination of equations (6) and (13), say, if the basic model is that all income change is multiplicative in nature. Various other combinations are possible, and their usefulness can be judged on a case-by-case basis.

Throughout this chapter we have focused on poverty impact per unit of deficit reduction. To complete the picture, we would need the consequence for poverty if the deficit is not reduced. For example, among the most important considerations in the reduction of subsidies are the adverse implications of the government deficit, monetary expansion, and inflation. To complement the analysis, we would need to think through the poverty impact of inflation.

One issue that arises in combining the effects of different instruments is that some effects would take longer to materialize than others. In simply combining the different effects discussed in earlier subsections, we would have to make the assumption that we were looking at the situation after the full effect had worked through. This is not just a problem for poverty analysis, of course. It is as much a problem for forecasting macroeconomic effects. The strategy suggested here is that the poverty analyst rely on the macroeconomist for the magnitudes of the macro effects over a given time horizon (e.g., the extent of expenditure reduction and the extent of change in the composition of output as between tradables and nontradables), and then use this information to arrive at poverty impacts.

Compensatory Measures and Targeting

Up to this point we have attempted to derive, under various assumptions, the poverty impact of adjustment measures. As we have seen, there are bound to be gainers and losers from attempts to alter the structure of the economy and to curtail aggregate demand. Our focus has been on the impact on poverty at the national level, that is, the net effect of the increase in poverty among losers and the decrease among gainers. However, it has been argued that this masks the dire position of those whose income is drastically cut, or those who face dramatically higher prices or unemployment, as a result of the adjustment process. Can there not be short-term compensation in these cases? The question arises not only in terms of the very poor, but also the not so poor who are articulate enough to oppose the adjustment strategy and do so successfully. However, in this discussion, we focus on the poor.

The crucial question is whether the compensatory measures can be targeted to the poor at little cost, and whether they can be designed so that their operation does not in fact impede the adjustment process itself. Another important question is whether the resources for the compensatory measures are to be made available externally or are to come from within the country. Let us suppose that someone previously employed in a nontradable or import-competing activity loses his job as a result of a devaluation or liberalization of the trade regime. If he stays in the labor market associated with the activity, we may suppose that he will eventually get employment at a lower wage as the market adjusts. He has the option of moving into an exportable producing activity, but (1) he may lack the necessary resources for migration if this activity is in the rural sector, or (2) he may lack the necessary training even if no migration is involved. In any case, his short-term position is made difficult by the lack of employment. Compensatory schemes that are temporary and directed to such individuals would not necessarily impede adjustment while providing short-term respite. Indeed, by retraining, they may well aid adjustment.

Compensatory measures may be used when a generalized food subsidy is removed for fiscal or efficiency reasons. A certain sum could be made available to be used to grant food subsidies targeted to the poor. One of the well-known examples of this is the retargeting of the Sri Lanka rice ration program after 1977. In fact, this method could be used not only to protect the poor who are in danger of losing a specific commodity subsidy but also to create a new subsidy for those out of work because of adjustment.

However, the problems with such compensatory schemes should not be overlooked. These are discussed in Besley and Kanbur (1988b) and are to be found in all attempts to "fine-tune" transfers to particular target groups. We may be able to identify the characteristics of losers on the basis of a priori reasoning supported by household surveys, but it is quite a different matter to identify those characteristics and monitor the scheme on the ground. The administrative costs of attempts at fine targeting can be large, as has been seen in developed countries (unfortunately, there is very little analysis of the costs of administering such schemes in developing countries). However, as discussed before, more generalized targeting, such as switching subsidies to foods consumed by the poor, may be possible. If external resources were available to achieve such retargeting it would certainly ease the pain of adjustment, but detailed country-specific analysis would be required to identify possibilities for such support.

Conclusions

The object of this chapter has been to sensitize the macroeconomist to the sort of issues that might arise in an analysis of the complications of adjustment programs for poverty. However, our focus throughout has been on identifying methodologies that have some hope of being made operationally feasible. The central methodology suggested here is one based on a *policy-relevant poverty profile* that can be used to translate the impact of policy instruments on the size and composition of national income into the consequence for poverty. In this context, the use of subgroup decomposable poverty indices is recommended, and we have given some examples of how they might be used. The extent to which feedback effects should be taken into account, that is, the extent to which the analysis should be general equilibrium in nature, is a question faced by the macroeconomist as much as the poverty analyst. The same is true of the extent of disaggregation entertained. However, our approach to both has been to accept the norm and findings of the macroeconomic analysis of IMF-supported programs, and then to use the output from this analysis in the expressions we have derived for poverty impacts. Of course, it would always be better, ceteris paribus, to have as complete a model as possible. But in the operational context, the shortcuts suggested here may prove useful.

Our approach does depend on the availability of data on the basis of which poverty profiles can be constructed. In the absence of such data, crude poverty rankings of sectors and socioeconomic groups based on secondary information might suffice. But it is a useful truism to note that without the data for poverty analysis, an analysis of poverty impacts cannot be done. However, it should be noted that the excuse of a lack of good-quality data to do poverty analysis is likely to become less and less acceptable over the next few years. The World Bank's Africa Region has launched a major program of data collection on the basis of household surveys that will eventually cover about 25 African countries. Côte d'Ivoire already has such data; Ghana and Mauritania have completed one year's survey activities; and Senegal is due to begin soon. Those involved in the design of IMF-supported programs will have considerable interest in this information as they begin to systematize and analyze.

References

Anand, Sudhir, and Christopher Harris, 1985, "Living Standards in Sri Lanka, 1973–1981/82: An Analysis of Consumer Finance Survey Data," Applied Economics Discussion Paper No. 84 (Oxford: University of Oxford Institute of Economics and Statistics).

Atkinson, A.B., 1987, "On the Measurement of Poverty," *Econometrica*, Vol. 55 (July), pp. 749–64.

Besley, Timothy J., and S.M. Ravi Kanbur, 1988a, "Food Subsidies and Poverty Alleviation," *Economic Journal*, Vol. 98 (September), pp. 701–19.

——, 1988b, "The Principles of Targeting," Policy, Research, and External Affairs Working Paper No. 385 (Washington: World Bank).

Bourguignon, François, William H. Branson, and Jaime De Melo, 1989, "Macroeconomic Adjustment and Income Distribution: A Macro-Micro Simulation Model," Technical Papers (International), No. 1 (Paris: OECD Development Centre, March).

Braverman, Avishar, and Jeffrey S. Hammer, 1988, "Computer Models for Agricultural Policy Analysis," *Finance & Development*, Vol. 25 (June), pp. 34–37.

Deaton, Angus, 1987, "The Allocation of Goods Within the Household: Adults, Children, and Gender," LSMS Working Paper No. 39 (Washington: World Bank).

——, and John Muellbauer, 1986, *Economics and Consumer Behavior* (New York; Cambridge: Cambridge University Press).

Donaldson, David, and John A. Weymark, 1986, "Properties of Fixed-Population Poverty Indices," *International Economic Review*, Vol. 27 (October), pp. 667–88.

Foster, James, and Joel Greer, 1984, "A Class of Decomposable Poverty Measures," *Econometrica*, Vol. 52 (May), pp. 761–66.

International Monetary Fund, Fiscal Affairs Department, 1986, *Fund-Supported Programs, Fiscal Policy, and Income Distribution*, IMF Occasional Paper No. 46 (Washington: International Monetary Fund).

——, Research Department, 1987, *Theoretical Aspects of the Design of Fund-Supported Adjustment Programs*, IMF Occasional Paper No. 55 (Washington: International Monetary Fund).

Kanbur, S.M. Rav61i, 1987, "Measurement and Alleviation of Poverty: With an Application to the Effects of Macroeconomic Adjustment," *Staff Papers*, International Monetary Fund, Vol. 34 (March), pp. 60–85.

——, 1990, "Poverty and the Social Dimensions of Structural Adjustment in Côte d'Ivoire," Social Dimensions of Adjustment in Sub-Saharan Africa Working Paper No. 2 (Washington: World Bank).

Kynch, Jocelyn, and Amartya K. Sen, 1983, "Indian Women: Well-Being and Survival," *Cambridge Journal of Economics,* Vol. 7 (September/December), pp. 363–80.

Ravallion, Martin, and Dominique van de Walle, 1988, "Poverty Orderings of Food Pricing Reforms," DERC Discussion Paper No. 86 (Warwick: University of Warwick Development Economics Research Centre).

Sen, Amartya K., 1976, "Poverty: An Ordinal Approach to Measurement," *Econometrica,* Vol. 44 (March), pp. 219–232.

——, and others, 1987, *The Standard of Living,* ed. by Geoffrey Hawthorn (New York; Cambridge: Cambridge University Press).

4

Economic Reforms, Social Safety Nets, and the Budget in Transition Economies

Ke-young Chu and Sanjeev Gupta

The economic transformation of former centrally planned econo-mies has been accompanied by large declines in output, significant changes in relative prices, and, at least initially, rapid increases in inflation and declines in living standards. Although much of the decline in living standards is attributable to the economic dislocations resulting from the breakdown of the trading regime, the breakup of the Baltics, Russia, and other former Soviet Union countries (BRO), and loose national financial policies, a significant part of it has stemmed from reform policies, which, in the short run, have increased the prices of essential commodities and reduced employ-ment opportunities.

The transition economies will have to persist with reform policies as only sustained and broad-based growth can raise living standards over the long term. In the meantime, to sustain the reform process, specif-ic policy measures will have to be adopted, and resources allocated, to mitigate the short-term adverse effects of reform policies on vulnerable groups.

The transition economies have sought to deal with the adverse effects of reform policies in a variety of ways. While economic trans-formation is still under way, some common elements of these efforts

Note: Reprinted from *Fiscal Policy and Economic Reform: Essays in Honor of Vito Tanzi*, ed. by Mario Blejer and Teresa M. Ter-Minassian (London and New York: Routledge, 1997), pp. 134–63.

The authors wish to thank their colleagues in the Expenditure Policy Division, Robert Hagemann, and an anonymous referee for helpful comments and Tarja Papavassiliou for computational assistance.

can be identified. A critical issue is the budgetary implications of social protection measures. This chapter reviews social protection experiences of different transition economies and, with the help of a stylized model, illustrates interactions between the measures adopted and the budget. Some lessons for the future are also drawn.

Social Protection and Transition Economies

Social Safety Nets

"Social safety nets" in this chapter are defined as the measures adopted to mitigate short-term adverse effects of economic reforms on the poor. These effects stem from price increases of essential goods and services and reductions in employment opportunities. Both effects are unavoidable in the course of economic transformation. Correcting relative prices is necessary to improve the allocation of resources, which reduces real incomes for some while increasing them for others. Strengthening the macroeconomic position requires reducing budgetary transfers or tightening bank credit, or both, which causes inefficient state enterprises to shed labor.

Many economies in transition have inherited extensive consumer subsidies for essential goods and services and other social protection arrangements (or social insurance and social assistance systems) that had been maintained to address normal life cycle contingencies such as old age, sickness, and disability and have only recently established unemployment benefits aimed at "normal" unemployment. However, in many instances, the reform-induced income changes can—and do—dominate normal life cycle and other income changes. Under the circumstances, the existing social protection instruments may not be adequate, and it may become necessary to integrate transitory social safety nets into reform programs. To this end, existing social protection instruments may have to be adapted or modified. Moreover, new measures may have to be introduced specifically to mitigate the reform-induced reductions in the incomes of the more vulnerable members of society. The nature and cost of social safety nets depend very much on living standards, demographic profiles, and the mix and sequence of reform policies in each country.

The depiction (Table 4.1) of the prereform conditions in selected countries, in most cases, is still valid, while the reform efforts are ongoing. As regards overall income levels, some were extremely low-income countries (Albania, Ethiopia, Lao People's Democratic Republic); others were middle-income countries (Hungary, Poland, and many BRO

Table 4.1. Demographic Structure and Living Standards in Selected Transition Economies, 1992

	Population	GNP per Capita[1]	Population Age 14 and under	Age 65 and over	Life expectancy at birth	Infant mortality rate per 1,000 births
	(In millions)	*(In U.S. dollars)*	*(In percent)*		*(In years)*	
Lower-income countries						
Many elderly						
Georgia	5.5	850	24	12	73	17
Many children						
Albania	3.4	415	32	5	73	28
Armenia	3.5	780	30	7	72	21
Azerbaijan	7.4	870	33	6	71	32
Ethiopia	52.5	110	47	3	49	128
Kyrgyz Republic	4.5	810	38	6	66	40
Lao People's Dem. Rep.	4.5	250	45	3	51	97
Tajikistan	5.7	480	45	4	69	49
Uzbekistan	21.8	860	42	4	69	44
Higher-income countries						
Many elderly						
Belarus	10.3	2,910	22	13	71	15
Bulgaria	8.9	1,330	20	14	71	17
Estonia	1.6	2,750	22	12	70	13
Hungary	10.4	3,010	19	14	70	16
Latvia	2.7	1,930	22	13	69	16
Lithuania	3.7	1,310	22	12	70	14
Poland	38.4	1,960	24	10	71	15
Romania	23.2	1,090	22	11	70	27
Russian Federation	148.3	2,680	23	12	69	20
Ukraine	51.9	1,670	21	14	70	18
Many children						
Kazakhstan	17.0	1,680	31	7	69	31
Macedonia, former Yugoslav Republic of[2]	2.1	1,452	25	8	72	29
Moldova	4.4	1,260	31	9	68	23
Turkmenistan	3.9	1,270	41	4	66	55

Sources: World Bank: Socioeconomic Time Series System, World Population, Population Structure and Vital Statistics; The World Bank Atlas 1994; and IMF staff estimates.

[1]Estimates for the Baltics, Russia, and other countries of the former Soviet Union states are preliminary and have changed substantially since 1992.

[2]Gross social product, which excludes the value of many services.

countries). The poor in the former group of countries had relatively low incomes and had little room to withstand reform-induced income losses. In comparison with the middle-income countries, the low-income countries had a relatively large number of vulnerable people to protect, but weak social policy institutions. This suggests that the low-income countries required a relatively large amount of resources for social safety nets but had little scope for adapting existing social programs for this purpose.

The demographic profile also influenced the nature of social safety nets and their financing. In some countries, a large proportion of the population was elderly (Belarus, Bulgaria, Hungary, and Ukraine), while in others the young tended to dominate the population (the Kyrgyz Republic, Lao People's Democratic Republic, Tajikistan, Turkmenistan, and Uzbekistan). Whereas the proportion of the working population that supported the financing of benefits to the elderly and the young was low in both groups of countries, protecting the old became a major issue in the former group, ensuring adequate protection for children was a principal concern in the latter.

The reform policy mix has also dictated the characteristics of social safety net instruments. A change in relative prices has required cash transfers (e.g., supplements to existing cash benefits) to the poor who were adversely affected by the higher prices. Consequently, whether or not some subsidies should be retained as a social safety net has been a major issue. Large cuts in transfers to loss-making enterprises, which have followed the price liberalization, inevitably reduced the demand for labor. At the same time, an increase in unemployment has required transfers to the new poor (e.g., through unemployment benefits or public works programs). Eastern European countries have shown tolerance for higher open unemployment, as evidenced by average unemployment rates that in 1993 ranged between 10.2 percent in Romania and 17.5 percent in Albania. However, most BRO countries other than those in the Baltic area have suppressed open unemployment, resulting in an average registered unemployment rate of less than 1 percent.[1] The Baltic area countries lie somewhere in between.

Targeting social safety nets to intended beneficiaries has not been easy, since it has been difficult to identify society's poor members and those whose welfare is adversely affected by reform measures. The administrative requirements to track all household incomes and assets have been formidable, particularly as informal sector activities have been growing. Furthermore, it has not been possible to establish new

---

[1]The phenomenon of disguised unemployment in transition economies is reflected in the enterprises' tendency to hoard labor, which has meant a cut in real wages for all workers. In a way, this shows the "flexibility" of labor markets to allow for an across-the-board real wage cut. The main difficulty is that this situation is not sustainable.

administrative structures during the transition period to deliver means-tested benefits. Targeting benefits on the basis of income has also been difficult because household incomes have been typically clustered around the poverty line—the income level that is often used to distinguish the poor from the nonpoor.

Existing Social Protection Institutions

Except for low-income African and Asian transition economies, most transition economies started with an extensive system of social protection, comprising general budgetary consumer and producer subsidies, provided through unrealistically low administered consumer prices, and cash benefits, including pensions, sickness and maternity benefits, and child allowances (Table 4.2). These benefits had universal coverage, regardless of the incomes of the beneficiaries. At the outset of the reform, most central European and BRO states formally abandoned the long-established system of guaranteed employment and instituted unemployment benefits. In African and Asian countries (Ethiopia and Lao People's Democratic Republic) reliance has been more on subsidies and informal social protection arrangements based on extended family ties.

Budgetary outlays on benefits provided by the government have varied across countries. Before reform measures were initiated in central European countries and BRO states, subsidies ranged from 1.3 percent of GDP in Latvia to 15.6 percent of GDP in Albania.[2] Outlays on cash benefits ranged between 8.6 percent of GDP in Albania and 20.1 percent of GDP in the BRO. The major cash benefit provided was pensions, the cost of which ranged from 6.3 percent of GDP in the BRO to 10 percent of GDP in the former Yugoslav Republic of Macedonia. Since no unemployment was officially recognized, there were no unemployment benefits. Two low-income countries (Ethiopia and Lao People's Democratic Republic) incurred relatively small expenditures on subsidies and cash benefits; the latter was confined to the formal sector employees. Expenditures on social protection in most transition economies have been financed through the government budget (subsidies and some child allowances) and payroll taxes, paid by both employers and employees (pensions, unemployment benefits, and sickness and maternity benefits). In most countries, extrabudgetary funds collect payroll taxes and disburse pensions, unemployment com-

---

[2]In Albania, this estimate includes large payments made to idle workers that, in some countries, are shown under other expenditure headings.

Table 4.2. Prereform and Postreform Subsidies and Cash Transfers in Selected Transition Economies
(As percent of GDP)

	Total Government Expenditure		Subsidies[1]		Cash Benefits		Pensions		Unemployment Benefits		Child Allowances		Other[2]	
	1990 or 1991[3]	1993[4]	1990 or 1991[3]	1993[4]	1990 or 1991[3]	1993[4]	1990 or 1991[3]	1993[4]	1990 or 1991[3]	1993[4]	1990 or 1991[3]	1993[4]	1990 or 1991[3]	1993[4]
Average	42.1	40.3	7.0	5.4	9.5	8.3	5.9	5.7	0.0	0.6	1.4	0.7	2.5	1.3
Lower-income countries														
Many elderly														
Georgia	33.0	46.3	...	33.3	6.0	0.6	3.9	0.5	0.0	0.0	1.7	0.1	0.4	0.0
Many children														
Albania	62.1	44.2	15.6[5]	2.6[6]	8.6	11.9	8.6	6.5	0.0	4.2	0.0	...	0.0	1.2
Armenia	28.0	68.6	1.5	8.4	...	7.0	...	7.0[7]	...	0.0	...	0.0	...	0.0
Azerbaijan	40.7	52.0	7.2	4.4	15.3	11.5	6.5	7.6	0.0	0.0	7.2	3.8	1.6	0.0
Ethiopia	46.9	34.3	0.7	0.0	3.0	4.7	1.3	1.3	...	0.0	...	0.0	1.7	3.4
Kyrgyz Republic	...	25.4	...	3.3	...	3.7	...	2.4	...	0.0	...	1.0	...	0.3
Lao People's Dem. Rep.	23.4	17.8	0.0	0.0	0.8	1.3	0.8	1.3	0.0	0.0	0.0	0.0	0.0	0.0
Uzbekistan	52.3	60.5	6.5	7.3	7.6	3.7	1.0	2.6	0.0	0.4	6.1	0.7	0.5	0.0
Higher-income countries														
Many elderly														
Belarus	...	51.9	...	14.3	...	9.8	...	6.3	...	0.9	...	0.3	...	2.3
Bulgaria	64.3	41.7	14.9	3.9	12.0	12.9	8.8	9.4	0.0	0.8	...	0.0	3.2	2.7
Estonia	31.8	33.9	2.5	1.3	10.4	8.8	2.6	5.6	0.0	0.2	0.3	1.8	7.5	1.1
Hungary	57.4	60.4	9.6	4.8	14.9	18.2	9.7	10.4	0.0	1.4	...	0.0	5.1	6.4
Latvia	31.0	26.7	1.3	1.2[8]	9.2	12.7	7.8	6.0	0.0	1.8	0.7	2.4	0.6	2.5
Lithuania	49.2	25.0	14.2	1.4	8.5	5.3	7.0	4.1	...	0.3	0.0	0.5	1.5	0.4
Poland	39.8	48.6	7.3	2.3	10.6	18.8	8.1	14.9	0.2	1.2	...	2.7	2.3	...
Romania	38.7	33.3	7.9	5.8	10.6	8.9	7.9	6.5	0.0	1.7	...	0.7	2.7	...
Russian Federation	...	34.8	...	0.7	...	6.4	...	5.5	...	0.1	...	0.6	0.0	0.0
Ukraine	53.9	73.4	13.0	12.1	9.7	8.2	9.7	8.0	0.0	0.2	0.0	0.0	0.0	0.7
BRO	50.9	...	15.0	...	20.1	...	6.3	...	...	...	...	...	13.8	0.0

Many children

Kazakhstan	31.4	22.9	...	2.3	3.9	0.7	3.9	0.3	0.0	0.0	0.0	0.2	0.0	0.2
Macedonia, former Yugoslav Republic of	40.4	43.9	0.0	3.2	17.5	18.4	10.0	11.7	0.5	0.6	0.0	0.5	6.9	5.6
Moldova	25.3	25.9	5.1	3.0	7.9	4.8	4.9	3.9	0.0	0.0	2.4	0.4	0.6	0.5
Turkmenistan	42.3	15.2	4.3	3.1	3.0	3.6	3.0	2.9	0.0	0.0	0.0	0.0	0.0	0.7

Source: IMF staff estimates.

[1] Producer and consumer subsidies for goods and services.

[2] Includes maternity and sickness benefits and social assistance programs.

[3] 1991 for Armenia, Azerbaijan, Estonia, Georgia, Latvia, former Yugoslav Republic of Macedonia, Moldova, Ukraine, and Uzbekistan. 1988 for the Baltics, Russia, and other countries of the former Soviet Union and 1990 for all other countries.

[4] Estimates for Bulgaria, Hungary, Kazakhstan, Lao People's Democratic Republic, Poland, Romania, and Uzbekistan. Preliminary actuals for Azerbaijan, Ethiopia, and Moldova. Budget figures for Latvia.

[5] Includes payments to idle workers of state enterprises amounting to 12.4 percent of GDP.

[6] Includes bread compensation for state enterprises.

[7] Includes child allowances.

[8] Heating allowance.

pensation, and sickness and maternity benefits. The combined payroll tax burden averaged 40 percent of the wage bill and exceeded 50 percent in one country (Ukraine).

Social Safety Nets and the Budget

A Stylized Model

The main features of the social protection arrangements and their financing in many transition countries can be captured in a simple stylized model that incorporates key aspects of the economies, demography, and social protection arrangements. This model can then be used to illustrate the budgetary implications of social safety net options.

First, the population, labor force, and employment have the following relationships:

$$N_t = (1 - u_t) L_t \tag{1}$$

$$
\begin{aligned}
POP_t &= N_t + BU_t + BY_t + BO_t \\
&= L_t [(1 - u_t) + u_t + by_t + bo_t]
\end{aligned} \tag{2}
$$

$$
\begin{aligned}
W_t &= w_t N_t \\
&= w_t (1 - u_t) L_t,
\end{aligned} \tag{3}
$$

where

$$L_t = \text{labor force;}$$
$$POP_t = \text{population;}$$
$$N_t = \text{employment;}$$
$BU_t, BY_t, BO_t =$ the number of unemployed, children, and elderly who are receiving unemployment benefits, child allowances, and pensions, respectively;
$u_t, by_t, bo_t =$ the number of unemployed, children, and elderly as ratios of the labor force (the last two are equivalent to child and old-age dependency ratios);
$W_t =$ wage bill of the economy; and
$w_t =$ average wage of the economy.

Different cash benefits may be expressed as follows:

$$CBO_t = cb_t BO_t \tag{4}$$

$$CBY_t = cb_t BY_t \tag{5}$$

$$CBU_t = cb_t BU_t, \tag{6}$$

where
CBO_t, CBY_t, CBU_t = the total amounts of pensions, child allowances, and unemployment benefits; and
cb_t = average cash benefit (assumed to be equal for pensions, child allowances, and unemployment benefits).

Second, the nonpoor and poor households consume two commodities—one is subsidized and the other is not. For simplicity, we assume that each employed worker earns an income above a minimum subsistence level for himself or herself and a spouse; when he or she has children, this income may reduce the average household income to below the minimum subsistence level. The child allowances are aimed at preventing the household from falling into poverty. We also assume initially that pensions and unemployment benefits are the only sources of income, respectively, for the elderly and the unemployed.[3] For our model, the worker and his or her spouse are considered to be nonpoor; others are poor.[4] The quantities consumed, prices, and production costs are denoted as follows:

q_{11}, q_{12} = average quantities of the subsidized commodity consumed by the nonpoor and the poor;
q_{21}, q_{22} = average quantities of the unsubsidized commodity consumed by the nonpoor and the poor;
p_{1t}, p_{2t} = consumer prices of the subsidized and unsubsidized goods, respectively;
c_{1t}, c_{2t} = production costs including normal profits of the subsidized and unsubsidized goods, respectively;
$c_{1t} > p_{1t}$; and
$c_{2t} = p_{2t}$.

The government subsidizes consumption of the first good by maintaining a below-cost sale price. The amount of subsidy may be expressed as follows:

$$SUBS_t = c_{1t} [1 - (p_{1t}/c_{1t})] [N_t q_{11t} + (BO_t + BY_t + BU_t) q_{12t}]$$
$$= c_{1t} [1 - (p_{1t}/c_{1t})] L_t [(1 - u_t) q_{11t} + (bo_t + by_t + u_t) q_{12t}]. \qquad (7)$$

---

[3]For the model, no distinction is made between the number of unemployed and those actually registered to receive unemployment benefits. In other words, all unemployed are assumed to be registered with official agencies.

[4]In transition economies, women's labor force participation is high. The model can easily be extended to include the working poor.

The extrabudgetary fund, financed through a payroll tax, provides pension and unemployment benefits.[5] The extrabudgetary fund's revenues and expenditures may be expressed as follows:

$$REV_t = tw_t (1 - u_t) L_t$$
$$= [T/(1 + \pi_t)^2] w_t [1 - u_t] L_t \tag{8}$$

$$EXP_t = CBO_t + CBU_t$$
$$= cb_t (bo_t + u_t) L_t \tag{9}$$

where

REV_t, EXP_t = revenues and expenditures of the extrabudgetary fund;

T, t = statutory and effective payroll tax rates, in percent of the wage bill; it is assumed that there is a *two-month* lag in tax collection;[6] and

π_t = monthly inflation rate.

Total spending on social protection by the consolidated general government may be expressed as follows:[7]

$$L_t \{c_{1t} [1 - (p_{1t}/c_{1t})] [(1 - u_t) q_{11t} + (bo_t + by_t + u_t) q_{12t}]$$
$$+ cb_t (bo_t + u_t) - [T/(1 + \pi_t)^2] w_t (1 - u_t)\} \tag{10}$$

with the first and the second lines in braces, { }, in equation (10) indicating, respectively, the amount of subsidy expenditures and the deficit of the extrabudgetary fund per person in the labor force.

The subsidy part of equation (10) illustrates two aspects of budgetary subsidies: their budgetary costs and their effects on household consumption. The unit subsidy $c_{1t} - p_{1t}$ (i.e., per kilogram) of the subsidized commodity is determined by the cost c_{1t} and the rate of cost recovery p_{1t}/c_{1t}, which is determined by government policy. In our simplified model, q_{11} and q_{12}, the average consumption of the subsidized commodity by the nonpoor and the poor, determines partly the extent of subsidy benefits provided to the nonpoor. The former (q_{11}) is greater than the latter (q_{12}); thus, the nonpoor benefit more than the poor from generalized subsidies administered through price controls.

The deficit of the extrabudgetary fund per person in the labor force is the difference between total expenditure and revenue per person, the former being the product of the average benefit and the number of

---

[5]Typically, in most transition economies, there are separate extrabudgetary funds to provide unemployment benefits and sickness and maternity benefits.

[6]t is the rate "effectively" faced by the payroll tax payers in the current time period. Because of the collection lag, t is lower than the statutory rate, T.

[7]In the formulation presented here, only the *deficit* of the extrabudgetary fund is considered to be a part of the general government expenditure.

beneficiaries, and the latter the product of the effective payroll tax rate and the wage bill. The deficit of the extrabudgetary fund gives rise either to central government transfers to the fund or the fund's resorting to bank borrowing.

Equation (10) shows the first-round fiscal effects of various exogenous and policy changes.

An increase in unemployment would affect the fiscal balance through the following channels: it would reduce subsidy expenditures for employed (nonpoor) workers but increase those for unemployed (poor) workers; at the same time, it would increase unemployment benefits and reduce the wage bill and thus the revenue for the extrabudgetary fund. These effects per person in the labor force can be shown as follows:

$$\{(c_{1t} - p_{1t})\,(-q_{11t} + q_{12t}) + cb_t\ - [Tw_t/(1 + \pi)^2]\}\,\Delta u_t\,, \tag{11}$$

where Δ denotes "an increase."

An increase in the average cash benefit would have the following fiscal effect:

$$(by_t + bo_t + u_t)\,\Delta cb_t. \tag{12}$$

Equation (10) also indicates what the government could do to reduce subsidies, while maintaining cash benefits for the poor. The government could eliminate subsidies by increasing the cost recovery rate to 1; this measure, however, would reduce the real incomes of the net consumers, including some of the poor, of the subsidized commodity.[8] Alternatively, the government could liberalize prices and establish a free market for the subsidized commodity and provide certain poor groups with limited cash transfers. The government could also maintain limited subsidies for the commodity targeted to certain groups. In the latter case, the amount of subsidies would still be determined by equation (10), but the government could limit subsidies by increasing the cost recovery rate and limiting subsidized quantities and the number of beneficiaries.

The net fiscal effect of reforming the social protection arrangements by eliminating subsidies and replacing them with cash benefits of an equal amount for pensioners, children, and unemployed workers would be:

$$-\Delta\,p_{1t}\,(1 - u_t)\,q_{11t}\,L_t \quad \text{or} \quad -(c_{1t} - p_{1t})\,(1 - u_t)\,q_{11t}\,L_t. \tag{13}$$

---

[8]The net consumers are those who consume more than they produce.

The savings would be large when the increase in the official price is large (i.e., when the prereform cost recovery rate was low) or the pre-reform subsidized quantity for the nonpoor is large.

The financial balance of the extrabudgetary fund—that is, the negative of the second part of equation (10)—is defined as:

$$REV_t - EXP_t = w_t \{[T/(1 + \pi_t)^2] (1 - u_t) - (cb_t/w_t) (bo_t + u_t)\} L_t. \quad (14)$$

For a balanced extrabudgetary fund, the following condition must be satisfied:

$$[T/(1 + \pi_t)^2] (1 - u_t) = (cb_t/w_t) (bo_t + u_t). \quad (15)$$

In the absence of unemployment and inflation, this is simplified to

$$T = (cb_t/w_t) bo_t, \quad (16)$$

which defines the statutory payroll tax rate needed to ensure balanced extrabudgetary operations as the product of the replacement rate (cb_t/w_t) and the old-age dependency ratio (bo_t). In the presence of inflation and lags in the collection of the payroll tax, the statutory tax rate must be high enough to offset the negative effect of collection lags on revenue. Then, in the presence of unemployment, inflation, and a collection lag of two months, the statutory tax rate to ensure balanced operations of the extrabudgetary fund would be

$$T = [(cb_t/w_t) (bo_t + u_t) (1 + \pi_t)^2]/(1 - u_t). \quad (17)$$

In this case, the statutory tax rate should be high enough to offset not only the negative effect of collection lags on revenue, but also the negative effects of unemployment on both revenue (reduced tax base) and expenditure (increased benefits to the unemployed).

Equation (17) shows key factors that would raise the payroll tax burden: an increase in unemployment (through a reduction in the wage bill or an increase in unemployment benefits), an increase in the old-age dependency ratio (through an increase in pension payments), an increase in the average unemployment benefit or the average pension, a decline in the average wage (through a reduction in the wage bill), a lengthening of collection lags, and an increase in inflation (through a further erosion of revenue).

Numerical Illustration

The relative importance of different variables in the model developed above can be assessed with the help of the following numerical illustration. The advantage of the illustration is that it gives a flavor of

Table 4.3. A Hypothetical Country: Annual Expenditures of an Average Individual in Poor and Nonpoor Households

	Total Food and Nonfood	Bread	Milk	Meat	Other Food Items	Total Food	Total Nonfood
Nonpoor							
Expenditure composition (in percent)	100.0	10.0	10.0	10.0	10.0	40.0	60.0
Quantity (in kilograms)		10.0	10.0	10.0	10.0	40.0	60.0
Price (in rubles per kilogram)		1.0	1.0	1.0	1.0		
Total expenditure (in rubles)	100.0	10.0	10.0	10.0	10.0	40.0	60.0
Income (in rubles)	100.0						
Savings (in rubles)							
Poor							
Expenditure composition (in percent)	100.0	20.0	20.0	12.5	17.5	70.0	30.0
Quantity (in kilograms)		8.0	8.0	5.0	7.0		12.0
Price (in rubles per kilogram)		1.0	1.0	1.0	1.0		0.0
Total expenditure (in rubles)	40.0	8.0	8.0	5.0	7.0	28.0	12.0
Income (in rubles)	40.0						
Savings (in rubles)							

social safety net measures that have the greatest impact on the budget, particularly in the short term.

Personal Expenditures

Table 4.3 displays expenditures of hypothetical nonpoor and poor persons on basic food and nonfood items. For analysis, the following assumptions are made initially: (a) a "nonpoor" person is a worker, whereas a "poor" person is a pensioner or a child; (b) there are 100 persons in the country: 50 workers, 30 pensioners, and 20 children; and (c) there is no unemployment.[9]

Whether a given household is poor or not would depend on the number of poor persons in each household (pensioners and children) and whether the average family income falls below the subsistence level. The nonpoor individual, on average, earns Rub 100 and spends

---

[9]The ratios of 30 percent and 20 percent for the number of pensioners and children to the total population, respectively, are indicative of the actual situation in many transition economies. For example, in 1992, the ratios of the number of pensioners to the population were 23 percent and 21 percent in Poland and Russia, respectively, because of low retirement ages and proliferation of special pensioners. The ratios of the number of children to the population were 24 percent and 22 percent, respectively, for these two countries.

Table 4.4. A Hypothetical Country: Budgetary Cost of Subsidies

	Total Food and Nonfood	Bread	Milk	Meat	Other Food Items	Total Food	Total Nonfood
		(In rubles per kilogram)					
Budgetary cost							
Retail price		1	1	1	1		1
Production cost		2	2	2	1		1
Subsidies	3	1	1	1	0	3	0
		(In rubles)					
Average per capita subsidy benefit							
Nonpoor	30	10	10	10	0	30	0
Poor	21	8	8	5	0	21	0
Total budgetary cost of subsidies							
Nonpoor	1,500						
Poor	1,050						
Memorandum items							
Population	100						
Nonpoor persons							
Working population	50						
Poor persons							
Pensioners	30						
Children	20						
Unemployed	0						

Rub 40 on food items (i.e., Rub 10 a year each on bread, milk, meat, and other food items) and the remaining Rub 60 on nonfood items.[10] In contrast, the poor person, on average, has an income of Rub 40, of which Rub 28, or 70 percent of income, is spent on food.[11] For simplicity, it is assumed that neither individual saves. Table 4.3 also shows quantities consumed by the members of two income groups. In absolute terms, the nonpoor person consumes larger quantities of food items than the poor.

Subsidies and Their Financing

Table 4.4 shows budgetary subsidies on food and nonfood items that benefit both poor and nonpoor persons. These subsidies arise because

---

[10]The currency unit, ruble (Rub), is used throughout for illustration.

[11]In 1993, the estimated share of food consumption in the household budget for the two lowest income deciles in the Russian Federation was approximately 80 percent; the share for the average household was 50 percent. (See appendix.)

the retail prices of bread, milk, and meat shown in Table 3 cover only 50 percent of their production costs. Budgetary subsidies of Rub 30 are provided to every nonpoor individual and Rub 21 to every poor individual. Total budgetary subsidies amount to Rub 2,550 a year, with the aggregate benefit equaling Rub 1,500 and Rub 1,050 for nonpoor and poor population groups, respectively.[12]

Cash Benefits and Their Financing

Pensions are financed through payroll contributions, and child allowances through the budget. The annual average wage is assumed to be Rub 100, and the average pension Rub 40, with the average child allowance equal to the average pension. The wage bill for the economy is thus equal to Rub 5,000. Pension and child allowance outlays amount to Rub 1,200 and Rub 800, respectively.[13]

The National Economy, the Budget, and Extrabudgetary Fund

It is assumed that annual nominal GDP amounts to Rub 25,000. The annual inflation rate is 1,000 percent, or 22.1 percent a month. Total budgetary revenues and expenditures amount to 30 percent and 40 percent of GDP, respectively.[14] Table 4.5 summarizes the overall fiscal position of this stylized economy.

---

[12]Many transition economies maintain unrealistically low agricultural producer prices and an overvalued exchange rate, giving rise to implicit subsidies. If the implicit subsidy is also Rub 1 per kilogram for the three items listed in Table 4.3 (i.e., bread, milk, and meat), the total benefit of the implicit subsidy and its distribution across income classes will be the same as for explicit budgetary subsidies. The major difference is that the cost of the implicit subsidy is borne by producers and not by the budget. The total annual cost of subsidies to the economy would then be Rub 1,500.

[13]In 1993, the ratio of the average pension to the average wage ranged between 30 percent and 60 percent. For example, the ratio was 36 percent in both Belarus and Russia. While the incidence of poverty is greatest among families with a large number of children, the amount of child allowances in most transition economies was less than 15 percent of the average wage in 1993 (e.g., Armenia, the former Yugoslav Republic of Macedonia, the Russian Federation). The wage bill as a ratio of GDP is assumed to be 25 percent in this model and lower than the labor share of GDP in many transition economies. The wage bill in this model, however, is shown net of payroll taxes and does not include in-kind or other wages that do not form the payroll tax base.

[14]Expenditures in relation to GDP assumed in the numerical illustration are close to the average of 42 percent of GDP prior to the initiation of reforms in transition economies (see Table 4.2).

Table 4.5. The Overall Budgetary Position
and the Extrabudgetary Fund

	In Rubles	As a Percent of GDP
Budget		
Revenue	7,500	30.0
Expenditure	10,000	40.0
Of which		
Subsidy	2,550	10.2
Child allowance	800	3.2
Overall deficit	2,500	10.0
Extrabudgetary fund		
Revenue[1]	1,114	4.5
Expenditure	1,200	4.8
Deficit	86	0.3
Memorandum items		
Average pension/average wage		
(in percent)	40.0	
Statutory payroll tax (in percent)	33.2	
Effective payroll tax (in percent)	22.3	

[1]Assuming a collection lag of two months and monthly inflation rate of 22.1 percent.

The economy spends 10.2 percent of GDP on subsidies, 5 percent of GDP on pensions, and 3.2 percent of GDP on child allowances.[15] The budgetary deficit is assumed to amount to 10 percent of GDP, whereas the extrabudgetary pension fund has a deficit of 0.5 percent of GDP.

Social Protection Options, Social Safety Nets, and the Budget

As stressed earlier in this chapter, the parameters of the stylized economy are representative of transition economies. Nevertheless, Table 4.6 displays the impact of variations in selected underlying parameters on the general government balance.[16] For instance, a change in the proportion of pensioners and children to the total population from

---

[15]In selected transition economies, the average spending on subsidies and child allowances was 7.0 percent of GDP and 1.4 percent of GDP in 1990 or 1991, respectively (see Table 4.2). Two countries spent 6 percent of GDP or more on child allowances.

[16]The following methodology assumes that the parameters underlying the hypothetical economy do not change significantly with the onset of economic reforms. Should these parameters (e.g., consumption pattern) change, the policy response would also have to be different from that enumerated here. However, the analysis presented in this chapter is essentially of a short-term nature. Most model assumptions are thus expected to hold, even when the economy has begun to reform.

Table 4.6. Summary of Budgetary Impact of Policy and Other Exogenous Developments in a Stylized Economy

	Effects on Fiscal Balance	
	(In rubles)	*(In percent of GDP)*
Prereform social protection expenditures		
Budgetary subsidies	2,550	10.2
Child allowances	800	3.2
Extrabudgetary fund revenue	1,114	4.5
Pension expenditure	1,200	4.8
Effects on the general government fiscal balance of:		
10 percent increase in the poor's consumption of bread, milk, and meat on subsidies	+105	+0.4
Change in proportion of pensioners and children from 30 and 20 percent to 20 and 30 percent on:		
Subsidies	0	0.0
Child allowance expenditures	−400	−1.6
Pension expenditures	+400	+1.6
Increase in unemployment from zero to 10 percent (or a Rub 500 reduction in the economy's wage bill) on:[1]		
Extrabudgetary fund revenue	−112	−0.4
Unemployment benefits	−200	−0.8
Effects on extrabudgetary fund revenue of:		
20 percent reduction in the statutory payroll tax rate, from 33.2 percent to 26.6 percent	−891	−3.6
One-month longer collection lag	−202	−0.8
20 percent reduction in inflation rate from 22.1 to 17.7 percent a month	+84	+0.3

[1]If unemployed workers receive wages without contributing to output (not an unlikely situation in some transition economies), there would be a positive effect of Rub 500 on the fiscal balance, if this leads to reduced budgetary transfers to state enterprises.

30 percent and 20 percent, respectively, to 20 percent and 30 percent would not have any fiscal impact.

The stylized model assumes no *unemployment.* So far, transition economies in the BRO have witnessed low open unemployment. However, since unemployment in these economies is expected to increase in the near term, the stylized model could be adapted to illustrate how the safety net for the unemployed would interact with budgetary policy.

Let us assume 5 of the 50 workers become jobless, implying an unemployment rate of 10 percent. If no change in the average wage were assumed, the wage bill would be reduced from Rub 5,000 to Rub 4,500. The payroll contributions to the extrabudgetary fund for pension payments would be reduced by Rub 112 (0.5 percent of GDP).

Table 4.7. Effect on the Cost of Living of the Nonpoor and the Poor

	Retail Price		CPI for the Nonpoor			CPI for the Poor		
	Old[1]	New[2]	Weight	Old[1]	New[2]	Weight	Old[1]	New[2]
Total	1.000		1.000	1.000	1.300	1.000	1.000	1.525
Food			0.400			0.700		
Bread	1.000	2.000	0.100	0.100	0.200	0.200	0.200	0.400
Milk	1.000	2.000	0.100	0.100	0.200	0.200	0.200	0.400
Meat	1.000	2.000	0.100	0.100	0.200	0.125	0.125	0.250
Other	1.000	1.000	0.100	0.100	0.100	0.175	0.175	0.175
Nonfood	1.000	1.000	0.600	0.600	0.600	0.300	0.300	0.300

[1]Before subsidy removal.
[2]After subsidy removal.

Moreover, unemployment benefits, replacing 40 percent of the average wage, would cost Rub 200 (0.8 percent of GDP). This alone would require the introduction of a 6 percent payroll tax, if this benefit were to be financed wholly from an extrabudgetary fund.

Subsidies

If retail prices were increased to cover the costs of food items for which there are explicit budgetary subsidies, the immediate impact would be to raise the cost of living for the nonpoor by 30 percent, on average, while raising it for the poor by 52.5 percent (Table 4.7). As a means of mitigating the effects on the poor, three policy options could be considered:

(1) Categorically targeted cash transfers equaling the amount of the explicit subsidy, Rub 21, could be given to pensioners and children in lieu of the subsidy.[17] This option would enable the poor to maintain their standards of living. The cash transfer could be delivered through the existing channels as supplements to pensions and child allow-

---

[17]It can be argued that in-kind transfers are superior to cash transfers, since the former assure a minimum provision of essential consumption items to the poor. This argument assumes that an effective administrative mechanism is in place to deliver in-kind goods, which is not always the case. Furthermore, experience has shown that commodities consumed mainly by the poor are difficult to identify. In contrast, the principal advantage of cash transfers is that they can be easily added to the existing benefit amounts without significant additional administrative costs.

ances. The budgetary cost of these transfers would be Rub 1,050 (4.2 percent of GDP) and would only partly offset the reduction in the budgetary cost of subsidies. Therefore, there would be a net budgetary savings of Rub 1,500 (6 percent of GDP).

In the absence of other policy measures, the deficit of the extrabudgetary fund would widen by Rub 630 (2.5 percent of GDP) because of higher pension payments necessitating increased budgetary transfers. However, the consolidated general government (central government and extrabudgetary fund) deficit would be lower than before. The central government could use part of the savings from the subsidy reform to finance the categorically targeted cash transfers and still achieve an improvement of the fiscal position. The composition of budgetary expenditure would also change; part of the savings from the subsidy reform would be offset by increased outlays of Rub 420 (1.7 percent of GDP) on child allowances.

(2) When relative prices change—as would be the case with the subsidy reform—the consumption pattern could be affected depending on price elasticities. In this case, to achieve even greater savings, the value of cash transfers to the poor could be reduced, say, to Rub 15, that is less than full compensation for the price increase.[18] The budgetary savings would amount to Rub 1,800 (7.2 percent of GDP). However, the demand for basic commodities could be expected to be relatively price inelastic, and consequently, their consumption would not change significantly immediately following relative price changes.

(3) The 30 percent increase in the cost of living of the nonpoor (i.e., wage earners in this model) could be too drastic. Wages might have to be raised. However, wage increases fully compensating the removal of the subsidy would achieve no improvement in the fiscal position if all workers were employed in the budgetary sector, although the removal of subsidies accompanied by price liberalization would improve the allocative efficiency. A drastic reduction in the subsidy might not be politically feasible. In these circumstances, subsidies could be phased out over a longer time period—say, two years—or a partial compensation could be given to wage earners. This would mean, however, that the budgetary savings would be smaller.[19]

---

[18]The assumption here is that the base period consumption levels were distorted by subsidies and that a correction in relative prices would reduce consumption of subsidized items.

[19]There are other ways to target benefits. For instance, the food subsidy could be targeted to the population in food-deficit regions, or it could be targeted to elderly or disabled workers, unemployed workers, and families with a large number of children.

Cash Benefits

As noted earlier, the stylized country has a permanent social security institution—the extrabudgetary fund—which is responsible for making *pension* payments. As also noted earlier, the subsidy reform could increase the extrabudgetary fund's deficit if pensioners were compensated for the cut in subsidies. The fund's widening deficit would require new revenue and expenditure measures, especially if the central government were unable to cover the deficit fully through transfers. At the same time, it would be necessary to ensure that pensioners earning minimum pensions were paid an adequate amount to subsist.

Initially, all pensioners were assumed to be poor. In reality, however, this may not be the case. Some pensions may exceed the subsistence income level, and others may be working—supplementing their pensions with wages. When reform-induced changes in real incomes become dominant, the link between social insurance contributions and benefits may have to be broken to place a substantially higher weight on the redistributive aspects of existing social protection arrangements.[20] It also becomes imperative to seek other measures that make the fund's existing expenditures more cost-effective and strengthen its revenue position. Various possibilities can be considered to restructure pension benefits while ensuring adequate protection for minimum pensioners.

First, the pension amount for working pensioners could be reduced. If some 25 percent of the 30 pensioners receiving an average pension worked, a 25 percent reduction in their pensions could save about Rub 75.[21]

Second, the replacement rate (i.e., the ratio between the average pension and the average wage) could be reduced, while the minimum pension is being maintained constant in real terms. This outcome could be secured by an indexation policy that would provide full compensation for price increases to earners of lower pensions but not to those receiving higher pensions. Another possibility would be to reduce explicitly the differential between the minimum and maximum pensions through the two-tiered pension system: the lower tier providing a minimum pension and a higher tier catering to those with rel-

---

[20]The link between contributions and benefits is already weak in many countries because, typically, payroll taxes are not paid by employees.

[21]Pensioners being denied a full pension might decide to stop working. This would reduce the wage bill and the payroll tax revenue to the pension fund, unless the vacated positions were filled by unemployed workers.

atively high wages and longer work history. At the extreme, a flat pension close to a subsistence income level could be provided. Such a system would have the advantage of ensuring a minimum pension to all pensioners at sustainable financial and administrative costs. The main drawback would be that it would uncouple social insurance contributions from pension payments. In the stylized economy, a reduction in the average replacement ratio from 40 percent to 35 percent would reduce pension expenditures by Rub 150, or 0.6 percent of GDP.

Third, because both statutory and actual retirement ages in most of these countries are low by international standards—generally 55 for women and 60 for men, with extensive provisions for early retirement—the possibility of gradually raising the retirement age could also be considered. Increasing the retirement age would be consistent with the current practice in almost all transition economies of permitting retired persons to work—usually on the same job they had prior to reaching the statutory retirement age.[22]

On the revenue side, the following possibilities could be considered. First, the two-month lag in revenue collection could be eliminated or shortened. If the lag were shortened by a month, the revenue position would improve by Rub 246 (or 1 percent of GDP). The impact of this measure on revenue would tend to be greater if the prevailing inflation rate were high.

Second, some transition countries apply lower rates of payroll tax to certain sectors (e.g., agriculture, self-employed) or enterprises with certain types of employees (e.g., the disabled). Further, some payments (e.g., vacation pay) may not be included in the base used for levying payroll taxes. If the payroll tax base were expanded to include all payments to employees and the tax base as a result expanded by 5 percent, additional revenue collected would amount to Rub 56.

Third, the effective yield from payroll taxes is also affected by weak enforcement procedures resulting in widespread evasion of payroll tax liabilities. A system of more frequent audits with increased and stringent penalties (in the form of interest payments on the amount due at real positive interest rates) would further enhance the extrabudgetary fund's revenue position.

In the stylized economy, there are 20 children receiving an *allowance* of Rub 40 each. Although categorically targeted, across-the-board payments to all children extend the benefit to both the poor and the non-

---

[22]This did not hold for the former Yugoslav Republic of Macedonia in 1993–94. In transition economies, the low retirement age took pressure off the labor market as jobs were guaranteed for everyone. Since these guarantees have been eliminated, there seems little rationale for keeping the retirement age low.

poor. A more appropriate option would be to increase the child allowance amount but restrict its award to families who are genuinely poor. However, as noted earlier, it is not always administratively feasible to target benefits based on family incomes. Some imperfect method would, therefore, have to be found to provide adequate income support to families with children.

Since poverty is frequently correlated with the number of children, one possibility would be to eliminate the allowance for the first child, except for the single-parent family. The drawback would be that it would fail to capture working poor families with one child. This would not be a problem if a second-tier safety net existed to fill the gap between the earned income and the minimum subsistence income. The other option would be to eliminate the allowance for relatively older children—say, above the age of 14—on the assumption that caregivers are better placed in their life cycles and that they do not have to withdraw from the labor force to care for the children.

An average unemployment compensation of Rub 40 is high. A reduction in the replacement rate to 30 percent would reduce the cost of unemployment benefits by Rub 50. Income-support programs for the long-term unemployed—in the form of public works—would further add to budgetary expenditures.[23] As unemployment rises, the need for financing unemployment benefits would also rise.

An increase in unemployment could be a result of cuts in either subsidized credits (quasi-fiscal expenditures) or direct budgetary transfers to loss-making enterprises. In these cases, the short-run budgetary analysis should take into account the savings resulting from cuts in credits and transfers; any long-run analysis should take into account the budgetary implications of possible efficiency gains for the economy and the concomitant effects on revenues and expenditures.

Table 4.8 summarizes the short-term budgetary impact of reform options enumerated above. It shows that the maximum budgetary savings occur when generalized consumer subsidies are replaced by targeted cash transfers.

Recent Social Protection Reform Experience

As noted earlier, transition economies began reforming under diverse economic, demographic, and institutional settings. Those con-

---

[23]Public works are not part of social insurance systems and, therefore, should not be financed out of the extrabudgetary fund's revenue.

Table 4.8. Summary of the Budgetary Impact of Social Protection Reform Options in a Stylized Economy

Return Options	Effects on Fiscal Balance	
	(In rubles)	*(In percent of GDP)*
Consumer subsidies		
Replace generalized subsidies with cash transfers targeted to pensioners and children	+1,500	6.0
Subsidies	+2,550	
Cash benefits	−1,050	
Pensioners[1]	−630	
Children	−420	
Extrabudgetary fund operations		
Benefit measures		
Reduce pensions to working pensioners by 25 percent[2]	+75	0.3
Reduce the replacement rate from 40 percent to 35 percent	+150	0.6
Revenue measures		
Broaden the payroll tax base by 5 percent	+56	0.2
Reduce the collection lag by one month	+246	1.0

[1]This would increase the extrabudgetary fund expenditures by the same amount, which could be financed through budgetary transfers. No unemployment is assumed.
[2]Twenty-five percent of the pensioners are assumed to be working for wages.

siderations, together with the speed of price reform and tolerance of open unemployment, influenced the nature and the financing of social safety nets in the reforming countries.

Many transition economies have reduced generalized subsidies and replaced them with different types of cash transfers, resulting in real food price increases. The other measures, introduced with a lag, often included cuts in transfers to public enterprises, which have forced the particularly inefficient ones to reduce production and employment. The restructuring and reform of state-owned enterprises have also contributed to unemployment. Eastern European transition economies have already experienced large increases in open unemployment—to more than 10 percent of the labor force. Others, however, have pursued policies to keep unemployment hidden; at the end of 1993, the average rate of registered unemployment in most BRO states was less than 2–3 percent.

Two major factors have been responsible for low open unemployment in the BRO states. Budgetary transfers and subsidized central bank credits have facilitated labor hoarding by enterprises. Moreover, inadequate unemployment benefits have made it difficult for an employee to give up a job that provides not only a wage but crucial nonwage benefits (e.g., health services). As a result, there has been large-scale underemployment, with a rising proportion of workers on short working days or on unpaid leave. In the presence of declining output, this phenomenon has reduced average labor productivity. In some countries (e.g., Romania), attempts have been made to reduce unemployment through early retirement schemes, with questionable fiscal and labor market consequences.

In many transition economies, exogenous shocks and loose economic policies have accompanied pricing reforms, aggravating the decline in living standards. These exogenous shocks ranged from increases in the prices of imported oil (Armenia, Belarus, and Ukraine) to natural disasters (the Kyrgyz Republic), civil strife (Georgia), imposition of trade embargoes (Hungary, former Yugoslav Republic of Macedonia, and Romania), and the disruption of interstate trade (all countries of the Council for Mutual Economic Assistance, BRO, and the former Yugoslavia). Loose financial policies—reflected in large fiscal deficits and high rates of credit expansion—caused prices to rise rapidly in many countries.

Reform measures, together with a worsening macroeconomic position, have had significant effects on the living standards of various population groups. It is not easy, however, to estimate these effects and assess social safety net needs, particularly since formal-sector activities have been declining, and informal-sector activities increasing. Recent household expenditure surveys (in the Kyrgyz Republic, Poland, and the Russian Federation) have indicated that, despite cuts in officially reported real incomes, the consumption of basic food items has not declined significantly or even increased, either because households have reduced nonfood expenditures drastically or because increases in informal sector incomes have offset the decline in formal sector incomes.[24]

Overall Mix of Subsidies and Cash Benefits

During 1990–93, most countries other than the Baltics, Russia, and other former Soviet Union countries listed in Table 4.2 reduced subsidies as a percent of GDP, with cuts ranging between 1.2 percent of GDP (Estonia) and 13 percent of GDP (Albania) and increased outlays on cash benefits, with increases ranging from 0.9 percent of GDP (Bulgaria, former Yugoslav Republic of Macedonia) to 8.2 percent of

---

[24]Recent reports from the Statistical Committee of the Russian Federation note that the official estimates of output may be understated by as much as 40 percent because of informal sector activity.

GDP (Poland). In many countries in this group, there was a reduction in the overall spending on social protection. There were, however, two exceptions: Romania, which has reduced both subsidies and cash benefits as a proportion of GDP, and Poland, which has increased overall social protection expenditures in relation to GDP.

BRO states have pursued a variety of strategies. Although most have reduced subsidies to below the 10 percent of GDP level that they registered in 1988, some have maintained persistently high levels of subsidies. For example, in 1993, subsidy expenditures were 8.4 percent of GDP in Armenia, 14.3 percent of GDP in Belarus, 33.3 percent of GDP in Georgia, 12.1 percent of GDP in Ukraine, and 7.3 percent of GDP in Uzbekistan.

Subsidies

As noted earlier, the initial reform measures included freeing prices of essential goods and services. For example, in early 1992, a number of BRO states raised the prices of many essential goods and services (e.g., bread, sugar, electricity, and gas) by a factor of between 3 and 6 (Kazakhstan, the Russian Federation, and Ukraine). Non-BRO European and Asian transition economies had also freed prices at the outset of the reform process (Poland, the Czech and Slovak Republics, Romania, and Lao People's Democratic Republic). Some countries were quicker in initiating liberalization of prices (Albania and Lithuania), whereas others retained some consumer subsidies (Armenia, Georgia, Romania, and Ukraine).

Some countries totally eliminated consumer subsidies (Estonia, Latvia, and the former Yugoslav Republic of Macedonia) or succeeded in containing these subsidies in a relatively short period of time (Albania, Bulgaria, and Poland), mitigating any adverse social consequences by increasing wages and various cash benefits for pensioners, children, and the unemployed. Others have replaced generalized subsidies with limited cash transfers to certain population groups (Albania, the Kyrgyz Republic, Kazakhstan, and Moldova). Some have introduced coupon schemes for a few essential commodities (milk, sugar, and vegetable oil) other than bread to provide limited quantities of these goods at subsidized prices to the population (Uzbekistan). While most transition economies have kept subsidy expenditures under the control of the central government, countries with decentralized systems of decision making have shifted subsidy costs to local governments (Poland and the Russian Federation).

The constraints on phasing out subsidies have been both political and administrative. Replacing generalized subsidies with subsidies targeted to vulnerable groups was difficult as a large number of political-ly influential middle- and upper-class income groups faced income losses. The bread subsidy was a particularly sensitive issue, especially in central Asian former Soviet Union states. Even in countries that reduced nonbread subsidies substantially, significant bread subsidies remained until recently (Armenia in 1994). The administrative require-ments for targeting, for example, through coupon schemes, have also posed a substantial problem. Countries have experienced leakages of the subsidized goods distributed through the coupon schemes. Even those countries that had introduced coupons for nonbread commodi-ties appeared reluctant to expand the system to include bread.

Replacing generalized subsidies with limited cash transfers to vul-nerable groups appears to be a promising approach to phasing out sub-sidies. Even in this case, however, there are a number of problems. For example, the pressure for a general wage increase to replace the lost income transfer can be intense. In many BRO countries, wages and var-ious cash benefits are often determined as multiples of the minimum wage. Therefore, an increase in the minimum wage, following the removal of subsidies and the consequent increase in prices, could imply no change in real wages and cash benefits—and a limited improvement in the fiscal position.

Even countries that have completely eliminated food subsidies have generally retained limited subsidies for selected services (e.g., a trans-portation subsidy in Estonia, at a cost of 1.2 percent of GDP in 1993; and a heating allowance for nonworking pensioners in Latvia, at a cost of 1.2 percent of GDP in 1993, which was borne by the Social Insurance Fund).

Although declining in most transition economies, producer subsi-dies to industrial enterprises and to agriculture continue to be provid-ed (former Yugoslav Republic of Macedonia, Romania, and the Russian Federation), often in an implicit form (Uzbekistan), with adverse effects on production efficiency and consumption decisions, and on the environment (e.g., by the increased use of subsidized fertilizers).

Cash Benefits

As subsidies for major goods and services consumed are phased out, cash benefits (mainly pensions, child allowances, and unemployment benefits) are becoming increasingly important instruments of social safety nets. At the same time, the increasing outlays on cash benefits have strained the financial positions of the budget and extrabudgetary funds, requiring a high rate of payroll contributions. The reform of cash benefits itself has therefore become an important issue. A major dilemma in this context has been the extent to which the provision of pensions and unemployment benefits should be based on social insurance principles.

In general, countries have continued to link pension payments to work history, although the dispersion between the highest and the lowest pension has narrowed as a result of the indexation mechanism (Armenia, the Russian Federation, and Ukraine). Only a few countries have adopted flat-rate pensions in the first years of transition (for non-working pensioners), but have now decided to link pensions to the work history of the beneficiary and the average wage growth in the economy (Latvia). Most countries, as yet, do not tax or reduce the pension income of working pensioners. In a few countries, working pensioners have not been given cash compensation when prices of basic goods (e.g., bread) were freed (Azerbaijan and Georgia). Some countries have moved to raise the statutory retirement ages for both men and women (former Yugoslav Republic of Macedonia and Romania), although these still remain below Western retirement ages. Many have also tightened early-retirement provisions (Albania, former Yugoslav Republic of Macedonia, and Poland).

Some tightening of eligibility requirements for unemployment compensation has also taken place to prevent misuse of the benefit (e.g., Estonia, where in addition to the requirement of a six-month work history, the applicant has to participate in public relief works for 10 days during a one-month period). Similarly, the duration of unemployment benefits has been shortened to obviate job search disincentives (Albania, former Yugoslav Republic of Macedonia, Poland, and Romania). This has been accompanied by a financial and administrative strengthening of social assistance programs (Albania and former Yugoslav Republic of Macedonia). However, the average unemployment benefit in relation to the prevailing wage remains low in many countries, creating disincentives for the unemployed to register (Armenia, the Russian Federation, and Estonia).

Child allowances have been maintained because families with children are considered to be vulnerable. In this respect, child allowances are considered targeted transfers. Child allowances are a particularly important element of the social safety net in many central Asian former Soviet Union states with a high child dependency ratio. There is widespread recognition, however, that not all families with children are vulnerable. Therefore, means testing of child allowances is also being attempted, although only notionally, to reduce the cost to the budget (the Kyrgyz Republic and former Yugoslav Republic of Macedonia). However, these countries face the usual difficulties of measuring with accuracy the income and assets of targeted families.

Countries with a very young population and with a high birth rate (Uzbekistan) face the conflicting pressures between child allowances as a safety net and as an incentive to have large families.

Attempts are under way in some countries to institute income support programs for individuals who fall below the poverty threshold (the Russian Federation). Other countries are either running this type of program relatively successfully (former Yugoslav Republic of Macedonia) or are planning to implement one soon (Estonia). Some countries (Albania, Latvia, and Poland) are also using the social assistance programs to provide income support to the long-term unemployed.

Summary and Conclusions

In the short term, social safety nets are meant to protect the vulnerable from the negative effects of reform measures. In this way, they enhance the sustainability and acceptability of reform programs. Using a stylized model and drawing on experiences of economies currently undergoing transition, this chapter has highlighted the interaction between social safety nets and the budget. One message that emerges is that increasing the cost-effectiveness of social safety net expenditures is not only a social policy issue but also an important consideration for macroeconomic stability and sustainability.

The other important message that emerges from the numerical example is that, in the short term, improved targeting of subsidies provides the maximum budgetary savings. For instance, in the stylized economy, the bulk of the estimated expenditure savings are a result of the improved targeting of the generalized subsidies. The numerical example also shows that significant financial savings are feasible from reforming pensions while improving their adequacy. Although the short-term impact of some measures (such as the raising of retirement ages) is relatively small, it can be quite significant over a period of time.

There has been some discussion that strengthening social safety nets in transition economies would require new foreign financing. The above analysis shows that this is not necessarily true, since possibilities exist for reducing the cost of ongoing programs and raising additional revenues without increasing the payroll tax.

This chapter has enumerated various options for reforming social safety net expenditures. Unfortunately, the survey of country experiences showed that, with the exception of limited rationalization of commodity subsidies, the success to date in improving the cost-effectiveness of other elements of safety nets has been rather limited. This could be partly because many countries, particularly in the BRO, are still in the initial stages of transition. Political considerations, too, have played a role—the individuals likely to lose benefits have prevented reforms from taking place.

What lessons can be drawn from the preceding analysis to ensure that the twin objectives of shielding the poor and ensuring fiscal sustainability are met in transition economies that are continuing with the reform process?

First, generalized commodity subsidies would have to be replaced with subsidies or cash transfers that are narrowly targeted to the truly needy. This would not only increase the efficiency of resource use but also improve the overall fiscal position. Also discussed have been various options that could be adopted, depending on administrative and other considerations. It appears that countries that reformed subsidies quickly have also succeeded in restraining their fiscal deficits.

Second, the rationalization of existing social protection mechanisms is critical. In the initial stages of reform, it is important to provide social protection to the population groups considered the most vulnerable. This means that in many cases the minimum benefit should be maintained at a subsistence level, while ensuring that the average benefit is financially sustainable. The net result could be a compressed or flat benefit structure, which—at least in the short term—breaks the link between contributions and benefits.

Third, structural reforms of cash benefits would also have to be implemented quickly to improve their financial viability. Unless retirement ages were raised and early pensions considerably tightened, the pressure on cash benefit expenditures would persist.

Fourth, much of the focus of policymakers in many transition economies has been on tailoring expenditures to available revenues. This concentration on the benefit side can lead to a neglect of the possibilities of increasing revenue without raising the statutory payroll tax rates. Steps to increase payroll tax compliance (and, therefore, the effective payroll tax rate), including, for example, reducing or eliminating exemptions and instituting real positive interest rates on unpaid obligations, would yield increased revenue receipts while removing distortions. Some institutional improvements, such as reducing or eliminating the lags in the transfer of the payroll tax to accounts of the benefit-disbursing agency and holding surplus funds in interest-bearing accounts, would also strengthen the financial position of the extrabudgetary funds that provide these benefits.

Finally, open unemployment in most transition economies has thus far been relatively low. As economic reforms gather momentum, the number of individuals who become openly unemployed—in contrast with the disguised unemployed—would be expected to rise. This would be a necessary condition for restructuring the enterprise sector in these countries. But a major consequence of increased unemployment is that the short-term need for social safety net expenditures would increase. Under conditions of a tight fiscal position, it would be necessary to improve the cost-effectiveness of existing social safety net expenditures to meet the contingency of higher unemployment.

Appendix
Average Consumption Per Person in Selected Transition Economies

	Lowest Two Income Deciles	Overall Population
	(In percent of total)	
Composition of household expenditures		
Lao People's Dem. Rep.[1]		
Food	42.9	42.2
Own produce	29.8	14.6
Clothing	3.1	3.6
Other	24.2	39.6
Romania[2]		
Food	31.0	32.6
Own produce	37.8	24.9
Clothing	10.4	12.2
Other	20.8	30.3
Russian Federation[3]		
Food[4]	79.3	50.2
Nonfood	17.5	46.8
Alcoholic beverages	3.2	3.0
	(In kilograms a month)	
Per capita household food consumption[5]		
Romania		
Bread and bread products	10.3	11.4
Corn flour	2.8	1.9
Meat and meat products	3.3	4.7
Beans	0.5	0.5
Potatoes	3.2	3.9
Russian Federation		
Bread products[6]	10.1	9.2
Potatoes	9.3	9.7
Meat and meat products	3.2	5.1
Milk	23.2	26.5

Sources: Authors' estimates, based on data provided by the authorities.
[1]Data are for urban households based on 1992–93 household expenditure survey.
[2]1992 data.
[3]1993 data.
[4]Household headed by a pensioner.
[5]Data on per capita food consumption are not available for Lao People's Democratic Republic.
[6]Lowest decile of the population.

References

Ahmad, Ehtisham, and Ke-young Chu, 1993, "Russian Federation—Economic Reform and Policy Options for Social Protection," in *Transition to Market: Studies in Fiscal Reform,* ed. by Vito Tanzi (Washington: International Monetary Fund).

Ahmad, Ehtisham, and others, eds., 1991, *Social Security in Developing Countries* (Oxford: Clarendon Press).

Atkinson, A.B., 1992, "The Western Experience with Social Safety Nets," Welfare State Programme Discussion Paper No. 80 (London: Suntory-Toyota International Economic and Related Disciplines).

Chu, Ke-young, and Sanjeev Gupta, 1993, "Protecting the Poor: Social Safety Nets During Transition," *Finance & Development,* Vol. 30 (June), pp. 24–27.

Fiscal Affairs Department, 1986, *Fund-Supported Programs, Fiscal Policy, and Income Distribution,* IMF Occasional Paper No. 46 (Washington: International Monetary Fund).

Grosh, M.E., 1995, "Towards Quantifying the Trade-Off: Administrative Costs and Incidence in Targeted Programs in Latin America," in *Public Spending and the Poor,* ed. by Dominique van de Walle and Kimberly Nead (Washington: World Bank).

Gupta, Sanjeev, and Robert Hagemann, 1994, "Social Protection During Russia's Economic Transformation," *Finance & Development,* Vol. 31 (December), pp. 14–17.

Halter, William A., and Richard Hemming, 1987, "The Impact of Demographic Change on Social Security Financing," *Staff Papers,* International Monetary Fund, Vol. 34 (September), pp. 471–502.

Heller, Peter S., A. Lans Bovenberg, Thanos Catsambas, Ke-young Chu, and Parthasarathi Shome, 1988, *The Implications of Fund-Supported Adjustment Programs for Poverty: Experiences in Selected Countries,* IMF Occasional Paper No. 58 (Washington: International Monetary Fund).

Kopits, George, 1992, "Social Security," in *Fiscal Policies in Economies in Transition,* ed. by Vito Tanzi (Washington: International Monetary Fund), pp. 291–311.

Mackenzie, G.A., 1988, "Social Security Issues in Developing Countries: The Latin American Experience," *Staff Papers,* International Monetary Fund, Vol. 35 (September), pp. 496–522.

Milanovic, Branko, 1992, "Distributional Impact of Cash and In-Kind Transfers in Eastern Europe and Russia," Research Paper Series No. 9 (Washington: World Bank, June).

Tanzi, Vito, 1978, "Inflation, Real Tax Revenue, and the Case for Inflationary Finance: Theory with an Application to Argentina," *Staff Papers,* International Monetary Fund, Vol. 25 (September), pp. 417–51.

———, 1987, "Quantitative Characteristics of the Tax Systems of Developing Countries," in *The Theory of Taxation for Developing Countries,* ed. by David M.G. Newbery and Nicholas Herbert Stern (New York: Oxford University Press for the World Bank).

———, ed., 1992, *Fiscal Policies in Economies in Transition* (Washington: International Monetary Fund).

———, ed., 1993, *Transition to Market: Studies in Fiscal Reform* (Washington: International Monetary Fund).

5

Social Protection in Transition Countries: Emerging Issues

Ke-young Chu and Sanjeev Gupta

The former centrally planned countries undergoing economic transition have experienced a sharp decline in output, income, and employment in recent years. This has resulted in severe hardships for many households, particularly those whose members include the elderly, young children, or the unemployed. The plight of these households has been further aggravated by extraordinarily high rates of inflation stemming partly from lax financial policies.

Although the output decline has been or is expected to be reversed in some countries, and inflation has been somewhat tamed, transition countries are now facing the challenge of securing adequate resources for social protection. Governments in these countries are confronted with severe financial and administrative constraints. While the shrinking formal sector is aggravating the difficulties governments face in mobilizing resources, the expanding informal sector is making it increasingly hard for governments to identify the poor and to administer targeted social protection programs. Furthermore, the provision of social benefits has become complicated as they cannot necessarily be provided through the place of employment. These developments have important implications for the design and financing of social protection programs for the transition.

Notes: Originally issued as IMF Paper on Policy Analysis and Assessment 96/5 (Washington: International Monetary Fund, May 1996). Also published in *MOCT-MOST*, Vol. 6 (Kluwer Academic Publishers, 1996), pp. 107–123.

The authors wish to thank Trevor Alleyne, Benedict Clements, Elliott Harris, Insu Kim, Henri Lorie, Georgiy Markosov, Edgardo Ruggiero, Jerald Schiff, and Ludger Schuknecht for helpful comments. They are also thankful to Tarja Papavassiliou for computational assistance.

This paper analyzes social protection issues concerning subsidies, pensions, unemployment, and other social benefits in transition countries, drawing on the recent experiences of ten of them: two Baltic countries (Estonia and Latvia), five other countries of the former Soviet Union (Armenia, the Kyrgyz Republic, the Russian Federation, Tajikistan, and Ukraine), and three eastern European countries (Albania, the former Yugoslav Republic of Macedonia, and Poland).[1] The focus of the analysis is on the social protection implications of the weakening financial and administrative capacity of these countries.

Recent Economic and Social Developments

The ten sample countries have diverse economic and social conditions. Some countries introduced economic reforms early (those in Eastern Europe) while others embarked on reforms only recently (those in the former Soviet Union). The Baltic countries are more advanced than Russia and other former countries of the Soviet Union in implementing economic reforms. Despite some dissimilarities in the ten countries, some broad common features can be discerned from the economic and social indicators displayed in Tables 5.1 and 5.2.[2]

Prior to the onset of reforms, in all ten countries, governments controlled virtually all prices and wages; guaranteed employment for all, at least in principle; and provided universal public pensions, child allowances, and other benefits for sickness, maternity, and childbirth. Governments did not have an explicit estimate of the economic costs of these benefits.[3] In general, consumer subsidies were financed partly through general taxation and partly through implicit taxation of producers (suppressed producer prices), while pensions, sickness, maternity, and childbirth benefits were financed through payroll taxes.

With the introduction of market-oriented reforms and the need for macroeconomic stabilization, governments faced more binding resource constraints, which were aggravated by the reduction in output and income. They sought to reduce the budgetary burden of subsidies by increasing the prices of the subsidized goods and services while mitigating the adverse effects of these price increases on household budgets through cash supplements to wages, pensions, and child

---

[1]The paper does not discuss health and education expenditures.

[2]Also see IMF (1995) for similar trends in other Eastern European and other former Soviet Union countries.

[3]This is because controls on all prices and wages meant that the cost estimates in the state budgets and extrabudgetary social funds were grossly distorted.

Table 5.1. Economic and Social Indicators in Selected Transition Countries

	Real GDP Growth			Inflation, Annual Average (In percent)			Life Expectancy at Birth	Calorie Consumption Per Capita			Food Consumption[1]		
	1993	1994	1995	1993	1994	1995	1993	1991	1993	1994	1991	1993	1994
Baltic countries													
Estonia	−5.5	−0.1	3.0	89	48	29	69	...	...	...	...	31.9	29.2
Latvia	−16.1	2.2	0.0	109	36	25	69	2,496	2,375	2,293	42.5	50.5	51.5
Russia and other former Soviet Union countries													
Armenia	−14.8	5.3	...	3,732	5,273	177	73	2,210	1,690	...	56.2	71.8	...
Kyrgyz Republic	−15.5	−20.1	1.3	1,209	278	43	69	2,527	2,552	2,427	38.5	46.3	46.8
Russian Federation	−12.0	−15.0	−4.0	896	302	190	68	...	...	...	...	...	...
Tajikistan	−11.0	−21.5	−12.5	2,195	350	610	70	3,445	2,868	2,895	...	...	...
Ukraine	−14.2	−22.9	−11.8	4,735	891	376	69	...	...	...	43.8	54.5	64.7
Eastern Europe													
Albania	9.6	9.4	8.6	85	23	8	72	3,115[2]	...	2,550	...	78.8	72
Macedonia, former Yugoslav Republic of[3]	−8.4	−4.0	−4.3	230	55	9	72	...	...	...	...	...	...
Poland	3.8	6.0	6.5	35	32	28	71	2,767	3,126	...	45.8	44.4	42.8

Sources: *Poverty, Children and Policy: Responses for a Bright Future*, Regional Monitoring Report No. 3, UNICEF (Florence, 1995); World Bank, *World Population Projections* (Washington, 1995); World Bank, Social Indicators of Development (Washington, 1995); and IMF staff estimates based on data provided by the authorities.
[1]Percent of consumption expenditure spent on food.
[2]The figure is for 1990.
[3]Revenue, expenditure, and social protection outlays as percent of GSP (Gross social product).

Table 5.2. Unemployment, Migration, and Demographics in Selected Transition Countries

	Registered Unemployment		Net External Migration		Percent of Population	
					Under 15	Over 55
	1993	1994	1993	1994	1994	1994
	(In percent)		*(In thousands)*			
Baltic countries						
Estonia	1.9	1.5	–13.8	–7.7	21.4	23.3
Latvia	5.8	6.6	–27.9	–18.8	20.9	24.9
Russia and other former Soviet Union countries						
Armenia	4.4	4.9	–20.9	–19.1	29.5	15.5
Kyrgyz Republic	1.7	4.1	. . .	. . .	37.9	11.5
Russian Federation	1.5	2.5	430.1	810.0	21.8	22.5
Tajikistan	1.2	1.5	. . .	. . .	44.5	8.5
Ukraine	0.3	0.4	50.0	–144.0	20.6	25.7
Eastern Europe						
Albania	22.3	19.2	. . .	. . .	31.9	12.4
Macedonia, former Yugoslav Republic of	20.0	18.7	. . .	. . .	24.5	17.5
Poland	14.9	16.5	–15.4	–19.0	23.5	20.2

Sources: *Poverty, Children and Policy: Responses for a Bright Future,* Regional Monitoring Report No. 3, UNICEF (Florence, 1995); World Bank, *World Population Projections* (Washington, 1995); World Bank, Social Indicators of Development (Washington, 1995); and IMF staff estimates based on data provided by the authorities.

allowances. Open unemployment has so far been largely suppressed, in part by providing only token unemployment benefits. But the high old-age or child dependency ratios have required these governments to set aside substantial resources for pensions or child allowances and limited the proportion of the population that contributed to payroll taxes. Estonia, Latvia, Poland, the Russian Federation, and Ukraine have a high proportion of the population above 55 years of age (between 20 percent and 26 percent). The Kyrgyz Republic and Tajikistan have a high proportion of the population below 15 years of age (around 40 percent).

Transition countries have reduced, but still maintain, budgetary subsidies for energy products, housing, and other communal and transportation services. As revenues for social funds have dwindled, governments have reduced average benefits more than minimum benefits. As a result, pension benefits have become largely flat, and have lost their envisaged link with recipients' earnings histories. In some countries, governments have substantial arrears in the payment of social benefits. Certain aspects of these benefits, nevertheless, remain generous, with loose eligibility criteria. For instance, in many countries, workers do not have to retire from a job upon reaching the statutory retirement age but can continue working; working pensioners continue to receive full pensions while receiving a salary and employer-provided benefits for health, education, and housing; the statutory retirement age is low by international standards; and many categories of workers can retire early. Individuals receive credit for pensions even while studying or staying home to take care of children. Workers are able to take subsidized vacations, and their sick leave benefits are financed out of payroll taxes, a situation that creates an incentive for abuse.

Output, Prices, and Living Standards

In 1994, transition countries continued to record a large decline in output. In six of the sample countries, the output decline accelerated. Only four registered an increase in output: Armenia and Latvia, for the first time since the beginning of market-oriented reforms, and Albania and Poland, which continued to bear the fruits of early reform efforts. In 1995, the output decline slowed in three countries, and two that experienced a decline in real GDP in 1994 began to grow. Inflation continued to persist, although a few countries have reduced inflation somewhat through tight financial policies. In 1993, five countries (Armenia, the Kyrgyz Republic, the Russian Federation, Tajikistan, and Ukraine) had an annual average inflation of about 1,000 percent or above; by 1994, the number of such countries declined to two. In 1995, there was a reduction in inflation in all countries, with the exception of Tajikistan.

The output decline together with the elimination of consumer subsidies on food items has reduced the real income of households. As a result, households are devoting an increasing share of their income to food (Armenia, Latvia, the Russian Federation, and Ukraine). In a few countries the caloric intake per capita fell (Latvia and the Russian Federation). Only two countries experienced a decline in the share of household income allocated to food consumption (Albania and Poland).

Population Movements

Many transition countries are suffering from the consequences of adverse political and social developments. Many have lost a significant proportion of their active population through emigration (Armenia,

Estonia, Latvia, Poland, and Ukraine) while others have been confronted with a large influx of refugees or a displacement of persons (the Russian Federation and Tajikistan) (Table 5.2). Armenia lost at least 350,000 mostly working-age persons (9.3 percent of the population) by the end of 1993, and another 200,000 persons (5.3 percent of the population) were displaced because of the conflict with Azerbaijan. Ukraine lost 144,000 persons (0.3 percent of the population) through emigration in 1994. Tajikistan has had a large share of the population displaced by civil strife. Since 1992, the Russian Federation has experienced a large influx of ethnic Russians from other republics. However, these official estimates of population migration are most likely underestimations of the actual movements of the population in these countries.

Informal Sector

Shrinking employment opportunities in the formal sector and pervasive government regulations are boosting informal sector activities. The migration of labor has increased private transfers between members of families. That informal sector activities and private transfers are now important is clear from household surveys, which point to the declining share of wages and government cash benefits in average household income. Table 5.3 displays the income structure of households in Armenia in 1993–94. In the first six months of 1994, formal sector wages and government cash benefits constituted less than 30 percent of average household income, with the remainder originating from other sources, such as informal sector activities and financial assistance received from relatives and friends. By contrast, the share of formal sector wages and government cash benefits in household income averaged 40 percent in 1993.[4] A similar pattern emerges for Ukraine, where a household expenditure survey for 1995 indicates that reported incomes on average were less than half of reported expenditures, indicating a large share of informal sector incomes and private transfers in supporting household expenditures.

---

[4]The financial assistance received from friends and relatives in Table 5.3 does not capture direct private transfers and humanitarian commodity assistance received from abroad, because households were not required to report incomes from these sources. Armenian households received an annual average income transfer of $210 per household in the form of commodity assistance in 1994, distributed by government agencies as well as by private and religious charities. In addition, an average household received private direct transfers of $40 from abroad. These transfers were large in relation to average monthly wages or cash benefits of less than $10.

Table 5.3. Income Structure of an Average Household in Armenia
(In percent)

	1993		1994	
	Average	First quarter	First quarter	First six months
Salaries and stipends	31.8	43.1	24.7	21.7
Other income	7.7	15.1	5.5	5.4
Of which				
Pensions	4.3	8.1	3.0	2.9
Stipends	0.3	0.5	0.1	0.1
Allowances, etc.	3.0	6.2	2.3	2.4
Remaining income[1]	60.5	41.8	69.8	72.9
Total cash income	100.0	100.0	100.0	100.0

Source: Armenian national authorities.
[1]Includes sale of services, informal sector activity, rents, and assistance received from friends and relatives; does not include humanitarian commodity assistance from abroad.

Tax System and Administration

Transition countries are maintaining some old taxes (payroll taxes) as well as introducing some new taxes (personal income tax and VAT). Statutory tax rates are high, and tax bases tend to be narrow, partly because of the informal sector activity. High statutory tax rates, combined with weak administration, have resulted in tax evasion and a buildup of tax arrears. For example, the combined statutory rate of payroll taxes ranges between 37 percent (the Russian Federation) and 52 percent (Ukraine). The capacity of transition countries to administer old taxes is fragile and has been severely weakened by an expansion of informal sector activities. Their capacity to administer new taxes is at an infant stage. Effective tax rates in these countries are, thus, only a fraction of the statutory rates.

Implications for Social Protection

Emerging Social Protection Issues

These developments have important implications for social protection. The increase in unemployment and underemployment and the reduction in real wages have boosted the number of households in need. The expansion of informal sector activities has reduced the number of taxpayers and made it more difficult for the government to identify the poor.

The decline in official incomes overstates the fall in living standards, making it harder to measure the number of households and individuals below a universally accepted poverty line. Single pensioners living alone, single parents, families with many children, individuals earning low or minimum wages, and unemployed persons not working in the formal sector are among the population groups that may have fallen below the poverty line in many of these countries. This, however, does not necessarily imply that the aggregate needs for social protection have increased; as argued here, there is ample scope for improving the targeting of existing benefits and using the resulting savings for shielding the truly vulnerable.

Unemployment and Underemployment

The collapse of output has drastically reduced the demand for labor. This reduced demand has increased open unemployment in some countries and underemployment in others. In 1993–94, registered unemployment ranged between 0.3 percent of the labor force in Ukraine, 2.5 percent in the Russian Federation, and 22.3 percent in Albania.[5] The data on registered unemployment mask the social impact of the decline in output and employment. Since the onset of reform in these countries, there has been a continuous decline in total employment. In the Russian Federation, total "official" employment, which stood at around 74 million in 1991, declined to 66.9 million by 1995 (Table 5.4). In Ukraine, total employment declined from around 25 million in 1991 to 22 million by the end of 1995. The workers who have "vanished" from the official employment statistics have either dropped out of the labor force, become unemployed, or entered the informal sector. For instance, it is likely that a significant proportion of the 6.7 million "vanished workers" in the Russian Federation have joined the informal sector.

At the same time, enterprises have been hoarding labor, which is reflected in the growing number of workers put on either short working days, partial pay, or unpaid leave. The incentive for workers to stay with their current employer, despite little or no monetary compensation, has stemmed both from the attraction of employer-provided housing, education, and health benefits and from the inadequacy of unemployment benefits. The incentive for employers to hoard labor has arisen from their legal obligation of granting severance pay and may also have arisen from the belief that the current sit-

---

[5]In early 1996, it increased to 3.3 percent in the Russian Federation.

Table 5.4. Trends in Employment in Transition Countries
(In thousands of persons)

	1991	1992	1993	1994	1995
Baltic countries					
Estonia	799	748	681	665	660
Latvia	1,397	1,350	1,265	1,205	1,191
Russia and other former Soviet Union countries					
Armenia	1,672	1,578	1,543	1,500	1,455
Kyrgyz Republic					
Russian Federation	73,600	72,300	71,000	69,600	66,903
Tajikistan	1,971	1,909	1,850	1,901	1,940
Ukraine	24,977	24,420	23,845	23,316	22,200
Eastern Europe					
Albania	1,400	1,021	954	1,083	1,144
Macedonia, former Yugoslav Republic of	737	755	762	763	747
Poland	16,300	15,400	15,000	14,800	15,126

Source: IMF staff estimates based on data provided by the authorities.

uation is transitory.[6] In a way, this is a reflection of the soft budget constraint facing many state enterprises. During 1993, the average number of days of administrative leave per worker in the Russian Federation rose from 14 days to around 23 days. In Ukraine, the number of workers on administrative leave was 2 million (8 percent of employment) in 1995; the number of workers receiving partial wage payments was 1 million.

An increasing number of individuals who are not employed in the formal sector or are not registered as unemployed are excluded from the provision of social benefits. In Ukraine, the unregistered unemployed are ineligible for the newly introduced housing subsidies and child allowances. While the rationale behind this policy appears to be that all individuals who are not registered as unemployed must be working in the informal sector, there is evidence that registration by the unemployed is not easy.

The difficulty in targeting benefits to those working in the informal sector is illustrated by the experience of the former Yugoslav Republic of Macedonia, where around 19 percent of the workforce (175,000) was

---

[6]In the Russian Federation and Ukraine, there is a requirement that the employer give the worker three months' notice prior to dismissal. There is currently a move in Ukraine to eliminate this requirement. In the former Yugoslav Republic of Macedonia, laid-off workers received six months' notice of termination in 1994.

registered as unemployed in 1993. Only 10 percent of the registered unemployed—mostly from bankrupt firms—received unemployment benefits. A significant proportion of the remaining registered unemployed were believed to be working in the informal sector. However, registration provided such workers with the benefit of health insurance—effectively supplementing their earnings. Many had emigrated to other countries for work because the unemployed were required to register only every six months; many returned to the country only when they required medical attention.

Financial Constraints

Social protection outlays in transition countries are coming under increasing financial pressure (Table 5.5). While these countries have eliminated or reduced generalized consumer subsidies on basic food items, the expenditure reduction in general has been achieved not through an improvement of expenditure efficiency and prioritization but through ad hoc cash rationing.

An important factor behind the expenditure squeeze in these countries has been weak revenue performance. Despite the implementation of discretionary revenue measures from time to time, the revenue-to-GDP ratio has declined for many countries, reflecting in part a significantly sharper fall in payroll taxes, which finance major social programs. The growth of the informal sector, payment of partial wages, and the phenomenon of unpaid leave have contributed to the narrowing of the revenue base. In addition, weaknesses in tax administration have drastically reduced tax compliance and effective tax yields. High statutory payroll tax rates are creating incentives for employers to shift some components of labor compensation out of the wage fund, which forms the payroll tax base. Labor payments have been made in-kind or even in the form of shares of enterprises (Ukraine). Differential rates or exemptions for different types of workers (self-employed, agricultural, and the handicapped) have further narrowed the tax base (the Russian Federation).[7]

Many transition countries had a relatively high old-age dependency ratio at the start of market reform (the former Yugoslav Republic of Macedonia, the Russian Federation, and Ukraine). The increase in unemployment, growth in informal sector activities, emigration of workers, and low retirement age have further reduced the number of

---

[7]For a discussion of social protection issues in the Russian Federation, see Gupta and Hagemann (1994); also reprinted as Chapter 13 in this volume.

Table 5.5. Social Protection Outlays
in Selected Transition Countries

	Total Budgetary Revenue[1]			Total Budgetary Expenditure[1]			Total Social Protection Outlays[2]		
	1992	1993	1994	1992	1993	1994	1992	1993	1994
				(As percent of GDP)					
Baltic countries									
Estonia	33.3	39.9	41.2	33.6	40.6	38.3	9.7	12.0	11.2
Latvia[3]	28.2	36.4	35.5	28.2	35.3	38.2	9.6	14.2	16.0
Russia and othe former Soviet Union countries									
Armenia[3]	20.8	20.8	15.8	51.7	82.9	44.1	23.2	23.7	15.8
Kyrgyz Republic	16.5	15.2	15.3	33.9	36.8	28.1	. . .	18.9	11.9
Russian Federation	29.4	28.7	24.5	38.9	34.8	35.1	10.0	8.5	8.3
Tajikistan[3]	26.6	27.1	15.2	57.8	52.1	26.5	13.9	17.5	10.9
Ukraine[3]	44.0	43.7	39.9	73.3	55.5	44.9	17.6	18.0	18.0
Eastern Europe									
Albania	19.3	24.5	25.2	47.6	44.6	41.0	14.4	14.5	12.2
Macedonia, former Yugoslav Republic of	38.6	40.9	53.4	48.2	54.5	56.6	28.3	30.8	21.2
Poland	43.8	47.6	45.6	50.4	50.5	47.5	22.7	21.5	22.8

Source: IMF staff estimates based on data provided by the authorities.

[1]General government revenue and expenditure, except Albania (central government); Armenia, the former Yugoslav Republic of Macedonia, Latvia, and Ukraine (Consolidated General Government).

[2]Includes outlays on explicit consumer subsidies, pensions, unemployment benefits, and child and other allowances.

[3]The 1994 figures for total budgetary revenue, total budgetary expenditure, and total social protection outlays are actuals for 1995.

working-age individuals who can contribute payroll taxes. For instance, in 1993, the ratio between the numbers of pensioners and workers had fallen to less than 50 percent in Armenia, the former Yugoslav Republic of Macedonia, and Ukraine. This ratio was above 60 percent in 1995 in Ukraine. In recent years, this development has contributed to a worsening of the financial position of pension funds of these countries.[8]

Consequently, the budget in many transition countries is unable to pay social benefits in time, to meet the legal obligation of transferring payroll taxes of government employees to the providers of social benefits, or to transfer budgeted amounts to social funds (the Kyrgyz

---

[8]The present situation presents an interesting contrast with surpluses generated by pension funds in earlier years. The value of those surpluses was quickly eroded by high rates of inflation (e.g., the Russian Federation).

Republic, Tajikistan, and Ukraine). In some instances, social funds are being asked to finance child allowances out of their payroll tax revenues (Ukraine). The decline in the compliance of payroll taxes has lowered their effective yields by 30–40 percent (Armenia, the Kyrgyz Republic, and the Russian Federation). In the absence of major policy initiatives, the near-term prospects for pension funds in these countries are bleak. As a reflection of a tight liquidity position in the economy, the pension fund of one country (the Kyrgyz Republic) is receiving part of the payroll tax collections in-kind (flour, canned meat) and has also begun to pay pensions in-kind, creating new problems for the fund. There appears to be no scope for raising payroll taxes further without having a substantial negative impact on wages or labor demand. Furthermore, in the present difficult climate, budgets cannot be expected to fill the gap between pension fund obligations and revenues; budgetary transfers, if any, have been erratic (e.g., the Kyrgyz Republic).

Payment Arrears and Inadequate Social Benefits

Falling revenues, together with the inability of social funds to restructure or rationalize benefits, have resulted in the emergence of arrears in benefit payments (e.g., the former Yugoslav Republic of Macedonia, the Kyrgyz Republic, the Russian Federation, and Tajikistan). A more pointed targeting of costly social benefits is being resisted, allowing relatively high-income groups to receive social benefits. Combined with dwindling resources, this has caused the average benefit size (e.g., a pension or cash compensation) for the truly needy to become small with little differentiation between the minimum and the maximum benefit. The lack of targeting has also resulted in a shortage of budgetary resources to finance programs to assist the poor (e.g., Armenia). For instance, in 1993, the maximum pension was two-thirds larger than the minimum pension in Ukraine and the average replacement rate (i.e., the average pension in relation to the average wage) was 43 percent. At the end of 1995, the maximum pension was merely 21 percent larger than the minimum pension, and the average replacement rate was reduced to 25 percent.

Remaining Subsidies

Many transition countries still maintain substantial subsidies for housing, other communal services, and transportation. Attempts are being made to reduce the budgetary cost of these subsidies by gradually raising tariffs while mitigating the adverse effects of higher prices on household income through targeted schemes (e.g., Ukraine). Nevertheless, estimates of the cost of these services do not fully reflect all input costs. For example, cost estimates for housing services in Ukraine do not take into account the depreciation of housing.

Information and Administrative Deficiencies

Many transition countries lack adequate information to assist them in policy formulation, particularly in three areas. Governments do not have adequate information on first, the number or composition of the needy—it is unclear how many workers are underemployed or how many among the unemployed or underemployed workers are engaged in informal sector activities; second, the number of persons receiving social benefits; and third, the number of enterprises that are obliged to pay payroll taxes.

The expansion of informal sector activities makes the identification of the poor increasingly difficult. The use of officially recorded incomes for determining eligibility is inappropriate because it could lead to a mistargeting of benefits. The large share of nonwage incomes in household income suggests that the average size of government cash benefits ought to take into consideration these nonwage incomes, including informal intrafamily transfers. Determining the size of government cash benefits entirely from wages or formal sector incomes would result in an overestimation of the budgetary costs of social protection. Moreover, public social protection payments could crowd out these private transfers, which are voluntary, efficient, and well targeted, making an important contribution to social protection in many transition countries.[9]

Some transition countries are seeking to target the social benefits only on the basis of formal sector income but are facing difficulties. In the Kyrgyz Republic, a whole range of benefits (bread compensation, child allowances, birth grants, and social pensions) were replaced by a single benefit on January 1, 1995, targeted on the basis of per capita household income to children under age 16 (under 18, if still in school), students, nonworking pensioners, the handicapped, and the unemployed. The principal objective behind the new benefit is to target the truly poor and thereby reduce its budgetary cost. Because this benefit's eligibility is based on official income and because the share of official income is declining, the number of eligi-

---

[9]For example, see Cox, Okrasa, and Jimenez (1993), and Cox, Eser, and Jimenez (1994) for such networks in Poland and the Russian Federation, respectively.

ble individuals as well as budgetary outlays are rising. Similar problems exist with the housing subsidy program introduced in Ukraine in May 1995, which limits household expenditures on housing and other communal services to 15 percent of declared family income. By the end of 1995, over 1.4 million households were receiving subsidies under this program.

Short- to Medium-Term Social Protection Reform Options

In transition countries, the primary objective of social protection programs at this time should be to provide minimal benefits for survival to the growing number of truly vulnerable households. It may not be possible for many of these countries to set more ambitious objectives in light of the severe financial and administrative constraints facing them.

Reforming the Eligibility and Benefit Structure

Most transition countries have so far resisted reforms of eligibility conditions and the structure of pension, unemployment, and other benefits. Needed reforms include raising the statutory retirement ages, rescinding the system of special pensions, and reducing pensions for working pensioners. To be eligible to receive pensions, individuals should be required to retire from their last job upon reaching the retirement age. Some countries have initiated partial reform of the structure of benefits (e.g., Estonia and the former Yugoslav Republic of Macedonia), but these reforms are unlikely to correct fully the imbalance in their pension systems. For instance, Estonia has raised the retirement age annually by six months for men and women (from their former levels of 60 for men and 55 for women) to a maximum of 65 for men and 60 for women. However, the country continues to provide early pensions, and credits toward pension eligibility for the time spent staying home to care for children or studying at the university. On the other hand, unemployment benefits are low in relation to the prevailing wage, whereas resources collected to assist the unemployed are being diverted toward granting questionable subsidies to individuals and enterprises (e.g., the Russian Federation). A reform of benefits would spread evenly the burden of adjustment across different population groups as well as generate resources for social protection. Unless the social protection system is reformed, some pensioners or the unemployed—or both—may end up bearing the brunt of the decline in income as reflected in the declining ratio of the average pension to the average wage and low level of unemployment benefits.[10] The long-term unemployed should be assisted, but not all of them need to receive benefits since some may be working in the informal sector. The issues that arise in targeting benefits in these circumstances are discussed below.

The design of social policies must take into account the decline in formal sector employment and the growing importance of informal activity. Social benefits, including child allowances and compensation for higher prices and tariffs, should also be accessible to informal and private sector workers and the unemployed who do not register for unemployment benefits.

Securing Financial Resources

Securing resources requires at least three measures. First, laws need to be strengthened to include in the wage fund the untaxed elements of labor compensation. Unless this is done, the payroll tax base would be eroded and there would be difficulties in financing social benefits in the near term with the current levels of statutory tax rates. Exemptions from the payment of payroll tax or differential rates for different occupations would have to be abolished. Second, all-out efforts need to be made to register new enterprises and businesses. This would improve financing for social protection by expanding the payroll tax base, strengthen the coverage of workers in the unregistered sector, and widen the tax base for other taxes, such as the VAT. Third, other budgetary expenditures must be prioritized. It is inefficient and inequitable to continue supporting low-priority budgetary programs and projects while squeezing social protection outlays.

Minimizing the Burden on Administrative Resources

Because of the difficulty of tracking incomes and growing informal sector activity, greater reliance would have to be placed on self-targeting mechanisms for the provision of benefits. Public works programs represent one such self-targeted social assistance program that requires an unemployed worker to tie his or her time to the receipt of food or wage. Other, simpler targeting mechanisms would have to be identified; these could target certain population groups such as pensioners, particularly older pensioners. In Ukraine, for instance, to ease the

---

[10]There is evidence that recorded income differentials in the Baltic countries have widened markedly to levels comparable with those of southern European countries (see Cornelius and Weder (1996)). This suggests the need for enhancing the targeting of different benefits.

administrative burden, the housing subsidy could target, among others, single pensioners living alone. However, some targeting methods could be counterproductive. Publishing the names of all beneficiaries, while potentially enhancing the targeting of benefits,[11] may stigmatize beneficiaries, forcing some truly needy to withdraw from social programs. Asking all recipients to collect benefits in person would tend to discriminate against the old and the handicapped, who may not be able to report to social agencies on a regular basis.

What is the likely financial impact of the above-noted reform options? Table 5.6 shows payroll tax revenue, pensions, unemployment benefits, child allowances, and social assistance, all expressed in relation to GDP for the ten sample countries.[12] They have been derived by using (mostly) 1994 average wages, total employment, the shares of the old and the young in the population, and the registered unemployed in these countries. For simplicity, it is assumed that these countries provide an average pension equal to 40 percent of the average wage, an average unemployment benefit equal to 30 percent of the average wage, an average child allowance equal to 15 percent of the average wage, and an average social assistance benefit equal to 20 percent of the average wage. The actual benefit amounts could be lower and the actual payroll tax compliance higher (e.g., the Russian Federation and Ukraine) than shown in Table 5.6.

The results are revealing. With the assumed levels of tax compliance and benefits, payroll taxes would clearly be insufficient to finance both pension and unemployment benefits. If payroll taxes were also used to pay some child allowances, the imbalance between available resources and needs would be substantially greater. A lowering of average benefits through incomplete indexation, the elimination of special pensions, or a raising of the retirement age for pensioners would reduce pension outlays. For instance, if pensions were limited to the population above the age of 60 through a benefit restructuring, with the average benefit amount held at 40 percent of the average wage, these countries would save between 1.2 percent of GDP and 3.6 percent of GDP (Table 5.7).[13] For instance, pension outlays for Estonia

---

[11]This has been successfully implemented in Sri Lanka.

[12]As most countries are using payroll taxes to finance pensions and unemployment benefits, the simulations reported here link outlays on these programs to payroll taxes. It is not necessary for a country to finance social programs from payroll taxes; general taxation can also be used for this purpose.

[13]Given the comparative static nature of the simulation, some caution needs to be exercised in interpreting this result. The retirement age is typically raised gradually (e.g., Estonia and the former Yugoslav Republic of Macedonia) and consequently, the financial savings would be realized only over a period of time.

Table 5.6. Simulation of Social Protection Resource Requirements, 1994

(As percent of GDP)

	Payroll Tax Revenue[1]	Payroll-Tax Financed Benefits			Child Allowances[4]	Social Assistance[5]
		Total	Pensions[2]	Unemployment benefits[3]		
Baltic countries						
Estonia	4.8	9.2	8.2	1.0	2.8	0.9
Latvia	7.5	13.9	12.7	1.2	4.0	1.3
Russia and other former Soviet Union countries						
Armenia	4.1	5.5	4.9	0.6	3.5	0.8
Kyrgyz Republic	5.6	6.1	5.6	0.6	6.9	1.2
Russian Federation	3.9	6.3	5.6	0.7	2.0	0.6
Tajikistan	6.8	7.4	7.1	0.3	13.9	2.1
Ukraine	4.3	7.8	7.8	0.0	2.3	0.8
Eastern Europe						
Albania	6.1	8.1	5.4	2.7	5.2	1.1
Macedonia, former Yugoslav Republic of[6]	9.4	16.7	12.4	4.3	6.5	1.8
Poland	5.7	11.6	9.1	2.5	4.0	1.1

Source: Authors' estimates.

[1]Assuming an effective payroll tax of 13 percent of the wage bill. The base for payroll taxation is typically the wage fund, which is narrower than the wage bill. Furthermore, the wage bill is derived by multiplying the average wage by employment. The latter is an overestimate because many workers are being placed on administrative leave and are not receiving wages. This has been taken into account by lowering the effective payroll tax.

[2]Based on population above the age of 55 and 40 percent of the average wage.

[3]Based on 30 percent of the average wage.

[4]Based on 15 percent of the average wage.

[5]Based on 20 percent of the average wage and assuming the poor equal 5 percent of the total population.

[6]As percent of GSP. Figures are for 1993.

would decline from 8.2 percent of GDP in Table 5.6 to 6.2 percent of GDP in Table 5.7. If payroll tax compliance (including coverage of in-kind income in the payroll tax base) were to be improved by 1 percentage point, payroll tax revenue would expand by up to 0.7 percent of GDP. For instance, Latvia's payroll tax revenue would increase from 7.5 percent of GDP in Table 5.6 to 8.1 percent of GDP in Table 5.7. The impact of increased unemployment, a higher level of child allowances, and increased demand for social assistance is also shown in the table.

Table 5.7. Resource Requirements for Social Protection Under Different Scenarios[1]

(As percent of GDP)

| | Increased Payroll Compliance[2] | Payroll-Tax-Financed Benefits | | | | Increased Demand for Social Assistance[6] |
		Total	Reduced pensions[3]	Increased unemploy-ment[4]	Increased child allowance[5]	
Baltic countries						
Estonia	5.2	7.3	6.2	1.1	3.0	1.1
Latvia	8.1	11.0	9.6	1.4	4.3	1.5
Russia and other former Soviet Union countries						
Armenia	4.4	4.4	3.7	0.7	3.7	1.0
Kyrgyz Republic	6.0	4.9	4.2	0.7	7.3	1.5
Russian Federation	4.2	4.9	4.1	0.8	2.2	0.7
Tajikistan	7.4	5.7	5.2	0.5	14.9	2.5
Ukraine	4.7	6.1	5.9	0.1	2.5	0.9
Eastern Europe						
Albania	6.5	6.7	3.8	2.8	5.6	1.3
Macedonia, former Yugoslav Republic of[7]	10.1	13.4	8.8	4.6	6.9	2.1
Poland	6.1	9.5	6.9	2.7	4.3	1.4

Source: Authors' estimates.

[1]The baseline for the simulations is given in Table 5.6.

[2]Assuming that the effective payroll tax increases to 14 percent, in comparison with 13 percent in Table 5.6.

[3]Based on population of age 60 and above, and 40 percent of the average wage in comparison with population of age 55 and above in Table 5.6.

[4]Increase in 1 percentage point in unemployment in comparison with Table 5.6, and benefit equaling 30 percent of the average wage.

[5]Increase in 1 percentage point in child allowance with benefit equaling 16 percent of average wage, in comparison with 15 percent of the average wage in Table 5.6.

[6]The proportion of the poor in the population is assumed to increase to 6 percent from 5 percent in Table 5.6, with the benefit equaling 20 percent of the average wage.

[7]As percent of GSP.

Summary and Conclusions

The efforts of transition countries to help households with vulnerable members of society are being stifled by severe financial and administrative constraints that have recently surfaced. In a number of countries, the formal sector is shrinking, and unemployment and underemployment are rising rapidly. The fast-contracting revenue base is threatening the ability of pension systems to provide even basic pension benefits. Increasing informal sector activity is also complicating the task of targeting different social benefits and providing adequate social protection to the vulnerable.

These countries need to respond quickly to the challenges. This is necessary to ensure macroeconomic stabilization and sustain the reform process. The remaining generalized subsidies, particularly for housing and communal services, would have to be better targeted to reduce their budgetary costs and to correct price distortions.

The simulations presented in this paper indicate that transition countries must restructure social benefits and take steps to improve compliance with payroll taxes. They should also develop ways to target social benefits to the truly vulnerable without taxing their limited administrative capacity. These tasks are not easy, but they are nevertheless essential. More broadly, they must achieve improvements not merely in social programs but also in tax policy and administration and in all public spending programs.

References

Ahmad, Ehtisham, and Ke-young Chu, 1993, "Russian Federation: Economic Reform and Policy Options for Social Protection," in *Transition to Market: Studies in Fiscal Reform,* ed. by Vito Tanzi (Washington: International Monetary Fund).

Chu, Ke-youngv, and Sanjeev Gupta, 1993, "Protecting the Poor: Social Safety Nets During Transition," *Finance & Development,* Vol. 30 (June), pp. 24–27.

———, 1997, "Economic Reforms, Social Safety Nets, and the Budget and Transition Economies" in *Fiscal Policy and Economic Reform: Essays in Honor of Vito Tanzi,* ed. by Mario I. Blejer and Teresa Ter-Minassian (London: Routledge).

Cornelius, Peter K., and Beatrice S. Weder, 1996, "Economic Transformation and Income Distribution: Some Evidence from the Baltic Countries," IMF Working Paper 96/14 (Washington: International Monetary Fund).

Cox, Donald, Wlodek Okrasa, and Emmanuel Jimenez, 1993, "Family Safety Nets During Economic Transition: A Case Study of Poland" (unpublished; Boston College).

Cox, Donald, Zekeriya Eser, and Emmanuel Jimenez, 1994, "Family Safety Nets During Economic Transition: A Study of Inter-Household Transfers in Russia" (unpublished; Washington: World Bank).

Gupta, Sanjeev, and Robert Hagemann, 1994, "Social Protection During Russia's Economic Transformation," *Finance & Development,* Vol. 31 (December), pp. 14–17.

International Economics Department, 1995, "Social Indicators of Development" (Washington: World Bank IED Socio-Economic Data Division)

International Monetary Fund, 1995, "Social Safety Nets for Economic Transition: Options and Recent Experience," IMF Paper on Policy Analysis and Assessment 95/3 (Washington: International Monetary Fund).

————, and the World Bank, 1993, "Social Security Reforms and Social Safety Nets," *Development Committee Report* No. 32 (Washington: World Bank, September 27).

United Nations Children's Fund (UNICEF), 1995, *Poverty, Children and Policy: Responses for Bright Future,* Regional Monitoring Report No. 3 (Florence, Italy: UNICEF International Child Development Centre).

World Bank, 1995, *World Population Projections: Estimates and Projections with Related Demographic Statistics* (Baltimore: Johns Hopkins University Press for the World Bank).

III
Country Studies

6

Bangladesh: Economic Reform Measures and the Poor

Padma Gotur

With a per capita income of about $200 in 1991, Bangladesh is one of the poorest countries in the world. More than half of its population—50 million people—live in poverty. The most vulnerable groups include small farmers, landless rural laborers, and workers in the urban informal sector. Health care, nutrition, and education standards are low, especially among women and children. The earning potential of most poor people is limited by their lack of skills, assets, and access to credit. Given its limited natural resources, high population density, and frequent natural disasters, Bangladesh faces an enormous challenge in its efforts to reduce poverty.

The only lasting way to reduce poverty is to ensure sustainable economic growth, by implementing policies to promote financial stability and the efficient use of resources. With this strategy in mind, the government launched a medium-term structural adjustment program in the mid-1980s, supported by the IMF under the Structural Adjustment Facility (SAF) and the Enhanced Structural Adjustment Facility (ESAF). The government's efforts have also been supported by the World Bank, other donors, and nongovernmental organizations (NGOs).

Adjustment efforts are likely, however, to have some adverse effects on the poor in the short run, arising primarily from increases in public pricing, lower subsidies, public enterprise reform, and deregulation of private sector activity. The government has put in place compensatory and targeted programs to mitigate these negative effects,

Note: This is an abridged version of IMF Working Paper 91/139 (Washington: International Monetary Fund, 1991).

although the massive numbers of poor people, on the one hand, and the shortage of budgetary resources, on the other, constrain the scope of these efforts. Although improved food availability remains the focus of targeted action under the SAF and ESAF programs, efforts are being made to reduce the constraints that impeded the development of a comprehensive social safety net in the past.

This paper evaluates the impact of the adjustment programs on the poor. It sets out the objectives of the government's economic reforms and the main elements of the SAF and ESAF programs. It then analyzes the impact on the poor of program-induced changes in relative prices as well as induced changes in production, employment, and income.

Economic Reforms and Structural Adjustment Programs

The programs under the SAF (1986/87, 1988/89) and ESAF (1990/91, 1992/93) reflect the government's emphasis on addressing poverty reduction mainly by promoting sustained economic growth. The government has adopted a policy program to (1) spur private investment through financial reform, exchange and trade liberalization, and industrial deregulation; (2) facilitate public investment by raising domestic revenues, curtailing government consumption, and improving project implementation; (3) protect the purchasing power of the poor by reducing inflation; and (4) improve human resource development by strengthening social programs and reorienting public expenditures. These policies aim at promoting labor-intensive agricultural, industrial, and export production, and economic diversification. At the same time, since the benefits of growth may not reach the poor in the short run, this policy framework has been supplemented by targeted programs that provide special assistance to the poor. The details of each policy measure are discussed in the next two sections.

During the SAF arrangement, growth and investment objectives were not realized because of the disruptions caused by severe floods, as well as slippages in the implementation of structural reform. Real GDP growth averaged only 3 percent, inflation remained at 10 percent, and per capita income did not increase in real terms. The SAF program, however, was successful in expanding the tradable goods sector, which created employment, and in reforming the agriculture sector, which laid the basis for the subsequent recovery of production and the improved availability of food. The ESAF program maintains the objectives of raising investment and reducing inflation with a view to achieving 5 percent real GDP growth. Higher incomes and profits resulting from higher investment are expected to improve per capita consumption while generating increased private savings. A more open and competitive economy, resulting from agricultural, financial, and exchange and trade liberalization, is expected to strengthen production incentives and create employment opportunities.

Program-Induced Changes in Relative Prices and Their Impact on the Poor

Although it is generally observed that the poor are hardest hit by changes in relative prices during adjustment, this is not so in Bangladesh because price distortions have not been severe. As a result, not only was the need for sizable adjustment reduced, but it was possible for the pace of adjustment to be gradual. The government recognizes, however, that, as adjustment efforts are intensified, there could be more pronounced short-term adverse effects on the poor, which would require compensatory measures.

The main changes in relative prices resulting from the adjustment programs are those stemming from increases in ration prices for foodgrains, prices of administered goods and services (e.g., energy and transportation), and excise taxes. The direct impact of these changes on the poor has varied, depending on the relative importance of the affected items in their consumption and the magnitude of the changes. The poor spend a high proportion (about 60 percent) of their income on food compared with the rest of the population, with more than half of such expenditure devoted to foodgrains. Given this consumption pattern, the changes in relative prices resulting from the program are estimated to have reduced the incomes of the poor by not more than 3–6 percent during 1986–91 (see Table 6.1).[1]

Increases in Foodgrain Prices

An important objective of the government's food policy under the structural adjustment programs has been to reduce food subsidies and the budgetary cost of food management operations, partly through an increase in ration food prices. Although the availability and cost of

---

[1]Price changes resulting from exchange rate changes are discussed later in the paper.

Table 6.1. Bangladesh: Impact of Program-Induced Changes on the Poor
(Annual average percentage change)

	Weight in Consumption (In percent)	Price Change				Income Loss	
		1983/84 1985/86	1986/87 1988/89 SAF program	1989/90	1990/91 First-year ESAF	1986/87 1989/90	1990/91
Ration foodgrain prices	33.0					2.2	2.3
Rice		7.2	5.9	8.6	7.0		
Wheat		6.9	5.7	8.7	7.0		
Petroleum products[1]	4.0	9.8	0.2	-0.9	85.0	0.2	2.5[2]
Kerosene		-2.3	—	5.8	91.8		
Gasoline		-2.4	—	-38.0	70.7		
Diesel oil		-0.1	—	5.8	91.8		
Liquefied petroleum gas		13.1		9.2	52.7		
Railway passenger fare	3.0	7.2	6.7	3.8	15.0	0.2	0.4
Electricity	2.0	9.0	6.6	7.5	6.5–16.7	0.1	0.3
Natural gas	1.0					0.1	0.1
Household		15.3	11.5	16.0	15.0		
Power and fertilizer		14.3	22.3	15.6	15.0		
Industry		12.0	11.9	16.7	15.0		
Commercial		20.5	21.9	7.5	15.0		
Total income loss						2.8	5.7[2]

Sources: Bangladesh authorities; and IMF staff estimates.

[1] Weighted average.

[2] In response to the 92 percent increase in kerosene prices, the poor are expected to substitute less expensive firewood for kerosene, as a result of which the net income loss would be 1.5 percent and the corresponding total income loss would be 47 percent.

food have a major influence on the standard of living of the poor, the impact of change in ration food prices alone on their income has been limited and is likely to remain so in the future. This limited impact is explained by the fact that the poor receive only 20 percent of their foodgrain consumption from the public food distribution system. Out of the 8 million tons of foodgrains consumed by the poor, only 1.5 million tons are obtained through the public system. The major share, 4.5 million tons, of their consumption is obtained from their own farm production, while the remaining 2 million tons are purchased from the private market. The urban poor receive a larger share of the food distributed by the public system and also depend more on the private market than the rural poor.

Within the poor groups, the ultrapoor receive the bulk of the 1.5 million tons distributed by the public system, which represents about half of their total consumption of foodgrains. About 60 percent of the 1.5 million tons is made available to them under the nonmonetized channels of the system as food wages paid for work rendered under the Food for Work and Vulnerable Group Development programs. Thus, the increase in ration prices undertaken in the adjustment programs applies to only 0.6 million tons or 20 percent of the food consumed by the ultrapoor.

Average ration prices for rice and wheat were both raised by only 6 percent annually during the SAF program, well below the rate of inflation. Assuming that these increases affect a third of the total income of the poor, their impact on the income of poor households would be to reduce it by about 2 percent annually. Under the first-year ESAF program, ration prices were raised by an average of 7 percent in July 1990. To improve the targeting of subsidies, prices were increased by 5 percent for distribution channels available to poorer groups and by 16 percent for channels available to the relatively well-off groups. The 5 percent increase in ration prices would reduce the income of poor households by less than 2 percent.

Although the ration price increases of recent years sought to reduce budgetary food subsidies, the latter increased considerably in 1988/89 and 1989/90 as higher international prices were not passed through to consumers. While the poor benefited to this extent, they would have been better off had the ration prices on those channels available to the nonpoor been raised in step with world price increases and the resulting budgetary savings applied toward programs for the poor. The differentiated ration price increase in 1990/91, coupled with a cutback in commercial food imports, will permit a substantial reduction in budgetary food subsidies, from 0.8 percent of GDP in 1989/90 to 0.6 percent in 1990/91.

Increases in Administered Prices

The rationalization of public enterprises under the adjustment pro-grams has led to increases in prices of several public goods and services, some of which imply higher consumption costs for the poor. This impact was limited during the SAF program because some planned price increases had not been implemented, and those that had been carried out accounted for only a small share of the consumption of the poor. During the SAF program, administered prices were increased for electricity (20 percent), natural gas (35 percent for household con-sumers), and transportation (10 percent). Gas and electricity prices were further increased by 16 percent and 8 percent, respectively, in 1989/90. The impact of the changes in transport fares and energy prices on the income of the poor during this four-year period, howev-er, is estimated at only 0.4 percent annually.

The government is raising prices more aggressively during the ESAF period to strengthen public enterprise finances. Increases that have already been implemented include prices of natural gas (15 percent), electricity (6–17 percent), railway fares (15 percent), and petroleum products (85 percent). However, even price increases of this magnitude for energy products, except for kerosene, have limited impact on the rural poor, although the urban poor are somewhat more affected by increases in transportation costs. In the case of kerosene, prices have been raised by 92 percent, largely reversing its previous cross-subsi-dization against other petroleum products, which the authorities believed had encouraged smuggling across land borders. This price increase will cause a reduction of 2½ percent in the real income of the poor. However, this effect is likely to be smaller to the extent that the poor would substitute less expensive firewood for kerosene.

Increases in Excise Taxes

The SAF and ESAF programs include, as part of the revenue mobi-lization effort, increases in excise taxes for sugar, tobacco, natural gas, and certain services, which result in higher prices. Such effects are not substantial for the poor since these goods together account for less than 10 percent of their consumption. During the SAF program, price increases on these items are estimated to have reduced the income of the poor by less than 1 percent annually. Further, the government usu-ally attempts to levy excises mainly on goods and services largely con-sumed by the better-off groups, including bank transactions, telephone services, and luxury consumer goods. To assist the poor, proposals in the original 1990/91 budget for higher excise duties on kerosene, which represent an estimated 4 percent of the total consumption expenditure of the poor, were subsequently withdrawn.

Program-Induced Changes in Production, Income, Employment and Their Impact on the Poor

The reform measures that induce changes in production, employment, and income consist of (1) agricultural policies; (2) tax reform; (3) public expenditure policies; (4) financial reform, exchange rate, and trade liberalization policies; and (5) public enterprise reform. In contrast to the limited adverse effects of relative price changes, program-induced changes in production, income, and employment are substantially benefiting the poor. Under the SAF program, such positive or beneficial effects were most evident in the impetus given to agricultural output and the diversification of export production. The implementation of measures under the ESAF program is expected to increase income and employment opportunities in both agriculture and industry.

Agricultural Policies

Agricultural policies have sought to raise foodgrain output. The government has taken measures to increase the role of the private sector in the distribution of inputs, including the liberalization of the fertilizer market and irrigation equipment imports, to strengthen research and extension services, and to extend the provision of rural credit. The crop replanting and intensification program launched in the aftermath of the floods included free distribution of fertilizer and seeds to small farmers, and assistance with procurement and repair of minor irrigation equipment. These policies benefit the poor by increasing food security, strengthening incomes, and generating employment opportunities. The productivity of small farmers is enhanced by their improved access to irrigation equipment and support services. As a result of the higher level of activity, additional jobs become available for farm laborers and sharecroppers. Moreover, landless rural workers and the urban poor gain from the resulting moderation of retail foodgrain prices.

Improvements in the public food distribution system have had a beneficial impact on farmers' incentives, production decisions, and poverty alleviation. A key objective has been to achieve greater stability of market prices; this has been realized partly through foodgrain imports and greater recourse to open market operations in foodgrains. The system has provided improved incentives for domestic producers through average increases in foodgrain prices of about 7 percent during the last four years. These policies have helped maintain prices paid to farmers by private traders. Beneficiaries have included the small farmers who market about 2 million tons of foodgrain annually.

Agricultural reform will continue to be stressed in the ESAF period. Planned measures aim at an increased share of agriculture in public development spending, flexible pricing, and a greater private sector role in distribution of inputs, improved extension services and research, and financial support for marginal farmers and landless groups. Public sector food procurement and distribution operations will be further improved to sustain market prices at economic levels and realistic support prices will be introduced for farmers. However, no political consensus has emerged for the implementation of land reform that could have potentially far-reaching implications for poverty alleviation.

Tax Reform

Extensive tax reform measures planned under the SAF and ESAF programs, including the introduction of the value-added tax, aim to improve the structure and elasticity of the tax system. These measures will strengthen economic efficiency and provide the additional resources needed to use available project aid, with potentially favorable consequences for output and employment. A major objective of the reforms is to remove impediments to higher private sector output, such as the current bias against export production. It is expected that, with the proposed changes, fiscal incentives for private investors, including tax holidays, could be reduced. These reforms would benefit the poor by promoting employment opportunities in more labor-intensive forms of production.

The poor are not likely to suffer much from an adverse effect of tax reform. The total tax burden of the poor is estimated at only 4 percent of their household income. Indirect taxes are levied mainly on commodities that have a substantial import content, and, in most cases, are not consumed by the poor. The introduction of the value-added tax in 1991, to replace a number of sales and excise taxes in a revenue-neutral manner, will broaden the tax base, but any additional costs to the poor in the short term will likely be more than offset in the long run by additional employment opportunities expected to result from the removal of distortions associated with existing consumption taxes.

Table 6.2. Bangladesh: Poverty Focus of Government Current Expenditure

	1983/84–1985/86 Average	1986/87–1988/89 Average	1989/90 Estimate	1990/91 Budget
	(In percent of total current expenditure)			
Human resource development	21.5	22.6	21.6	21.6
Education	15.8	16.9	16.2	16.2
Health and population	5.7	5.7	5.4	5.4
Subsidies	6.6	4.8	14.0	13.5
Food	6.2	3.7	9.4	8.0
Vulnerable group development and relief	4.2	6.0	4.5	2.5
Agriculture and water development	3.9	3.8	3.8	3.7
Total	36.2	37.2	43.9	41.3
Excluding agriculture and water development	32.3	33.0	40.1	37.6
	(In percent of GDP)			
Human resource development	1.6	1.9	2.0	1.9
Education	1.2	1.4	1.5	1.4
Health and population	0.4	0.5	0.5	0.5
Subsidies	1.1	0.4	1.3	1.2
Food	0.6	0.3	0.8	0.7
Vulnerable group development and relief	0.1	0.5	0.4	0.2
Agriculture and water development	0.3	0.3	0.3	0.3
Total	3.1	3.1	4.0	3.6
Excluding agriculture and water development	2.8	2.8	3.7	3.3

Sources: World Bank, *Bangladesh: Managing the Adjustment Process—An Appraisal*, World Bank Economic Report No. 8344 (Washington, March 1990); Bangladesh authorities; and IMF staff estimates.

Public Expenditure Policies

Public expenditure policies support poverty alleviation efforts by raising the allocations for human resource development, welfare, and agriculture and water resource management. Poorer groups will also benefit from the flood control program, which will promote better early warning systems, medical services, and food security in the event of disasters. However, expenditure on social programs remained limited during the SAF period (Tables 6.2 and 6.3). Current and development spending was limited to 2 percent of GDP for education, 1 per-

Table 6.3. Bangladesh: Poverty Focus of Government Development Expenditure

	1983/84–1985/86 Average	1986/87–1988/89 Average	1989/90 Estimate	1990/91 Budget
	(In percent of total development expenditure)			
Human resource development	9.4	10.5	14.6	19.2
Education	4.1	5.0	6.1	10.1
Health and population	5.3	5.5	8.5	9.1
Social welfare	0.5	0.6	0.5	0.8
Agriculture, water resources, and rural development	26.9	20.5	26.3	24.1
Total	36.8	31.6	41.1	44.1
Excluding agriculture and water resources	9.9	11.1	14.8	20.0
	(In percent of GDP)			
Human resource development	0.7	0.8	0.9	1.3
Education	0.3	0.4	0.4	0.7
Health and population	0.4	0.4	0.5	0.6
Social welfare	0.1	1.0	—	0.1
Agriculture, water resources and rural development	1.2	1.4	1.6	1.6
Total	2.8	2.2	2.5	3.0
Excluding agriculture and water resources	0.8	0.8	0.9	1.4

Sources: Bangladesh authorities; and IMF staff estimates.

cent of GDP for health and population control, and 0.5 percent of GDP for relief and welfare. Moreover, the effectiveness of the already under-funded social programs was further constrained by poor targeting and other infrastructural deficiencies.

Several of the problems encountered in the SAF period are now being addressed. A careful prioritization of development expenditures is being undertaken to ensure that available resources are concentrated on the highest-priority projects, including poverty-oriented programs. In cooperation with the donor community, the government will fully fund programs for the expansion of primary education and health and family planning services. The allocation for human resource development in the 1990/91 budget has been increased to 20 percent of total development spending, almost double its share in the final year of the SAF program, while its share in current expenditure has been maintained. Additional expenditure on agriculture and water resource development should help expand job opportunities for the poor in rural areas.

Financial Reform, Exchange Rate, and Trade Liberalization Policies

These policies are expected to generate additional employment opportunities, especially in export-oriented and import-substitution activities. Indeed, during the SAF period, improved competitiveness, resulting from earlier exchange rate depreciation, promoted rapid growth in the ready-made garments industry. The expansion of this industry is estimated to have created employment for some 500,000 persons, mainly previously unemployed women. The ESAF program continues the emphasis on strengthening the export base in labor-intensive goods, primarily through tight financial policies and structural reforms. Given the potential for exports of electronics, toys, luggage, and leather products, export volume is projected to show strong growth and generate 350,000 additional jobs. These gains can help offset the employment losses resulting from public enterprise, import, and tariff reforms.

Public Enterprise Reform

The SAF and ESAF programs include measures to reduce the financial losses of public enterprises by cutting labor and other costs, tightening financial control, and improving profitability. Only limited progress was made under the SAF program in these areas but efforts will be intensified under the ESAF program. The proposed reforms of jute and industrial enterprises, in particular, emphasize employment rationalization, the closing of uneconomic units, privatization, and increased competition from the private sector. The most important of these actions, which relates to the public sector jute mills, could reduce employment by one-third, or 30,000 people, equivalent to 5 percent of the total public sector workforce. To mitigate such consequences, the government is examining the option of using part of the resulting budgetary savings to provide unemployment compensation and retraining to displaced employees.

Targeted Programs and Nongovernmental Organizations

Targeted programs reflect the priority assigned to ensuring food availability for the poor, while reducing budgetary food subsidies, primarily by withdrawing benefits available to the relatively better-off nonpoor. During the SAF period, two programs—the *Food for Work* program, which provides wages in the form of food for temporary rural workers, and the *Vulnerable Group Development* program, targeted at disadvantaged women and children—were expanded to account for 40 percent of the total amount of the food distributed by the Public Food Distribution System. These schemes have reached about three million persons, including 500,000 women, with at least three-fourths of the poor receiving assistance. The budgetary costs of these programs were 35 percent of total rice subsidies and over 80 percent of total wheat subsidies in 1989/90, or two-thirds of total budgetary appropriations. In the event of natural disasters, such as the floods and cyclones of 1987/88 and 1988/89, these programs are temporarily expanded. In addition, this focus of targeted programs has been broadened during the ESAF period to include literacy, health, and skill-acquisition components, which would enhance the income-earning capacity of participants in these programs.

Recognizing the budgetary, technical, and administrative constraints that affect targeted programs, the government has encouraged greater NGO participation in this effort. There are about 400 NGOs operating in Bangladesh—along with 12,000 voluntary social welfare agencies—which assist the poor, especially women, by providing credit, training, primary education, basic health care, nutrition, and family planning facilities. The focus of the activities of many NGOs has been shifting from emergency relief to development-oriented programs, especially those aimed at improving employment and income in rural areas.

Conclusion

The main thrust of the Bangladesh Government's strategy of poverty reduction has been to strengthen output growth and ensure food security. Increasingly, however, its attention has also turned to improving human resource development and the efficiency of targeted programs, with a greater role provided to NGOs. Nevertheless, poverty will remain a pervasive problem. Any progress achieved should therefore be regarded as only the beginning of a major effort that will need to be expanded in scope, demand greater resources, and continue over many years.

7

Social Protection, Labor Market Rigidity, and Enterprise Restructuring in China

Zu-liu Hu

An unpleasant trade-off facing policymakers in economies in transition is how to reconcile market efficiency and social protection. These economies have inherited from the central planning era a large, inefficient state-owned sector, which employed the bulk of the total labor force. During the process of transforming these state-owned enterprises into competitive, efficient, profit-oriented firms, many of the existing workers, who have been taking lifetime employment for granted, have suddenly confronted the risk of losing their jobs. In the absence of an adequate social safety net, high unemployment can cause enormous economic hardship to the vulnerable, as well as a strong backlash against market-oriented reforms.

China started its economic reform in the late 1970s.[1] The initial phase of the reform, which abolished collective agriculture—the People's Communes—and reestablished the family farming system was remarkably successful. At the beginning of the urban industrial reform, however, China realized that it was a far more difficult task than rural reform. A key difference between rural and urban areas was the different labor market structure. The family farming system granted farmers complete freedom in job choice, labor supply, and decisions concerning saving for old age. Responding to market signals, farmers could move freely from traditional farming to rural-township and village industries, or to construction and other tertiary sectors in cities. They

---

Note: Originally issued as IMF Paper on Policy Analysis and Assessment 94/22 (Washington: International Monetary Fund, 1994).

[1]For reviews on China's experience with economic reforms, see Perkins (1988), Blejer and others (1991), and Bell, Khor, and Kochnar (1993).

Table 7.1. China: Role of the State Sector in Urban Employment
(In tens of thousands of workers)

Year	Total Urban Labor Force	State Sector	Collectives	Individual Businesses
1978	9,514	7,451	2,048	15
1982	11,428	8,630	2,651	147
1986	13,292	9,333	3,421	538
1990	14,894	10,346	3,549	835
1992	15,630	10,889	3,621	1,120

Source: Chinese authorities.

were outside China's formal social safety nets even before they were liberalized from collective farming, so they were not bound by the cradle-to-grave socialist welfare system that applies to the urban, state-owned sector. By contrast, there was no such labor market flexibility in China's state-owned sector. China's state-owned sector played a dominant role prior to reforms, especially in China's highly centralized urban economy, accounting for 77 percent of China's gross industrial output, and employing 78 percent of the total urban labor force in 1978 (Tables 7.1 to 7.3). If the government was to impose the same

Table 7.2. China: The Evolving Role of the State and Nonstate Sectors
(Percentage share of total gross industrial output)

Year	State-Owned Sector	Nonstate Sector
1978	77.6	22.4
1979	78.5	21.5
1980	76.0	24.0
1981	74.8	25.2
1982	74.4	25.6
1983	73.3	26.7
1984	69.1	30.9
1985	64.9	35.1
1986	62.3	37.7
1987	59.7	40.3
1988	56.8	43.2
1989	56.1	43.9
1990	54.6	45.4
1991	52.9	47.1
1992	48.1	51.9

Source: *State Statistical Yearbook of China* (Beijing, 1993).

Table 7.3. China: Changing Distribution of the Industrial Labor Force in State and Nonstate Sectors

(Percentage share of total industrial workers)

Year	State-Owned Sector	Nonstate Sector
1978	51.5	48.5
1979	50.9	49.1
1980	49.7	50.3
1981	50.0	50.0
1982	49.7	50.3
1983	49.1	50.9
1984	46.3	53.7
1985	45.2	54.8
1986	44.0	56.0
1987	43.7	56.3
1988	43.8	56.2
1989	44.7	55.3
1990	45.0	55.0
1991	44.9	55.1
1992	44.2	55.8

Source: *State Statistical Yearbook of China* (Beijing, 1993).

kind of market discipline and hard budget constraint on state-owned enterprises, some enterprises would have to be closed down and their employees would lose their jobs. The government, although committed to market-oriented reforms, was not prepared to accept massive unemployment and the associated social and political risk. In the end, China took a cautious and gradual approach to enterprise reforms. The objective was to strike the right balance between improving enterprise efficiency and minimizing the social cost of restructuring. Over the 1980s China introduced, in a piecemeal fashion, measures to reform its labor market and social security system. It is only in the early 1990s, however, with appropriate market and social infrastructure already in place, and with the accumulated experience of more than a decade of trial and error with urban reform, that China began to launch full-scale enterprise reforms. While these initiatives have yet to demonstrate their full impact and effectiveness, the outcome so far has been encouraging.

China's experience, consistent with those of other reforming economies, suggests that, without removing rigidities in the labor market, the social and economic costs of necessary enterprise restructuring in terms of unemployment may be too high to be politically sustainable. Reforming the social safety net is crucial to increase labor market flexibility and to pave the way for transforming the state-owned sector.

Barriers to Enterprise Reform

The literature on economies in transition tends to emphasize that the main problem with state-owned enterprises in these economies lies in their public ownership and the associated inefficiency, and thus advocates rapid privatization as the panacea. A closer examination of China's prereform conditions and experience, however, suggests that the traditional labor market structure and social security system may be even more important barriers to enterprise reform.[2]

Wage Setting and Employment in the State-Owned Sector

Under the traditional employment system in China, the state simply assigned workers to enterprises. Since state-owned enterprises were obligated to provide jobs, and hiring decisions had no relation to their labor demand, firing was virtually nonexistent. The result was over-staffing in most enterprises. Similarly, potential job market entrants had no need to look for jobs. Although the state attempted to match a worker's skills to his job assignment, this administrative matching, like the rest of central planning, did not work well. Wages, like commodity prices and interest rates, were set by the state and usually fixed for long periods of time. There was little sectoral variation in compensation across industries and professions. Base wages were entirely determined by seniority, and total compensation did not correspond with work effort. Since pay was not linked to performance, workers had little incentive to increase productivity.

Enterprise as Provider of Social Protection

State-owned enterprises were obligated to provide their workers with a range of social services, including housing, pensions, and medical insurance. Unlike in the developed market economies, the social security system in China was based on individual enterprises. There were three pillars of social protection in China: guaranteed job security, subsidized housing, and pension benefits.

Guaranteed Job Security

Once a worker was assigned to an enterprise, from day one he was guaranteed lifetime employment. The system of lifetime tenure may

---

[2]For a survey on China's evolving social security system, see Ahmad and Hussain (1989).

have achieved an important social function, but it also had adverse consequences on enterprise efficiency. Instead of encouraging corporate loyalty, synergy, and greater work effort, as, arguably, occurred in Japan, the system of lifetime employment in China may have actually distorted work incentives and decreased work effort, owing to the so-called iron rice bowl effect. What was lacking was a competitive external environment and a rational wage structure. In China, the fixed, uniform wage-setting policy severed the link between pay and performance. Extreme egalitarianism failed to motivate workers.

Guaranteed Housing

Enterprises were responsible for providing their employees with accommodation, usually at subsidized rents. Since housing was constructed and owned by the firm, it was impossible for a worker to keep his house should he, in the unlikely event, switch jobs to a different firm. Based on survey data, a study by this author shows that in China's big cities, housing was the single most important determinant for a worker, given a choice, to accept one job over another.[3] Since housing constituted such an important part of a worker's remuneration package, he had an aversion to losing it. Therefore, nonportable housing benefits offered to a worker may also have forced him to get stuck with a particular firm. It is estimated that the annual job turnover rate in Chinese cities is less than 1 percent, and the mobility of nonagricultural households is estimated to be less than 4 percent, compared with an annual mobility rate of 10–20 percent in Korea.

Pension Benefits

Enterprises were also responsible for income maintenance for their own retirees. The expenditure on retirement benefits was financed by the firms' current revenues rather than by past or current contributions. China's older industrial firms tended to have a much heavier burden of retirement outlays because they had more retired workers to support. Like housing benefits, pensions were paid by individual firms and were therefore nontransferable.

Other social benefits provided by China's state-owned enterprises included:

- free medical benefits;
- liberal sick and maternity leave policy;

---

[3]See Hu (1989).

- day care and schools;
- library, sports, and entertainment facilities; and
- subsidized food and other consumer goods.

The traditional system of social protection had, therefore, tied workers to the firms that employed them. Enterprise-based, nontransferable social security benefits, together with fixed wage setting and a system of permanent employment that relied on administrative job assignment, created substantial labor market rigidity in China. These characteristics of China's employment and social security systems discouraged labor mobility by adding fixed adjustment costs, and led to a substantial loss of efficiency in the state-owned sector.

China's unique "city residence registration" *(Hu-Kou)* system effectively eliminated labor mobility between rural and urban areas. Millions of well-educated rural youth had been denied opportunities to work in the modern industrial sector, leading to underutilization of a sizable stock of China's human capital. Within the state-owned sector, the lack of labor mobility may also have caused further efficiency costs because of widespread mismatch between workers and jobs.

Although the social benefits offered by state-owned enterprises to their workers were both extensive and generous, a critical program was missing from the old system—there was no unemployment insurance. While it was not needed in China's old system of guaranteed job security, the lack of such insurance has become the major obstacle to enterprise restructuring. Without this important social protection system, market-oriented reforms would inflict poverty and human suffering on the jobless, resulting in the loss of public support for economic reform.

Linkages Between Labor Immobility, Social Protection, and Enterprise Reform

The surge of rural industry and private business in China during the last decade has put strong competitive pressures on the state-owned sector. In recent years, a third of state-owned enterprises (SOEs) have been loss-making. Financially troubled SOEs have suddenly found themselves facing the threat of bankruptcy and reorganization. Public enterprises are struggling to shoulder the social responsibility for their workers, and at the same time to survive competition from a fledgling but dynamic private sector.

Why does the labor market matter for enterprise restructuring? Is not a change of ownership and control, say, through privatization, all that is required to revitalize China's ailing state sector? Clearly, in

China's new competitive environment, a leading reason for SOEs to lose ground is that they have high costs. With gradual price decontrol and increased autonomy in making production and investment decisions, the profitability of SOEs becomes increasingly dependent on their cost structures. There is no noticeable difference in the net cost of capital between SOEs and China's rural and township enterprises (TVEs).[4] SOEs, however, have substantially high labor costs caused by overstaffing and the heavy burden of providing social benefits to their workers. To improve the economic performance of China's state-owned sector, a first step would be to relieve SOEs of the burden of social services and to increase labor market flexibility.

A comparison of SOEs and TVEs illustrates the importance of labor market reform. Like SOEs, and contrary to the misconception held by some Western economists, China's TVEs are not strictly privately owned; rather, most are owned and controlled by local governments or collectives. While there exist a host of factors that can help explain the success of TVEs, a chief advantage enjoyed by them is the flexibility of the rural labor market. Almost all TVE workers are short-term contractual employees or seasonal laborers who receive no permanent job guarantee. Wages are flexible and market-determined. There is a close link between pay and performance, so workers are well motivated and productivity growth is high. Firms' hiring decisions depend entirely on their demand for labor. They can readily adjust the size of the workforce to changing market conditions. Unlike SOEs, these TVEs provide few social services directly to their employees. In particular, the provision of housing is optional because workers of TVEs are ex-farmers and already own their homes. By contrast, the traditional social security system inhibits enterprise restructuring because it prevents labor mobility and produces a lock-in effect on employment.

The external factors faced by China's SOEs and TVEs—taxes, regulations, and macroeconomic conditions—have gradually converged over time since economic reforms began. One area that remains strikingly different, however, is the labor market structure. The differences in employment, wages, and social security system may be among the factors that help explain the contrasting economic performance of the state-owned sector and township and village enterprises.

Enterprise-based, nontransferable social security benefits, guaranteed lifetime employment, and the absence of a public unemployment insurance program have presented substantial risks and large opportu-

---

[4]SOEs in China do face higher nominal tax rates than TVEs. The effective tax burden on SOEs, however, is unlikely to differ substantially from that on TVEs, considering SOEs' easy access to soft "policy loans" and to government budgetary subsidies.

nity costs associated with adjustments in the labor market. This system of social security has led to overstaffing and high labor costs in most state-owned enterprises, and adversely affected their profitability. If excess labor in the state-owned sector cannot be released and absorbed into the private sector, then China's strategy of commercialization without privatization for reforming SOEs will stand little chance of success.

Chinese Experiments with Social Security and Labor Market Reforms

In contrast to the sweeping rural reforms introduced and implemented in 1978 and 1979, and the dramatic foreign trade and investment reforms of 1983 and 1984, China's enterprise reforms have been slow and late. The stop-and-go pattern was indicative of the hesitation of the Chinese leadership about reforming the state-owned enterprise sector. Although the government may have been reluctant to give up its commitment to the dominance of public ownership in China's economy, a more important reason for the delay has been the deep concern about massive unemployment and social instability likely to be caused by drastic enterprise reform measures. Apparently, the government has concluded that the social and political costs were too high to attempt a "shock therapy" approach to China's state-owned sector.

This cautious, gradual approach to enterprise reform may have brought about some unexpected benefits. For one thing, China has had ample time to experiment with and carefully evaluate various reform proposals in a few selected enterprises and several designated cities. Through slow-paced trial and error, valuable lessons have been learned and experience gradually accumulated. Without guidance of any formal theory, a practical strategy has nevertheless emerged—to start with labor market reform and social security reform—so that the necessary conditions, including legal and institutional requirements, can be created to support full-fledged enterprise reforms.[5]

---

[5]Most of the enterprise reform initiatives to date have aimed at improving the incentive structure for both SOE managers and workers and removing labor market rigidities. The reform measures in China are vividly characterized as smashing three "irons": (1) "iron rice bowls" (guaranteed job assignments, pay, housing, pension, medical, and a host of other benefits for SOE workers); (2)"iron chairs" (permanent job positions in permanent state enterprises, with no layoff or bankruptcy risk); and (3) "iron wages" (uniformly distributed, fixed wage payments that are not linked with job performance and productivity).

Reform of the Wage System and Employment

An area identified as one of the first targets of reforms was the irrational wage system in the state sector. The Chinese authorities were convinced that some changes in the rigid, egalitarian wage policies were long overdue and making these changes could generate immediate efficiency gains without incurring big social risks. The reform measures emphasized improving work incentives within state-owned enterprises. Wage policies were allowed to be more flexible, and bonuses, once condemned as capitalist, were introduced in 1978 as a component of workers' total compensation. SOEs were granted discretion in determining the amount of bonus to be paid to individual workers, and were encouraged to link pay to workers' performance. Wage gaps were permitted to widen, reflecting job performance differentials as well as workers' seniority. Concerned about general wage inflation under the more flexible wage system and the weak relation between firms' wage growth and productivity growth, the government introduced in 1984 a system of aggregate wage controls, which linked the total sum of wages and bonuses an enterprise is entitled to distribute to its employees to certain performance indicators such as gross profits or sales volume. Recently, the Chinese authorities have attempted to further liberalize direct control over total wages. The goal is for the government to play only a supervisory role in the future.[6] Trade unions, which traditionally have been inactive in the wage-setting process, will be given a role as the workers' representative in negotiations with SOE management over remuneration and work conditions.

Since the mid-1980s, SOEs have been gradually given more hiring autonomy. An important step leading to greater labor market flexibility was taken in 1986 when the "labor contracting system" was introduced, under which all new employees in SOEs would be hired on a contractual basis for a period usually lasting from three to five years. The introduction of labor contracts marked a shift from permanent jobs to more flexible "contracting," breaking away from the tradition of lifetime tenure. In contrast to the obligated permanent job offers in the past, these hiring contracts do not guarantee automatic renewal or job extension when they expire. With a finite duration of employ-

---

[6]In July 1992, the Chinese government issued the "Regulations on Transforming the Operating Mechanism of State-Owned Enterprises," with the intention of putting into effect the "Enterprise Law" enacted in 1988. These regulations specify 14 management rights that would henceforth be exercised by the state enterprises. Three of these clearly defined rights pertain to the labor market: the right to assign labor, the right to have personal management, and the right to set wages and bonuses.

Table 7.4. China: Percentage Share of Contract Workers in Total Workers

Year	Total Urban Labor Force	State Sector	Collectives	Individual and Foreign Businesses
1983	0.6	0.6	0.3	. . .
1984	1.8	2.0	1.0	8.1
1985	3.3	3.7	2.2	11.4
1986	4.9	5.6	2.7	14.5
1987	6.6	7.6	3.6	18.1
1988	9.1	10.1	5.8	20.7
1989	10.7	11.8	7.0	25.1
1990	12.1	13.3	8.1	26.3
1991	13.6	14.9	8.9	28.0
1992	17.2	18.9	11.0	29.8

Source: Chinese authorities.

ment, workers face the risk of joblessness and tend to work harder to stay on the job. Managers find it easier to monitor workers' performance, and appropriately reward or punish workers according to their performance. SOEs are, therefore, given considerable discretion in selecting employees and in making retention decisions upon expiration of labor contracts.

By 1992, the number of contract workers *(He Tong Gong)* in the state-owned sector had risen to 21 million, accounting for 19 percent of the total workforce in the state-owned sector (Table 7.4). The proportion was larger for state-owned industrial enterprises, with contract workers accounting for 27 percent of total workers in 1992. In Shanghai, contract workers accounted for 33 percent of total workers in the city's combined state-owned sector. As a complement to the labor contracting system, a labor arbitration system is being developed to resolve labor disputes. To replace gradually the old system of administrative job assignment by the government bureaucracy, numerous employment agencies, such as labor service companies, are being established in Chinese towns and cities to help place first-time job seekers in the labor force.

Even more significantly, managers of SOEs have been granted the legal authority to lay off redundant or incompetent workers. In practice, however, it is rare for managers to exercise their power to dismiss workers. Rather, they tend to feel morally obligated to keep unsatisfactory workers employed, and make efforts to reassign workers with poor performance to less important or lesser-paid positions. Instead of laying off all redundant workers, manufacturing enterprises have sought to create service-oriented subsidiaries to reemploy those workers.[7] In general SOEs still have the social responsibility to maintain jobs. Laying off workers is considered only as a last resort to improve efficiency and profitability. It remains to be seen how far China is willing to go to accept more unemployment as market forces may dictate.

Introduction of a Bankruptcy Law

In 1986, China enacted a bankruptcy law, the first ever in the history of the People's Republic, which came into effect in 1988.[8] The bankruptcy law has just begun to play a significant role in providing a set of incentives to managers to improve enterprise performance and allocate business risks among interested parties. In the immediate ensuing years, however, few actions were taken to apply the bankruptcy law to financially troubled state enterprises. Mainly because of concern for the implication for unemployment, the government was reluctant to allow the bankruptcy law to be fully implemented. Instead, the government intervened to bail out troubled firms by injecting cheap credit and subsidies, writing off or assuming their debt liabilities, in cases where losses were caused by policy factors, such as price controls. For those unprofitable firms whose financial losses were mainly due to poor management, the government would reshuffle management and force a reorganization by arranging a merger with another better-performing state enterprise.[9] As more SOEs became unprofitable and debt-ridden, which demanded huge increases in government subsidies and widened the government fiscal deficit, the Chinese authorities have become more willing to let loss-making state-owned enterprises go bankrupt. In 1992, the People's Courts handled 2,685 bankruptcy cases nationwide, a 365 percent increase since 1991. A large number of those that failed were state-owned. In the coming several years, the Chinese government plans to lift subsidies and all the special protection measures for SOEs so that SOEs become fully responsive to market forces. At the same time, measures will be taken to ensure management autonomy and rights of state-owned enterprises. While some SOEs

---

[7]*China Daily* (July 12, 1993) reported that China's giant state-owned metal company, China National Nonferrous Metals Industry Corp., planned to slash 330,000 jobs over the next several years. However, few if any of the workers to be laid off will actually end up jobless because they will simply be transferred from the company's core business, metalworking, to other newly established, job-creating service subsidiaries.

[8]For an excellent summary of the evolving legal framework for enterprise reform in China, see Lichtenstein (1993).

[9]Leasing and privatization have also played an increasingly important role in recent years. Many state-owned department stores and other stores, for example, have been leased out to private individuals. In many cities, foreign investors are allowed to bid and restructure existing unprofitable state-owned enterprises.

may eventually succeed in adapting to China's increasingly competitive, market-oriented economy, other SOEs are expected to fail the test, and more bankruptcies are likely to follow.

A constraining factor in China for applying the bankruptcy law, protecting enterprises' autonomy in both hiring and firing decisions, and imposing hard budget constraints on SOEs was the lack of an adequate social safety net for displaced workers. As noted above, the traditional social protection system in China was enterprise-based, which locked workers into their workplaces. Over time, this constraining factor has become a severe obstacle to the restructuring of China's state-owned enterprises. Increasing labor market flexibility, a necessary condition for the transformation of the state-owned sector, entails overhauling China's social security system. With the introduction of the labor contracting system, provisions had to be made for the transfer of retirement benefits, because a worker could no longer rely on being attached to one enterprise throughout his or her working life. Provision also had to be made for income support for those workers whose contracts were denied renewal and who were unable to find new jobs quickly.

Establishment of Unemployment Insurance

To facilitate the needed trimming of the redundant workforce in the state sector, and implementation of the bankruptcy law, the role of social unemployment insurance is critical. The package of labor market reforms introduced in 1986 included the establishment of an unemployment insurance (UI) scheme as a natural complement to the labor contracting system. The main elements of the unemployment insurance legislation are closely linked with the proposed labor market reform measures. The legislation addresses eligibility criteria, benefit levels, funding, and administration. Workers eligible for unemployment benefits include (1) workers of bankrupt enterprises; (2) workers made redundant by near-bankrupt enterprises during reorganization; (3) contract workers whose contracts have expired or been canceled; and (4) workers dismissed for disciplinary reasons. The eligibility criteria are thus compatible with the structural changes in China's labor market and overall economy. The UI legislation sets a two-year duration for benefits and a nominal replacement ratio of up to 75 percent of standard earnings.[10] Enterprises are required to contribute 1 percent of their payroll to UI funds. The UI scheme has the feature that the funds may be used to finance job training and job creation programs

---

[10]Standard earnings are defined as the claimant's average monthly standard wage over two years before his or her unemployment.

administered by local labor bureaus and their affiliated labor service companies, which have the mandate to assist new entrants, and more recently, job losers, in identifying employment opportunities.

Since the unemployment insurance is established as social insurance rather than an employer-liability program, it is mainly administered at the city- and county-government level, not at the enterprise level. There have been several attempts in China to establish pooled unemployment insurance programs at the provincial level, further moving away from enterprise-based social protection. The regulations on Unemployment Insurance for State Enterprises Employees were enacted in April 1993, and provide for the establishment, management, and operation of unemployment insurance funds. The UI program, as contained in the existing regulations, covers only the state-owned enterprise sector. In some cities, such as Shengzhen and Qingdao, which have moved furthest on reforms, UI has been extended to cover temporary and self-employed workers and workers in joint ventures and foreign-funded enterprises. The government's goal is to expand the coverage of the unemployment insurance system in the near future. In particular, unemployment benefits will be provided to all the involuntarily unemployed regardless of cause, and coverage will be extended to employees in collectively owned and foreign enterprises nationwide. It would be most desirable for China to extend the UI coverage to employees of TVEs and private businesses as well, whose share in the total workforce has surged over the last decade.

The timely introduction of unemployment insurance has introduced a critical program into China's social safety net, facilitating the release of "excess workers" from the overstaffed state sector, and helping to contain the social and economic costs associated with transformation to a market economy. During the first three years since the inception of the UI programs, there were annually an average of 30,000 workers who claimed UI benefits. This number more than tripled in 1990 and 1991, with the deepening of labor market and enterprise reforms. About 200,000 SOE workers in 1992 benefited from UI programs. The number of UI recipients have been so far quite small relative to the total workforce in China's state sector. But this number may start to rise in the next decade, depending on the current extent of "surplus labor" in the state sector, the proposed extension of UI coverage, and the growth prospects of the Chinese economy.

Housing Reform

Transforming state-owned enterprises into autonomous operating economic entities also requires development of alternative means of providing for the housing of their employees. The obligatory provision of employee housing by SOEs has not only created labor market rigidity, but also added a heavy social burden to SOEs in comparison to their private sector counterparts, such as township and village enterprises and foreign-owned enterprises. Since the late 1980s, China has made some limited progress in housing reform. A consensus has been reached that the provision of housing is not an essential function of state enterprises or government and that it could be better carried out by the private sector. The initial reform measures comprised upward rent adjustments aimed at reducing the housing subsidy in the state sector. More recently, the focus of reform has shifted to privatizing the public housing stock by selling housing units to state employees. Several legal developments, including the 1988 amendment of the Chinese Constitution, the revision of the 1986 land law, and national regulations concerning urban land use, land transfer, and property rights, have had a positive impact on the development of the real estate market in China. As widely recognized, these legal developments are necessary to replace enterprise provision of housing to workers with a market-based delivery of housing. Real estate development companies have been forming rapidly in the past several years; and have been involved in constructing and selling residential property to Hong Kong residents and Taiwan investors. Although the number of domestic customers who purchase residential housing has been growing, these buyers tend to be China's nouveau riches—prosperous private businessmen. Selling housing units at market prices to SOE employees has proven more difficult because of their low wage income and the lack of home financing. In some cities municipal housing funds have been set up—to be funded from the issue of savings bonds and proceeds from the sale of the existing state-owned housing stock—for the construction of affordable housing for urban residents in general and SOE employees in particular. Mortgage financing companies are also being established, with the pension funds as the primary source of funding.

Development of the Service Sector

China's rapidly expanding private sector has in fact presented opportunities for restructuring the state-owned enterprises through the creation of new jobs and the development of a housing market. These factors help to mitigate the lock-in effect in China's labor market because released surplus labor is quickly absorbed into the fast-growing private sector and housing becomes better available to new employees and transferred or relocated workers.

As part of the solution to the problem of excess workers in SOEs, the government has attached great importance to the development of the tertiary sector, which in 1992 employed fewer than 20 percent of China's total labor force and accounted for about 28 percent of GNP. This sector is generally more labor intensive than manufacturing and is viewed as having great potential for absorbing surplus labor in the state sector. In July 1992, the government published its "Decisions on Expediting the Development of the Tertiary Industry," which spell out a set of policy measures to boost the service sector, including transforming state-owned tertiary enterprises into profit-oriented businesses, decontrolling prices and offering credit and tax incentives. A policy measure of special importance is to encourage civil servants in government organizations and workers in SOEs to resign and establish private businesses in the service sector.[11] The government hopes that in the remainder of the 1990s the service sector will generate a large number of new jobs, essentially playing a role similar to that played by the township and village enterprises in absorbing the surplus labor in the rural area during the past decade.

Relaxation of Restrictions on Migration

Other initiatives to increase labor market flexibility in China include relaxation of restrictions on migration of rural labor to cities. Temporary city residence permits are issued to allow rural labor to provide a wide range of services in urban areas. Restrictions on regional mobility are being gradually lifted for university graduates and professionals. In recent years the government has also emphasized the role of training. The Ministry of Labor and its local labor bureaus, as well as enterprises themselves, have established numerous training centers, retraining programs, and technical and vocational schools to improve workers' skills and adaptability to the changing labor market.

Pooling of Pensions

A key objective of social security reform in China is to relieve individual enterprises of full, direct responsibility for their workers' retirement pensions by establishing funds that pool resources and risks among enterprises and across regions. Experimentation with pension pooling began in 1986 in several cities, including Shanghai and

---

[11]The Chinese press describe the voluntary exodus out of the state sector to the private sector by using a colorful phrase, *"Xia Hai,"* meaning "plunging into the sea (of commerce)."

Table 7.5. China: Economic Growth and Unemployment

Year	Total Urban Unemployed (10,000)	In Which: First-Time Job Seekers	Share of First-Time Job Seekers	GNP Growth Rate	Urban Unemployment Rate
					(In percent)
1952	376.6	. . .	. . .	. . .	13.2
1957	200.4	. . .	. . .	. . .	5.9
1978	530.0	249.1	47.0	11.7	5.3
1980	541.5	382.5	70.6	7.9	4.9
1981	439.5	343.0	78.0	4.4	3.8
1982	379.4	293.8	77.4	8.8	3.2
1983	271.4	222.0	81.8	10.4	2.3
1984	235.7	195.9	83.1	14.7	1.9
1985	238.5	196.9	82.6	12.8	1.8
1986	264.4	209.3	79.2	8.1	2.0
1987	276.6	235.1	85.0	10.9	2.0
1988	296.2	245.3	82.8	11.3	2.0
1989	377.9	309.0	81.8	4.4	2.6
1990	383.2	312.7	81.6	4.1	2.5
1991	352.2	288.4	81.9	8.2	2.3
1992	360.3	299.8	83.2	13.0	2.3

Source: Chinese authorities.

Shenzheng. In recent years, retirement funds have been established at the municipal level in most cities and some at the provincial level. Employers and employees are required to contribute a certain percentage of the payroll toward these funds.[12] These mandatory retirement funds are generally modeled on the Central Provident Fund of Singapore. Retirement pension pooling has eased the financial burden on many state enterprises of supporting the growing number of retirees. Pension pooling has also helped maintain workers' retirement benefits when changing jobs and, hence, improved the conditions conducive to greater labor mobility.

Table 7.5 suggests that the transition to a market economy in China has not sparked high unemployment. The officially measured urban unemployment rate stood at 2.3 percent in 1992, and the number of the unemployed in urban China actually declined from 5.3 million in 1978 when the reform was commenced, to 3.6 million in 1992. First-time job seekers, consisting mainly of recent secondary school graduates, accounted for about 80 percent of the total urban unemployed. While a variety of factors, including strong economic growth and bud-

---

[12]In Shanghai, for example, the contribution rates by both enterprises and workers are set at 5 percent of the wage bill.

getary subsidies to keep unprofitable SOEs afloat, have so far prevented massive urban unemployment in China, increased labor market flexibility has also clearly played a positive role in keeping the unemployment rate low.[13]

As China's social security reform continues, it is important to establish a system of social protection for all employees regardless of the ownership structure of their employer, hence achieving greater social equity and a "level playing field" among enterprises of different ownership in China's socialist market economy.

The Chinese authorities have noted the necessity of transferring social responsibility from enterprises to the government. The new fiscal reform measures, introduced at the beginning of 1994, aim at enhancing the role of the government in social protection and other social services such as education and health care. However, the lack of clear assignment of fiscal responsibilities among different levels of government in China presents risks to transferring government functions from enterprises to the appropriate levels of government.[14] Currently, for instance, it is the subnational governments—provincial and, most important, municipal—that are responsible for the financing and administration of both retirement funds and unemployment funds. The stated goal, however, is to establish a unified national social security system encompassing old-age pensions and unemployment insurance at the central government level.

Conclusions

Labor market rigidity induced by traditional social protection mechanism creates barriers for enterprise restructuring and privatization in economies in transition. Lessons from many of these countries' experience suggest that increasing labor market flexibility through social security reform is necessary to meet the challenge of making a smooth transition to a market economy.

In the past decade, China has made some important progresses in reforming its social security as well as the wage and employment systems. These developments have substantially facilitated labor mobility,

---

[13]Paradoxically, in spite of the rapid development of rural TVEs, the problem of rural unemployment may have become more acute. The fast growth in agricultural productivity and relaxed restriction on migration of rural labor to cities have produced a large pool of rural unemployed labor.

[14]For a discussion on issues and options for reforming social expenditure assignment in China, see Hu (1995).

helped protect workers' well-being, and helped sustain social support for economic reforms. China still faces formidable risks and challenges, however. Much more remains to be done to transform China's state-owned sector and to deal with the threat of potentially large unemployment in rural as well as in urban areas. Nevertheless, with the emergence of a strong, dynamic private sector, and the gradual creation of conditions favorable to reforms, China should now be relatively well poised to launch full-fledged enterprise reforms.

References

Ahmad, Ehtisham and Athar Hussain, 1989, "Social Security in China: A Historical Perspective," in *Social Security in Developing Countries,* ed. by Ehtisham Ahmad, and others (Oxford, England: Clarendon Press).

Bell, W. Michael, Hoe Ee Khor, and Kalpana Kochhar, 1993, *China at the Threshold of a Market Economy,* IMF Occasional Paper No. 107 (Washington: International Monetary Fund).

Blejer, Mario, and others, 1991, *China: Economic Reform and Macroeconomic Management,* IMF Occasional Paper No. 76 (Washington: International Monetary Fund).

China, State Statistical Bureau, *State Statistical Yearbook of China,* various issues (Beijing: State Statistical Bureau of the People's Republic of China).

Hamer, Andrew Marshall, 1992, "China: Implementation Options for Urban Housing Reform," A World Bank Country Study (Washington: World Bank).

Hu, Zu-liu, 1989, "Housing Benefits and Occupational Choices in Urban China" (unpublished; Cambridge, Massachusetts: Harvard University).

―――, 1995, "Social Expenditure Assignments in China: Issues and Responses," in *Reforming Intergovernmental Fiscal Relations—An International Perspective,* ed. by Ehtisham Ahmad, Gao Qiang, and Vito Tanzi (Washington: International Monetary Fund).

Lichtenstein, Natalie G., 1993, "Enterprise Reform in China: The Evolving Legal Framework," Policy Research Working Paper No. 1198 (Washington : World Bank).

Perkins, Dwight Heald, 1988, "Reforming China's Economic System," *Journal of Economic Literature,* Vol. 26 (June), pp. 601–45.

8

Colombia: Economic Adjustment and the Poor

Claire Liuksila

In the mid-1980s, faced with a rapidly deteriorating economic and financial picture, Colombia undertook a strong adjustment program. By putting the economy on a sounder footing, the government felt that the population in general stood much to gain from the program in the medium run. But it also recognized the likely short-run hardships for low-income groups.

How did the adjustment program affect the poor? This chapter attempts to answer this question by laying out the events that led to the adoption of the program. It then describes the major ingredients of the program and policies that the Government of Colombia adopted to protect the poor. The impact of the program on the poor is illustrated by a practical methodology that embodies the main ingredients of the program. Finally, the chapter ends with a concluding section and some caveats.

Economic Events

Colombia's economy began to show signs of a serious deterioration in the early 1980s, when real economic growth averaged only 1.6 percent, sharply down from the 4.9 percent annual rate seen during 1975–80, and the public sector and balance of payments deficits widened markedly. This was due both to outside factors, principally the decline in international coffee prices, and to expansionary domestic policies.

Note: This is an abridged version of IMF Working Paper 91/81(Washington: International Monetary Fund, 1991).

The intensification of exchange and trade restrictions was a central element of the authorities' initial strategy to stem the loss of net international reserves over 1982–84. By early 1984, 83 percent of all items in the tariff schedule were subject to prior licensing, 16.5 percent were on the prohibited import list, and only 0.5 percent of items could be imported without any administrative control. To reinforce this policy, the authorities accelerated the rate of depreciation of the peso against the dollar and adopted fiscal revenue measures in 1983 and 1984. These steps helped to reduce the fiscal and external current account deficits somewhat in 1984, but the deficits still remained unsustainably large. By the mid-1980s, the economy was marked by an overvalued exchange rate and a distorted price system.

The 1985–86 Adjustment Program

In response to the continuing economic and financial deterioration, the authorities adopted a comprehensive adjustment program that was supported by a monitoring arrangement with the Fund and adjustment loans provided by the World Bank that were designed to support structural reforms in trade policy, agriculture, and related areas. The program included a broad range of measures affecting virtually all areas of economic policy.

External Policy

The external policy measures included (1) a cumulative (1985–86) 30 percent depreciation of the real exchange rate; (2) a significant liberalization of import restrictions—by the end of 1986 nearly 70 percent of goods could be imported freely; (3) broadening of the tax base for import duties; (4) reduction of export incentives granted through tax credit certificates; and (5) imposition of an 8 percent surcharge on most imports.

Fiscal Policy

In addition to (5) above, revenue measures included (1) abolition of some sales tax exemptions; (2) prepayment of 20 percent of future income tax liability for companies and individuals with incomes in excess of 2 million pesos; (3) a range of measures designed to raise revenue from income and investment taxes; (4) elimination of the special income tax deduction for Carboco and the special discount for Empetrol, two state monopolies; (5) an increase of 50 percent in the stamp tax and its indexation to the consumer price index; (6) a cumulative increase of 35 percent in the gasoline tax, and (7) gradual elimination of transportation subsidies.

Policy measures on the expenditure side included (1) a reduction in current expenditure of 1 percent of GDP; (2) capping the weighted average salary increases of central government workers at 10.5 percent;[1] and (3) cuts in noninterest current and capital expenditure and social spending.

Monetary Policy, Wage Policy, and Other Price Measures

A tight monetary policy was adopted that involved increases in preferential lending rates to reduce the subsidy element. In 1985, the minimum wage was increased by 20 percent, in line with projected inflation for the low-income consumer price index. Other price measures included raising electricity, water, and telephone rates by 35–40 percent in 1985 and by a further 2 percent in 1986.

Government Policies to Protect the Poor

By realigning the relative prices of foreign and domestic goods, reducing inflation, and improving economic growth, the government hoped to raise living standards in both the short and the long run. These policies were expected to benefit everyone, including the poor. At the same time, however, the government recognized that certain measures of the adjustment program could hurt lower-income groups in the short run. These included an increase in the cost of imports due to the large depreciation of the exchange rate and the imposition of an 8 percent import surcharge; large increases in gasoline prices and public sector tariffs; the elimination of transportation subsidies; the removal of certain exemptions from the sales tax; and a sharp reduction in real terms in the public sector wage bill.

Against this background, the government opted for new measures to protect lower-income groups and to intensify the existing antipoverty programs. These measures took the following forms.

Wage Policies

As stated earlier, the minimum wage was increased by 20 percent as were wages of public sector workers at the bottom of the wage scale.

---

[1]Higher increases of up to 20 percent were allowed for lower-paid employees.

Adjustment of the minimum wage has been traditionally an important social policy tool in Colombia, a country in which wage indexation is widespread. While generally adjusted annually, the minimum wage is set at a very low level, just equivalent to the income required to keep an individual above the government's definition of the "poverty line."

Although there is no direct evidence concerning the relevance of the minimum wage for the poor, recent studies indicate that the adjustment of the minimum wage explains a significant portion of the increase in average wages in construction, the public sector, and the informal sector—activities in which the poor might be expected to be more heavily represented. Moreover, the adjustment of the minimum wage has apparently had a moderate, but increasing, influence on the growth of the average wage in rural areas where poverty tends to be high.

Selective Exemptions from Import Surcharge

A number of goods were exempted from the 8 percent surcharge, most notably food and fertilizers. There are no data on the importance of imports and imported production inputs in the food consumed by low-income groups. However, this measure, although not well targeted, was intended to mitigate the effect of the surcharge on low-income groups.

Antipoverty Programs

The government also continued to channel resources into one of its core poverty alleviation programs—the DRI (Program for Integrated Rural Development)—which concentrates on providing basic services and financial resources to small farmers. After 1986, a number of other antipoverty programs were launched, including:

- the Plan for National Rehabilitation (PNR)—a program that focuses on providing the basic necessities for the poorest 10–12 percent of the population and includes land distribution, improvements in infrastructure, and increased public services;
- the Better Homes for Children (HBI)—an innovative and successful World Bank-supported program that combines supplemental feeding and day care for children in poor communities with the education and training of their mothers; and
- the Plan for the Eradication of Absolute Poverty (BEPA)—a program aimed at poverty in urban areas; and a variety of other programs designed to improve the basic education, health, and housing of the poor.

Economic Impact of Adjustment Program

This chapter only attempts to examine possible first-round effects of the adjustment program on the poor. It does not question the basic policy thrust of the adjustment program. It does not attempt to measure what the program's impact might be in the longer run, nor conjecture what the position of the poor might have been in the absence of adjustment. Moreover, with the data available, it is difficult to pinpoint the impact of the program on the poor in general or on different socioeconomic segments within the category of those classified as poor. Bearing in mind these limitations, a two-step analysis is used to assess the impact of the program on the relative position of the poor. First, an estimate of first-round price and income effects is made without the benefit of ex-post information, that is, as if the program were being initiated now. Second, the estimates are then contrasted with the actual results for 1985–86.

First-Round Impacts on the Poor

The adjustment program contained a number of measures that affected prices. The evidence suggests that the depreciation of the exchange rate, the imposition of the 8 percent import surcharge, the broadening of the tax base on the sale of imported goods and the reduction in the implicit level of import duties raised the total domestic cost of imports by 20.8 percent in 1985 and by 30.6 percent in 1986 (Table 8.1). By weighting the increased cost of imports by the share of imports in aggregate demand, and assuming a complete and relatively quick pass-through of the higher cost of imports to domestic prices, one can conclude that these measures may have added 3.3 percentage points to the consumer price index (CPI) of low-income households in the first round of price adjustment in 1985, and 4.5 percentage points in 1986 (Table 8.2). An alternative approach to gauging the impact of higher import prices on domestic prices would be to use the calculated elasticities derived from various econometric studies that have investigated the relationship between import prices and domestic prices. These studies generally found that a 10 percent increase in the cost of imports raised domestic prices between 1 percent and 2 percent.[2] Using this methodology, the increase in the domestic cost of imports calculated in Table 8.1 would raise consumer prices between 2 and 4 percentage

---

[2]A survey of these studies appears in Santiago Herrera, "Relaciones de Causalidad Entre la Tasa de Cambio, los Precios y los Salarios: Alguna Evidencia Sobre el Caso Colombiano 1950–83," *Ensayos Sobre Política Económica,* No. 7 (June 1985).

Table 8.1. Colombia: Calculation of Program-Induced Price Effects on Import Prices

(In billions of pesos)

	1984	1985	1986
Value of imports (c.i.f.)	452.9	587.9	748.3
Taxes levied on imports, net of exemptions	74.0	122.3	193.6
Customs duties	45.3	53.7	85.0
Tax on sale of imports	25.8	40.8	62.7
Surcharges[1]	2.9	27.8	45.9
Total domestic cost of imports	526.9	710.2	941.9
(Percent change)		34.8	32.6
Program-induced effect on import prices	n.a.	109.7	217.6
Exchange rate[2]	n.a.	84.2	175.2
Discretionary tax element			
Customs duties[3]	n.a.	−1.1	3.7
Tax on sale of imports	n.a.	3.1	0
Surcharge: 8 percent	n.a.	23.5	38.7
Surcharge: 2 percent	n.a.	0	0
		(In percent)	
Implicit increase in the domestic cost of imports caused by exchange rate and discretionary tax measures		20.8	30.6

Sources: IMF staff estimates; and Contraloría de la República, *Informe Económico* (1985 and 1986).
Note: n.a. denotes not applicable.
[1]Includes both 8 percent and 2 percent surcharges.
[2]Calculated with the nominal effective exchange rate.
[3]Change in implicit tariff.

points in 1985, and by 3.1 to 6.2 percentage points in 1986. This is similar to the results obtained with the method employed in Table 8.2.

The 40 percent average increase in electricity, water, and telephone rates would have added a further 1.9 percentage points to the index in 1985, while the 26.8 percent increase in these public sector tariffs in the following year would have raised the CPI for low-income households by 1.3 percentage points. Assuming that the reduction in transport subsidies was passed through fully to higher bus fares, this measure would have raised consumer prices by 0.9 percent in 1985 and by 0.5 percent in 1986. The elimination of the VAT exemption for soft drinks could be expected to have had a very small impact on prices in 1985 and no impact in 1986. Assuming an underlying rate of inflation of about 20.5 percent for the other items in the CPI, it is estimated that the CPI for low-income households would have risen by about 21.5 percent in 1985 and by 21.8 percent in 1986.

There are a number of obvious pitfalls in this type of analysis. First, as stated earlier, the analysis attempts to measure first-round price

Table 8.2. Colombia: Estimation of Program-Induced Price Effects on Low-Income Households[1]

(In percent, annual averages)

	1985		1986	
	Change	Price impact	Change	Price impact
1. Import costs	20.8	3.3	30.6	4.5
2. Gasoline price	15.0	0.6	20.0	0.8
3. Elimination of VAT exemption for soft drinks	10.0	0.1	—	—
4. Electricity	40.0	1.0	26.8	0.7
5. Water	40.0	0.8	26.8	0.5
6. Telephone	40.0	0.1	26.8	0.1
7. Reduction of transport subsidies	32.9	0.9	17.2	0.5
8. Total induced effects		6.8		7.1
9. Other goods and services[2]	20.5	14.7	20.5	14.7
10. Total change in CPI (10 = 8 + 9)		21.5		21.8

Source: IMF staff estimates.

[1]To calculate the price impact, with the exception of import costs, the change in the price of the relevant article was multiplied by its weight in the low-income CPI. For imports, the price change was multiplied by the weight of imports in aggregate demand.

[2]This represents an extrapolation from past trends. The trend value for other goods and services was derived by regressing the log of the index for these items on a time trend over the period 1965–84.

effects only. Second, it assumes that the expenditure pattern implicit in the low-income consumer price index is valid for all poor households. The evidence appears to indicate that the poor spend a much larger proportion of their income on food than is suggested by the low-income CPI. Third, with the available data, it is not possible to differentiate by broad categories of goods the impact of higher import costs on prices and to match this with the expenditure patterns of those classified as poor. Fourth, as food represents nearly half of the low-income CPI, and probably considerably more of the expenditure of the very poor, exemption of food items from the 8 percent import surcharge could have helped to soften its impact on low-income groups. However, because of data limitations it is not possible to disentangle the negative impact on the poor of the import surcharge from the positive impact owing to exemption of some items (including food) from the surcharge. Finally, the analysis is based on the assumption of constant markup, which may not be valid since the pace of economic activity was expected to slow down following the implementation of the adjustment program.

In designing the adjustment package, an attempt was made to maintain the purchasing power of the lower-income groups by providing for a 20 percent average increase in the minimum wage in 1985. In addition, the ceiling of 10.5 percent on the average increase in public sector wages was weighted to give a higher-than-average increase to lower-paid employees. For those at the lowest end of the wage scale, the increase amounted to 20 percent.

As part of the effort to improve the public sector balance, current expenditure was to be cut by 1 percent of GDP in 1985, but no further cuts were planned for 1986. This led to a reduction in social expenditure of 0.9 percent of GDP in 1985 and 0.4 percent in 1986. Most of the reduction took place in education expenditures, transport subsidies, and housing expenditure. Public transfers (direct income support) rose by only 7.4 percent in nominal terms in 1985, implying a decline of 12.6 percent in real terms with a projected inflation rate of 20 percent. There are no sufficient disaggregated data to discern whether this real decline in transfers was an across-the-board cut or was limited to certain programs. However, to the extent that the poor's income from transfers did fall, and considering that such transfers represent about 16.5 percent of the income of the poorest 10 percent of the population and 14 percent of the income of the next poorest group, this decline in real terms would have represented in 1985, all things being equal, a reduction in real income for these two groups of 2.0 percent and 1.8 percent, respectively. These trends were reversed in 1986; public transfers increased broadly in line with inflation while the minimum wage was raised in line with actual inflation observed during 1985.

Although the depreciation of the exchange rate was expected to affect negatively the buying power of the poor in the first instance through its effect on prices, it could be presumed to have had a positive impact on the earnings of the poor in the traded goods sectors, particularly for agricultural small holders but also for wage earners through its second-round effects on employment and perhaps also on wages. Unfortunately, there is no hard evidence to support this intuitive conclusion.

In summary, the first-round effects of the 1985 stabilization program, on balance, could have resulted in a relatively small reduction in the real incomes of the poor because the negative first-round price effects would have been largely offset by the 20 percent increase in the minimum wage and by the positive impact of the depreciation of the exchange rate on the tradable sector.

Macroeconomic Impacts: Objectives Versus Outcomes

Economic developments during 1985–86 turned out to be better than targeted, partly as a result of favorable external factors. Real GDP grew by 3.1 percent in 1985, compared with a projection of 2.0 percent under the program. The low-income CPI rose by 22.7 percent on average compared with 21.5 percent based on first-round price effects. Most of the acceleration of inflation in 1985 seems to have been due to a sharp increase in food prices. However, the rate of growth of housing costs, which includes expenditures for electricity, water, and telephone services, also accelerated from 12.9 percent in 1984 to 14.9 percent in 1985, about in line with the 1.9 percentage point increase calculated as a first-round impact. The rate of increase in the cost of clothing and other items included in the low-income CPI actually decelerated in 1985 compared to the previous year (Table 8.3). These figures make it difficult to pinpoint the impact of higher import costs on domestic prices. The acceleration in food prices was apparently only weakly linked to the depreciation of the exchange rate and had more to do with supply shortages.

Looking at other indicators, the unemployment rate in the formal sector stabilized, but there was a major deterioration in real wages in all sectors ranging from a decline of 8.2 percent on average for public sector workers to 2.9 percent for wages in manufacturing. Wages in agriculture fell by around 4 percent on average in real terms in 1985. In contrast, minumum wages in agriculture and in services fell only slightly, by 1.4 percent. To the extent that trends in the minimum wage are representative of developments in the earnings of the poor, the incomes of the poor would have been relatively better protected than other groups during the adjustment period.

While it may be tempting to speculate what the position of the poor might have been had the adjustment effort not taken place, or about the long-run effects of the adjustment program on the relative position of the poor, there is insufficient information for such an analysis and, in any case, it is beyond the scope of this chapter. One could imagine that, in the absence of adjustment, ceteris paribus, the expansionary financial policies pursued in the early 1980s would have led to even higher rates of inflation, while the severe distortion of relative prices caused by inappropriate external policies would have further weakened economic growth. This combination, through its negative effects on real incomes and employment, would have had an adverse impact on all income groups, and on the poor in particular.

Any attempt to trace the impact of the adjustment measures in the long run is complicated by the sharp recovery of coffee prices in 1986. All things being equal, it would seem safe to assume that the adjustment, particularly the realignment of the exchange rate, placed the economy in a better position to benefit from the subsequent coffee boom and maintain balanced growth in the longer run.

Table 8.3. Colombia: Developments in the Components of the Consumer Price Index

(Average annual percent change)

	General Index	Middle-Income Index	Low-Income Index
All items			
1984	16.1	18.3	18.3
1985	24.0	21.8	22.7
1986	18.9	21.6	20.7
Food			
1984	19.6	18.6	19.6
1985	27.7	28.2	27.9
1986	23.7	24.5	23.3
Housing			
1984	12.9	11.7	12.9
1985	15.5	15.2	14.9
1986	14.8	15.7	14.0
Clothing			
1984	17.9	17.6	18.1
1985	16.3	15.5	16.7
1986	19.1	17.7	19.6
Other			
1984	24.6	24.7	24.6
1985	19.3	19.3	19.3
1986	22.9	22.6	22.8

Source: Colombian Statistical Office (DANE), *Boletín de Estadística* (Bogotá, various issues).

Conclusion

The simple estimate of the first-round price effects suggests that the initial negative impact of the adjustment program was probably largely cushioned by the government's action on the minimum wage, by the exemption of food from the 8 percent import surcharge, and by the fact that the items that increased in price as a result of the measures taken under the program accounted for only just over one-fourth of the goods and services included in the low-income CPI. In fact, the actual increase in the low-income CPI in 1985 was very similar to that predicted. In addition, the perceived negative distributional effects of the program were narrowly concentrated during 1985. By 1986, under the influence of the coffee boom, real wages had recovered strongly, as had growth and employment, and by 1988 there was a further improvement in the distribution of income.

Because of data limitations and the methodology employed, this chapter can give only a fairly rough indication of the impact of the

1985–86 program on the incomes of the poor. For future studies, it would be desirable to have direct data on the expenditure patterns of poor households, rather than having to rely on proxies, such as the weights of the low-income CPI.

More important, because of data limitations, this chapter has been unable to quantify the presumably negative impact of the depreciation of the exchange rate on the incomes of the poor in the traded goods sector, which can be substantial given the size of the depreciation. Finally, in a middle-income developing country such as Colombia, the poor are in fact quite heterogeneous. Not only are there important differences in the characteristics of the poor with respect to urban versus rural poverty, but there is also considerable differentiation within these two groups. It is therefore difficult to generalize about the impact of program-induced price measures on the poor as a group.

9

Jordan: Restructuring Public Expenditures and Protecting the Poor

S. Ehtisham Ahmad

Jordan suffered from unsustainable macroeconomic imbalances, particularly with respect to the fiscal and trade deficits, during the mid-1980s. Necessary adjustments have been constrained by the need to protect the poor and those on relatively low fixed incomes from the effects of relative price changes. Thus, while there has been a substantial depreciation of the Jordanian dinar, the less-than-proportional pass-through of price changes, particularly for imported food items and energy, has led to increased pressure on budgetary subsidies. In this paper we examine possibilities for reducing subsidies in a manner that protects the poor. We also examine other elements that would be necessary for an effective provision for the poor and vulnerable in Jordan. Many of the recommendations in connection with subsidy reduction and the protection of the poor have been put in place. It would be interesting to follow up with work on the implementation and its effects, as a guide to policymakers not only in Jordan but also in other countries for which similar policies might be considered.

Macroeconomic Imbalances

Jordan experienced a GDP growth rate of 8 percent a year during 1978–82, which was not sustainable. The relatively high levels of government expenditure, over 50 percent of GDP on average during 1978–82, had led to overall deficits in excess of 30 percent of GDP, two-

Note: Originally issued as IMF Working Paper 91/82 (Washington: International Monetary Fund, 1991).

thirds of which (or around $1 billion a year on average) was financed by external grants. With a slowing of growth in the region in the mid-1980s, and a concomitant reduction in the level of grants (which declined to around $550 million by 1988), the regional recession affected Jordan severely, with growth dropping to 1.2 percent by 1985, and becoming negative by 1988. There was also an increase in the "after-grants" budget deficit from around 12 percent of GDP in the early 1980s to over 15 percent in 1988; the budget deficit "before grants" remained high at about 25 percent of GDP in 1988.

Compounding the budgetary crisis was a critical external debt-servicing situation. Jordan's total debt (disbursed and undisbursed) outstanding by 1989 amounted to about 180 percent of GDP. Debt-service payments as a ratio to exports of goods and services rose to 28 percent in 1988 before declining to 18 percent in 1989 as a result of rescheduling. This has exacerbated a precarious balance of payments situation. In addition, with the delinking of the West Bank from Jordan in mid-1988, there was substantial capital flight that created speculative pressures on the Jordanian dinar (JD). Reserves fell to about two weeks of imports by the end of 1988.

The response to the reserve and balance of payments situation has been a depreciation in the value of the currency from JD 0.33 per U.S. dollar in mid-1988 to JD 0.673 = $1 in March 1990. Since virtually all of Jordan's food is imported, the effect of a limited pass-through of the effects of the depreciation of the dinar on domestic consumer prices has led to an increase in expenditure on food budgetary subsidies from about 1 percent of total expenditures in 1985 to 7.3 percent for 1989 (preliminary estimates). There has been a reduction in total government expenditure as a proportion of GDP from 46 percent in 1985 to around 41 percent in 1989, and, correspondingly, there has been an absolute and a relative decline in capital expenditures both in relation to GDP (9.1 percent to 7.7 percent) and to total expenditures (20 percent to 19 percent) over the same period. To the extent that this jeopardizes the country's future growth potential, the reduction in capital expenditures will make the process of recovery for Jordan more difficult.

Jordan has had fairly stable revenues, which have averaged around 25 percent of GDP. But the revenue system is generally inelastic and the government has had to resort to discretionary measures to keep the revenue-to-GDP ratio from falling. Structural measures on the tax side have been initiated, with IMF support, but some of the burden of adjustment is likely to bear on the expenditure side, particularly in the short run. The adjustment would be facilitated, however, if the poor might be protected from or compensated for any adverse real income effects.

The Poor and Their Characteristics

There are two sources of data on the characteristics of households in differing circumstances and on the incidence of poverty in Jordan: the 1987 Household Income and Expenditure Survey conducted by the Department of Statistics and the Health, Nutrition, Manpower and Poverty Household Survey for 1987. Unfortunately, more recent data are not available. We shall use the quantities consumed by household groups from these surveys in assessing the incidence effects of price changes on particular groups.[1]

We do not attempt to estimate caloric requirements or very precise poverty lines for Jordan but work with the poorest deciles, juxtaposed against the richest two deciles, to establish a relatively clear picture of how these different household types might be affected by particular policy options. Note, however, that the Ministry of Planning has estimated minimum consumption requirements for 1987 to be equivalent to JD 15 per capita a month, which corresponds to the mean expenditure levels of the poorest 20 percent of the population (of just over 3 million people). Since real incomes have fallen in the post-1987 period, relevant target groups, as far as the government is concerned, would roughly correspond to those in the lowest two or three deciles of the population.

For policy, it is important to identify with which broad groups the government is likely to be concerned. In Jordan, these include (1) low-wage employees, particularly in the public sector; (2) the unemployed; and (3) those unable to participate in the labor market. It is clear that low-income public employees, with earnings up to JD 170 a month, are at or below "poverty thresholds," given their relatively large family sizes (often up to ten members a household). Relative price changes, which adversely affect the minimum consumption expenditures of such groups, would thus exacerbate the problem and result in a large number of households being classified as poor. Thus, a prime policy objective would be to tailor relative price changes in such a manner as to protect the minimum consumption expenditure of low-income households, including the current poor and those who are at risk of being pushed deeper into poverty.

The 1987 Poverty Survey suggests that there are a number of distinct groups within the ranks of the unemployed that will require different

---

[1]These should, in principle, be modified by the effects of the price changes on consumption patterns, but economy-wide demand derivatives (or estimates of aggregate changes in demand, given price adjustments) are not presently available for Jordan. The analysis, presented in a disaggregated form ranked by various expenditure deciles, thus represents the first-round effects of the price changes.

policy responses. The first is a group of middle-aged or aging males (45 or over) who are not likely to be educated beyond the preparatory level and who have worked in manual occupations. They are at the greatest risk of poverty, as they tend to be heads of households without alternative means of livelihood or support. The second is a group of young, educated entrants to the workforce, both male and female. While the export of educated manpower has been one of the mainstays of the Jordanian economy, owing to the remittances generated (prior to the current upheavals in the Middle East), traditional values dictate that females are less likely than males to be part of this expatriate labor force. The rate of unemployment for females was 28 percent in 1987, as against 13 percent for males, and most of the unemployed females were educated and under 25 years of age. However, given the structure of family support, this group is less likely to be at risk of poverty than the ones described above.

Given the labor market conditions in Jordan, an area of policy concern appears to be to protect the minimum living standards of the poor; this is likely to involve the overall design of subsidies and consumer prices. It is also important to provide for groups unable to participate in retraining or the labor market, including the relatively elderly, nursing mothers, and poor children. Old-age pensions and targeted transfers, often in kind, are therefore likely to be important. Finally, the government may wish to ensure a minimum income for the currently unemployed, and for those who are likely to become unemployed as a result of the restructuring of the public sector. Here, measures to use the proposed Development and Employment Fund effectively may well be crucial.

Food Subsidies and Protecting the Poor

Under the current system of consumer price and subsidies, domestic prices for a range of food items have been left unchanged, despite the large depreciation of the Jordanian dinar since 1988. This has led to a growing subsidy for food items amounting to around 2 percent of GDP in 1989, exacerbating the already serious overall budgetary deficit. The program presented below suggests that there is considerable scope for reducing this bill in a manner that protects the poor and the lower-middle classes and eliminates production and consumption distortions. The proposed program consists of:

- short-term measures that, given price changes, the introduction of rationing for limited items, and a degree of targeting, would reduce food subsidies;

- compensatory mechanisms to offset any negative impact of commodity price "corrections" through direct transfers to the vulnerable and through wage adjustments; and
- a medium-term reform of the pension and social security system to promote greater equity and efficiency and the pooling of risk across generations.

Current System

A consumer subsidy could be defined as the difference between the price the consumer actually pays and the total cost of delivering the commodity to the retail outlet. For an imported food item, the total cost would include the c.i.f. import price, a margin for the cost of trade and transport, and a profit margin for the wholesalers and retailers. A budgetary subsidy, on the other hand, is the difference between the c.i.f. cost of importing, plus the trade and transport cost of delivering to the wholesaler and the price charged to the wholesaler.

Of the total budgetary subsidy of JD 98 million in 1990,[2] 76 percent is likely to be on wheat, sugar, and rice; the remaining 24 percent on milk, maize, sorghum, and barley (Table 9.1). The largest subsidy, amounting to JD 39 million, or a little less than half the total outlay, is for 0.4 million tons of *imported* wheat, which is delivered to millers for JD 35 a ton while costing JD 130 a ton. Imported wheat also bears the highest consumer subsidy rate of 146 percent. Jordanians are able to buy flour at JD 75 a ton while the cost of importing, transporting, and milling the wheat is estimated to be about JD 185 a ton. *Sugar* is another essential consumption item that is heavily subsidized, with a consumer subsidy rate of 140 percent and a projected budgetary outlay of JD 25 million for 1990. *Rice* is the other major food item bearing a consumer subsidy rate in excess of 100 percent. The budgetary outlay on subsidizing meat products has recently been reduced. There is no budgetary subsidy on imported lamb and only a small budgetary subsidy on imported beef. However, the price of domestically produced meat is substantially higher than that of imported meat. This price differential is partially offset by subsidized inputs, such as barley and maize used as domestic animal feedstock.

Reforming the Present System: A Rationale for Limited Rationing

It is possible to reform the existing system of administered prices and bring about a substantial reduction of budgetary outlays. This

---

[2]Estimated *before* the reform measures taken by the authorities during the year.

Table 9.1. Jordan: The System of Subsidies in 1990[1]

Item Imported A	Projected Consumption B	Cost of Supplying Wholesalers			Resale Price to Wholesalers[2] F	Retail Cost[3] G = E*1.09	Consumer Price H	Consumer Subsidy Rate (H − G/H)*100	Budgetary[4] Subsidies (F − E)*B
		CIF price[5] C	Transport cost D	Total E = C + D					
	(In thousands of tons)	(Jordanian dinars a ton)	(Jordanian dinars)	(Jordanian dinars a ton) →				(In percent)	(In millions of Jordanian dinars[6])
Rice	70	278	8	286	125	310	140	−121	11
Wheat									
Imported	400	122	8	130	35	185	75	−146	38
Domestic	25			125	80	179	140	−28	1
Sugar	140	300	8	308	128	336	140	−140	25
Milk[7]	585	17	1	18	11.5	19.6	12	−63	4
Lamb									
Imported	11			1,586	1,690	3,286	1,800	⋯	⋯
Domestic	9						2,500 to 4,000	Input subsidy	
Beef									
Imported	11	1,475	90	1,565	1,050	1,935	1,400	−38	6
Domestic	2						2,500		
Maize	155	95	8	103	75	103		−37	4
Sorghum	155	61	8	69	55	69		−25	2
Barley	160	96	8	104	60	104		−73	7
Total subsidy									**98**

Sources: Jordanian authorities; and IMF staff estimates.

[1] Estimates of subsidies *before* the reform measures that were introduced during 1990.

[2] Resale price to wholesaler is the price at which the government sells the imported or domestically procured item to the wholesaler.

[3] The retail cost = cost of supplying the wholesaler + a profit margin of 9 percent. This formula is used for most commodities. For wheat, milling costs of JD 35/ton and a profit margin of 12 percent are assumed. For maize, sorghum and barley, there is no retail margin because these items are not retailed.

[4] Budgetary subsidy = cost of supplying wholesalers – the price to the wholesaler.

[5] The price is quoted in dollars a ton and the exchange rate used is $1 = JD 0.675.

[6] Figures are rounded to nearest million.

[7] All quantities for milk are expressed in terms of thousands of cartons of 12 kilograms each. Prices in JD/carton.

involves limiting the use of general subsidies, introducing rationing for selected items, and taxing items consumed mainly by the rich.

General Subsidies

A general subsidy implies that consumers could potentially purchase unlimited quantities of an item at the subsidized price. If budgetary outlays are limited through shortages, a system of ad hoc rationing operates through queues, which are either random or favor the rich and well connected. In principle, only inferior goods justify a general subsidy. At present, however, the general subsidies on a range of commodities, as described above, make substantially greater income transfers to the rich and middle classes than to the poor, and also represent open-ended budgetary commitments. It is only for imported Zero No. 1 flour that a greater than proportionate benefit accrues to the bottom 10 percent or 20 percent of the population (Table 9.2). This is the only potentially suitable item for a general subsidy. For a given budgetary outlay, there are substantially greater transfers to the richest, than to the poorest deciles, for commodities such as high-quality local flour, bread, sugar, and, in particular, rice and meat. However, political and administrative realities suggest that a general bread subsidy is likely to remain in Jordan in the medium term. This can, however, be targeted by increasing the bran and fiber content of the subsidized bread, leading to more cost-effective transfers in the longer run.

Rationing

Rationing would be more cost-effective than a general subsidy for "normal" goods since it can provide limited, although equal, benefits to all and hence limit budgetary outlays. It also has useful "insurance" properties since the availability of given quantities at predetermined prices ensures that such goods are not priced beyond the means of the poor. Nonetheless, in the case of a JD 1 subsidy outlay, in principle, only 200 fils would accrue to the bottom 20 percent; the remaining 800 fils may be viewed as a "cost" or leakage if the transfer objective is the most important consideration. In determining the choice of commodities to ration, the item should be important in the consumption baskets of the poor. In Jordan, rice and sugar, which involve large outlays and are normal goods, fall into this category. For rice, additional targeting may be achieved by restricting rationing to relatively low-quality varieties, with higher-quality rice being sold on the open market without subsidy, or by using a tax to achieve a degree of cross-subsidization.

Table 9.2. Jordan: Benefits Relating to One Jordanian Dinar in General Subsidy by Commodity

Item	Deciles						
	1	2	3	4	9	10	Total
Flour							
Zero No. 1	0.145	0.101	0.128	0.121	0.090	0.100	1.000
European	0.149	0.088	0.089	0.141	0.088	0.074	1.000
Mixed	0.076	0.118	0.119	0.099	0.079	0.060	1.000
Local	0.062	0.087	0.079	0.101	0.103	0.078	1.000
Bread	0.075	0.087	0.089	0.096	0.111	0.133	1.000
Rice							
United States	0.032	0.050	0.028	0.041	0.187	0.362	1.000
Other	0.048	0.060	0.073	0.083	0.145	0.146	1.000
Mutton imports	0.010	0.023	0.028	0.048	0.187	0.342	1.000
Veal imports	0.035	0.049	0.065	0.075	0.167	0.185	1.000
Sugar	0.060	0.077	0.086	0.110	0.123	0.115	1.000

Sources: Jordan, Department of Statistics, *Household Income and Expenditure Survey* (1987); and IMF staff estimates.

Note: In this analysis, it is assumed that a general subsidy of JD 1.000 is allocated to *each* of the above commodities. The resulting benefits are described for the lower four deciles and the highest two deciles. If the benefit exceeds JD 0.100, then the subsidy provides more than proportional benefits. A uniform ration would generate equal benefits to all deciles (if not targeted further). In the Jordanian case, only a general subsidy on flour (either Zero No. 1 or European varieties) would be more progressive than a ration.

To ensure the availability of essential food items at "reasonable prices," the government has proposed a system of in-person registration for food stamps. Food stamps, purchased in advance, would be redeemable at retail outlets. An honor code or stigma could prevent the wealthy from taking advantage of the stamps. Under this option, it is expected that the subsidy would be reduced by 60 percent. Resale of rationed items is not, in principle, a disadvantage. This system improves on the current one, which involves either an open-ended commitment by the state to provide subsidized supplies to satisfy excess demands, or random rationing with shortages. Not too much should be expected of rationing, however, and unless the self-targeting works well (so as not to exclude the poor while preventing the rich from benefiting), rationing is still an inefficient means of transferring income on a permanent basis to the poor. The main advantage of rationing is as a "protective" short-term instrument for major relative price changes. More direct mechanisms would be preferable and more cost-effective in the longer run.

During periods of scarcity or adjustment, price and income stabilization objectives often involve assured supplies at stable prices but do not invariably imply extensive subsidies. Higher free market prices reflecting conditions of excess demand would make it easier to adjust prices upward toward international prices (or social opportunity cost) for importables such as rice and sugar. The government has agreed with the IMF that this process should take place in the medium term, at which point rationing would become redundant. Nonetheless, the need for price stability remains, and this can be achieved through a combination of stock and trading policies.

Taxable Items

Poorer income groups consume little meat, so there is little justification to subsidize this set of commodities. At current prices there is considerable excess demand for meat by the middle classes, and limited quantities of imported meat are in fact subject to informal rationing. This suggests that the retail price of meat could be raised, which would be desirable for a number of reasons. First, it would be possible to make a substantial profit, which in turn could be used to cross-subsidize food commodities that are more important in the consumption basket of the poor. Second, raising domestic meat prices would curtail consumption, which is nutritionally beneficial. Third, the present low prices have resulted in price differentials with neighboring countries and have led to extensive smuggling. Finally, raising the price of imported meat would also allow an increase in the present low price of domestically produced meat. This would also allow the government to eliminate the subsidy on imported maize, sorghum, and barley, which are used as animal feedstock.

Reforming Food Subsidies

Milk is particularly useful for nursing mothers and young children, and targeting by income status may not be desirable. It would be desirable, however, to target subsidized milk to primary schools and to clinics that cater to pregnant women, nursing mothers, and infants. This would increase the attractiveness of such clinics and assist in the dissemination of information on hygiene and preventive care. Neither a general subsidy nor the rationing of this commodity is needed. The targeted provision should be accompanied by *unrestricted* market clearing prices for all other types of milk. The overall subsidy could thus be reduced to JD 0.9 million, from a projected level of JD 3.8 million.[3]

---

[3]This calculation is roughly based on the ratio of primary school children and nursing mothers to total population.

Wheat and bread comprise the main food expenditure items for the poorest quintile in Jordan, but only around 6 percent of total expenditures. Much of the wheat is imported (400,000 tons out of the total consumption of 425,000 tons in 1989/90) and is sold to mills at a highly subsidized price.[4] A 12 percent profit is permitted, and bread from bakeries is priced at JD 0.075 a kilogram (kg) for "normal" loaves. This price may not be changed very easily. Notwithstanding short-run political constraints, the JD 40 million subsidy involved suggests that measures to target consumption of subsidized flour and bread should be explored. One possibility is to shift the subsidy to high-bran "brown" bread. Increasing the percentage of extraction would reduce the subsidy per se and, in addition, may make subsidized bread less attractive to better-off households.[5] If the objective is to target transfers to the poor, subsidizing imported low-quality flour provided directly to consumers may be the more cost-effective alternative. This is likely to lead to a reduction in the aggregate consumption of flour, if flour is sold to bakers at cost, leading to a contraction in the demand for bread. This option may not be politically feasible. Also, if there is a shift in demand patterns, the general subsidy may continue to pose budgetary problems, and could also have negative balance of payments implications.

While rice is important in the consumption baskets of the poor, it is clearly a normal good (consumption rises from 16 kg per capita a year for the lowest decile to 52 kg per capita a year for the richest) and is an appropriate item for rationing. Lower-quality, cheaper supplies could be targeted rather than the high-quality California variety. On 54,000 tons (assuming full take-up by all Jordanians), the subsidy would amount to around JD 5 million (as against JD 11.27 million projected for 1990). The remaining demand for rice could be for higher-quality rice at cost. Given that effective prices are higher than the controlled price of JD 0.14 per kg, the true price of rice would be less than the nominal price differential of JD 0.16 per kg between the present and proposed benchmark prices.

Sugar is also appropriate for rationing given that it is an "essential," albeit normal, commodity, which reflects current consumption patterns of the poor and the rich. A ration entitlement could be set at 18 kg per capita a year at the current price of JD 0.140 per kg. The subsidy

---

[4]Import prices range from JD 110–130 a ton, whereas wheat is released to the mills at JD 34.7 a ton.

[5]It was estimated that there could be a JD 1 million reduction in the bread subsidy if the percentage of extraction were to be increased from 78 percent to 80 percent.

on 54,000 tons of rationed sugar (again assuming full take-up) would amount to JD 10 million, rather than the JD 25 million projected for 1990 under a general subsidy. If the remainder is sold at cost, it would necessitate a price rise of JD 0.2 per kg. A degree of cross-subsidization is possible if open-market sales are subject to the standard rate of sales tax above the cost price.

With respect to *meat prices and input subsidies,* it would be desirable to eliminate all input subsidies immediately, allowing mutton, beef, and chicken prices to adjust to the new cost structure and changing patterns of domestic demand and trade. The price increases would not affect poorer consumers, since they do not consume large quantities of imported meat. Indeed, the poorest income groups purchase between one-half and two-thirds of their mutton requirements from higher-priced domestic supplies. Low meat prices benefit mainly the rich. If the prices of imported meat were raised to the level of domestic prices (e.g., through appropriate import duties), not only would the disincentive for domestic production be removed, but the measure would generate additional revenue of JD 28 million. In addition, there could be a further saving of JD 13 million with the abolition of input subsidies on barley, sorghum, and maize.[6]

Among the limited sets of options considered here,[7] a rise in the price of commodities consumed primarily by the rich could be used to finance the system of subsidies needed to protect the living standards of various target groups. This is a progressive alternative to financing subsidies through printing money and inflation.

Consequences of Reform

Effect on Consumers

The effect of the reform program on consumers is taken as the money loss resulting from the price changes assumed. The poorest 10 percent of the population would suffer a loss of JD 5.5 per capita a year (see Table 9.3). This is equivalent to around 3 percent of the gross expenditures of this group. For employees in the public sector, salary

---

[6]It was not possible to estimate the effects of input price changes on the price of domestically produced meat products and, consequently, these effects have not been incorporated into the distributional impact mentioned in the next subsection.

[7]In principle, we would need to examine all commodity taxes and subsidies to determine the appropriate balance between commodity pricing options (see E. Ahmad and N. Stern, "Taxation for Developing Countries," in *Handbook of Development Economics,* Vol. II, ed. by Hollis B. Chenery and T.N. Srinivasan (Amsterdam: North Holland, 1988)).

Table 9.3. Jordan: Distributional Impact of Price Changes
(In Jordanian dinars)

	Deciles (by per capita expenditures)					
	1	2	3	4	9	10
Food prices and rationing package						
Per capita a year	5.509	8.217	12.950	18.900	45.060	68.030
Per household a month	4.660	6.622	9.173	13.140	22.490	26.870

Sources: Jordan, Department of Statistics, *Household Income and Expenditure Survey* (1987); and IMF staff estimates.

Note: It is assumed that quantities consumed remain unchanged at survey levels. For the food price reform package, see previous tables.

adjustments of around 3 percent would compensate for the price changes. The richest decile would suffer a loss of around JD 68 per capita a year, or about 15 times as much as the poor.[8]

Effect on the Budget

In the absence of reforms, the aggregate subsidy is likely to be about JD 98 million for the current year. If the program of price changes and food rationing discussed above is implemented as a package, the total budgetary subsidy could be brought down by about a third, to JD 66.5 million, without adversely affecting the poor households (see Table 9.4). For political or administrative reasons, the government may wish to phase in some of the options over a longer period.

Finally, the suggested program can be thought of as a core strategy, which could be logically extended as follows. The suggested rationing of sugar and rice is likely to halve the subsidy, at the minimum. Further targeting, through coupons and quality differentials, is likely to reduce this subsidy even further. In addition, there may be some scope for cross-subsidization by taxing the free-market sales of both sugar and rice, and by using cheaper-quality supplies for rationing. Similarly, targeting the flour and bread subsidy is likely to generate further savings. These additional measures would increase the progressivity of the package. Eliminating input subsidies for the domestic production of meat would also lead to substantial budgetary savings while removing production distortions. Given the relative scarcity of meat products,

---

[8]These estimates are based on the quantities consumed, as reported in the Household Income and Expenditure Survey for 1987, which is the latest available; the assumption is that the quantities consumed were unchanged in 1990.

Table 9.4. Jordan: The Revenue Impact of Possible Reforms for Food Items[1]

Item	Suggested Reform	Quantity A	Cost of Supplying Wholesalers B	Price Charged to Wholesalers C	Current Consumer Price D	Assumed Consumer Price E	Subsidy (−) Tax (+) (C − B)*A
		(In thousands of tons)	(In Jordanian dinars a ton)				(In millions of Jordanian dinars)
Rice							
Superior	Allow free market sale	16					0.0
Inferior	Ration as proposed	54	210	125	140	140	−4.6
Wheat	Continue with the present system				75	75	−39.1
Sugar	Ration	54	308	128	140	140	−9.7
	Allow free market sale	86					0.0
Milk	Provide free to target groups	52,800 cartons	18 JD/carton	—			0.9
Lamb	Sell imported lamb at a profit or place a tax on imports	11	1,586	3,286	1,800	3,500	+18.7
Beef	Sell imported beef at profit or place a tax on imports	11	1,565	1,935	1,400	2,300	+4.1
Maize	Raise prices to eliminate subsidies						0.0
Sorghum	Raise prices to eliminate subsidies						0.0
Barley	Raise prices to eliminate subsidies						0.0
Total subsidy with reform							**31.5**

Source: IMF staff estimates.

[1]It is assumed that free market quantities will remain unchanged. In reality, higher prices will result in lower consumption, with lower import requirements. Furthermore, it is intended by the authorities that the system of ration registration will result in lower subsidy outlays. Additional targeting of general bread subsidies could also lead to lower subsidies on major wheat outlays.

and the excess demand by higher-income classes, there is a strong case for protecting relatively poor domestic producers through the imposition of tariffs and sales taxes on imported meat. This would remove price differentials between imported and domestic production.

Additional Provision for the Poor and Direct Transfers to the Needy

Among the poorest groups in Jordan are widows, orphans, the disabled, and the elderly with no extended family support. A proposed *zakat tax* would be earmarked to provide for such individuals at the local level, where costs of identifying such individuals are minimal. Identification of the needy and direct provisioning are illustrations of cost-effective targeting. The tax base would be wealth, including gold hoards, cash, and fixed assets. The imposition of the tax would likely increase the propensity to invest in productive assets and would have a positive overall effect on savings.

The reform of *public sector pensions* and the extension of *social security benefits* are of high priority, given a net amount of JD 65 million spent on public pensions in 1989 and the substantial projected rate of increase. As the amounts involved are on the same order of magnitude as the total subsidy bill, pension reform requires careful analysis and is extremely important for the medium-term fiscal and budgetary strategy, as well as for equity purposes. Given that social security funds generate huge surpluses because of the relatively young profile of workers covered, there may well be a case for extending coverage to include many workers presently in the public sector. This would ease the transition from a productive structure dominated by the public sector to one more reliant on the private sector.

Wage adjustments are likely to be accompanied by a reduction in *public sector employment,* which accounts for about 50 percent of the workforce. Measures to provide income maintenance through retraining and employment would be important as a means of ensuring a more effective transition to a higher level of private activity. However, additional employment provisions would have to be self-targeted through below-market wage rates. Care has to be taken not to increase the bureaucracy in this process of providing "targeted" unemployment support. The proposed Development and Employment Fund could be used to finance this activity. Apart from the purely "transfer" aspect of the program, the portfolio of projects chosen should be justifiable in terms of economic criteria for longer-run sustainability and growth. As discussed above, unemployment among middle-aged and elderly, illiterate or semiliterate (largely unskilled) workers with large numbers of dependents is a serious problem. Further, unemployment among educated entrants to the labor force, particularly females, is also a matter of concern, although the latter are likely to have some extended family support. Employment provision for this group differs significantly from that for relatively elderly, illiterate agricultural or manual workers.

The facilitation of investment opportunities and schemes targeted toward females with some skills is likely to be of increasing importance. The experiences of countries in South and East Asia with comparable educational levels and infrastructure are likely to be relevant. To ensure the protection of the poorest, investment measures would need to be supplemented by employment provision through public works at low wages (including possible in-kind payments) for the truly destitute, and with local transfers to those unable to participate in the labor market (as through the *zakat* schemes). The responsibility of the state should not extend beyond the provision of a minimum guarantee to those without assets or family support.

Prospects for Reform

The Jordanian government has introduced some of the measures discussed in this paper. A rationing scheme for sugar, rice, and milk, was made operational with effect from September 1, 1990. For rice and sugar, the quantities being rationed are 1.5 kg/month a person. The price schedules are similar to those shown in Table 9.1, with the subsidized price at current levels, and the nonration price set so as to realize small profits (JD 340/ton for sugar, and JD 280/ton for rice). Rather than targeting milk through schools and health clinics, a ration has been introduced. The Jordanian authorities estimate that rationing sugar, rice, and milk will lead to an annual reduction in subsidies of around JD 22 million. No attempts have been made to target the wheat or bread subsidies, although the overall outlays are reported to be lower on account of falling international wheat prices. Prices of imported beef and mutton have also been set to cover retail costs, but no element of tax has so far been introduced. There has also been a reduction, which the Jordanians estimate will be on the order of JD 3 million on an annual basis, in the subsidy on barley and sorghum used as animal feed. The direction of reform is to be welcomed, although there is still some scope for further action. It would be useful to conduct an expost evaluation of these measures in due course.

It is apparent that expenditures on subsidies can be reduced substantially without adversely affecting the poor. The principles involved in a restructuring of administered prices, with large implicit or explicit subsidies, are of general applicability in the context of transition to a more market-oriented system. As seen in Jordan, these measures have to be considered in the context of the real income levels of the poorest, keeping in mind appropriate measures to protect those who are unable to participate in the labor market. Setting reforms in motion should improve the ability of the country to weather external shocks and crises.

10

Assessing the Impact of Structural Adjustment on the Poor: The Case of Malawi

Ronald Hicks and Odd Per Brekk

This case study of Malawi illustrates a practical approach for assessing the impact of structural adjustment policies on poverty. Malawi initiated a structural adjustment program in 1987, which, since mid-1988, has been supported by the IMF through an arrangement under the Enhanced Structural Adjustment Facility (ESAF), the first such program with an IMF member country. The pervasive nature of poverty in Malawi was recognized in formulating the ESAF-supported program. Social and demographic indicators for Malawi are shown in Table 10.1. Five principal factors were viewed as obstacles to poverty abatement in Malawi: (1) limited employment opportunities; (2) low physical productivity of land and labor, leading to low agricultural output; (3) poor health and educational services, which undermined the development of efficient and productive human capital; (4) rapid population growth, which created severe pressure on land resources; and (5) minimal income transfers. The macroeconomic objectives of the ESAF-supported program—the resumption of high-quality sustainable economic growth, the maintenance of a viable external position, and price stability—were aimed at providing impetus to improved economic welfare, which would benefit all groups in the economy, including the poor. Similarly, the program's structural policies—most notably import liberalization, tax reform, and reforms of the agricultural and financial sectors—were intended to improve efficiency and longer-term eco-

---

Note: This chapter is an abridged version of IMF Working Paper 91/112 (Washington: International Monetary Fund, 1991).

Table 10.1. Malawi: Social and Demographic Indicators[1]

Area	118,428 square kilometers
Population	8.2 million
Rate of growth	3.3 percent a year
Density	69 persons per square kilometer
Population characteristics	
Life expectancy at birth	47 years
Share of population under 15 years	47 percent
Infant mortality	148 per thousand
Crude birth rate	54 per thousand
Crude death rate	19 per thousand
Urban population	14 percent
Labor force	
Total labor force	3.4 million
Women in labor force	1.4 million
Overall participation rate	43 percent
Health	
Population per physician	11,334
Population per nurse	3,106
Access to piped safe water	
Rural population	50 percent
Urban population	97 percent
Nutrition	
Daily caloric supply per capita	2,009
Protein intake per capita	57 grams per day
Education	
Adult literacy	41 percent
Primary school enrollment	66 percent
Secondary school enrollment	4 percent

Source: World Bank (1990b).
[1]Most recently available data as of 1991.

nomic growth across a wide spectrum of the economy and provide a stimulus to employment, including jobs for the poor. At the same time, it was recognized that the process of economic adjustment and structural change could have short-run adverse effects across the economy, including ramifications for the poor and disadvantaged who were less able to cope. These concerns required giving consideration to modifying policy instruments, or perhaps taking specific remedial measures to ease the burden of adjustment for certain population groups.

The principal focus here is to ascertain the short-run impact of adjustment policies on prices and incomes as they affected the poor in Malawi under the ESAF-supported program initiated in 1988. In this context, the chapter discusses various economic policy measures designed to alleviate possible short-run adverse effects of the macro-economic and structural reform measures on poor groups. It should be borne in mind that while economic reform measures could adversely affect some of the poor, the same measures could also result in immediate benefits for other poor groups and in the longer run the poor may suffer more in the absence of reform measures.

Characteristics of the Poor in Malawi

Classification

The World Bank (1990a) identified two categories of the poor in Malawi, the "poor" and the "core poor"—or the poorest group—with the poverty line based on minimum nutritional requirements. According to this criterion, about one-half of the population is classified as living below the poverty line, with the core poor close to 20 percent of the population (Table 10.2).

Based on the 1987 census and evidence from surveys, the World Bank (1990a) identified three groups of the poor—poor smallholders, poor estate workers, and urban poor. Almost 50 percent of the total population in Malawi is composed of poor smallholders; another 4 percent are poor estate workers; and about 1 percent constitute the urban poor. Poverty in Malawi is essentially rural, pertaining mostly to smallholders and, to a much lesser extent, estate workers. Based on minimum nutritional requirements, the incidence of urban poverty is of far less importance. The high incidence of extreme poverty suggested by these data is reflected in social indicators such as low life expectancy (47 years), high infant mortality (148 per thousand), low adult literacy (41 percent), and low productivity in the smallholder agricultural sector.

Poor smallholder households include all households cultivating less than one hectare, the smallest size considered compatible with satisfying basic nutritional needs without relying on income transfers, and one-half of households farming between one and one and a half hectares. The smallholder "core poor" are defined as those households farming less than one-half hectare. These poor farmers generally concentrate on producing traditional maize, which is the staple in their diets, and root crops. Improved varieties of maize and cash crops, such as groundnuts, are cultivated to a limited extent.

The agricultural production of *estate worker households* differs markedly from that of smallholders. The primary products of estate agriculture are tobacco, tea, and sugar. The World Bank (1990a) estimated that about one-half of the estate worker households were poor,

Table 10.2. Malawi: Poverty Incidence[1]

	Population			Households		
	Total poor	Core poor	Other poor	Total poor	Core poor	Other poor
	(Proportion of total population excluding refugees, in percent)					
Total	55	20	34	51	20	31
Smallholders[2]	48	18	31	46	18	28
Estates						
Laborers	4	2	2	4	2	2
Tenants	1	1	—	1	1	
Urban	1	—	1	1	—	1
	(Proportion of subsector, in percent)					
Smallholders[2]	60	22	38	66	26	40
Estates						
Laborers	67	34	34	47	20	26
Tenants	64	41	23	53	30	23
Urban	9	—	9	7	—	7

Sources: World Bank (1990a). The World Bank data for each subsector are derived from the following sources: Smallholders, *Annual Sample Survey of Agriculture*, 1987/88; Estates, *Estate Household Survey 1983*; Urban, *Urban Household Expenditure Survey*, 1979/80; and Population, *1987 Census*.
[1]Poverty definition based on indicators for nutritional intake.
[2]"Poor" smallholders are defined as households cultivating less than one hectare; "core poor" smallholders are defined as households cultivating less than one-half hectare.

when judged on satisfaction of basic nutritional requirements. The incidence of poverty was higher among tenant estate households (about one-half). In contrast to smallholder and estate worker households, only 7 percent of *urban households* could be considered poor.

While no statistical information is available regarding the informal sector in Malawi, it is not believed to be large in the urban areas, partly because formal marketing activity is relatively efficient for a wide range of goods and services. In the rural areas, informal sector activity is thought to be significant among the self-employed and part-time workers, with a distinct seasonal pattern.

Sources of Income

Table 10.3 provides details relating to the sources of income of poor *smallholders*. Own-farm (subsistence) agricultural production provides a little over 70 percent of the income of smallholders in the core poor category, rising to about 90 percent for those households with higher incomes and larger plots. Off-farm activities—self-employment, paid agricultural labor, and other labor—constitute about 10–20 percent of

Table 10.3. Malawi: Smallholder Composition of Income
(In percent)

	Core Poor	Other Poor	Nonpoor
Total	100.0	100.0	100.0
Own-farm agricultural production	72.6	86.7	93.7
Food remittances[1]	3.6	0.9	
Cash remittances[1]	4.2	1.8	1.8
Paid other off-farm activities	9.3	6.5	—
Paid agricultural employment	6.3	2.4	—
Self employment	4.0	1.7	4.5

Source: World Bank (1990a).
[1]For the nonpoor, the figure for cash remittances includes any income that may come from food remittances.

income for poor smallholders. The poorest segment of the population supplements its income to a larger extent than other groups by paid employment and other off-farm activities, as well as food and cash transfers from household members who migrate to other sectors of the economy because of the low productivity on the smaller farm plots.

For *estate workers* (both laborers and tenants), the World Bank (1990a) estimated that some three-fourths of their income was derived from permanent labor income (almost 80 percent in the case of the core poor in the estates, and just over 70 percent in the case of the other poor). The remainder of their income was from other wage income, with incomes from own-farm agriculture—in contrast to smallholders—being minimal.

For *urban households,* wages were the principal income source, including income from self-employment, household enterprises, and other informal activities.

In sum, subsistence agricultural production of traditional maize and root crops was the predominant source of income for the poor in Malawi. Wage income was the main source of income for the poor estate workers and also for the small group of the urban poor.

Expenditure Patterns

The information available with regard to spending patterns of the poor in Malawi is limited. Comprehensive household expenditure surveys have covered urban areas only,[1] whereas the majority of the poor

[1]Roe and Wycliffe (1989).

reside in rural areas. Broad-based surveys of expenditure patterns for estate workers and smallholder farmers do not exist, and only very limited information exists with regard to smallholders and estate workers.

Smallholders and Estate Workers

A limited survey of smallholder expenditure in Zomba South showed that expenditure on food accounted for more than 50 percent of total spending of the poorer smallholders in that area (Peters and Herrera, 1989). The proportion spent on food declined to 40 percent in the higher-income groups. Spending on household goods and services, including clothing, accounted for most of other expenditures for all income groups. For estate households, food was again the principal spending component, constituting, as estimated by the World Bank (1990a), about 65 percent of total spending for both poor estate laborers and tenants. However, transfer payments to their home villages amounted to an estimated 6 percent of expenditure for poor estate households, whereas such payments were negligible for smallholders.

Urban Poor

The 1978/80 Urban Household Expenditure Survey covered 3,000 households in four cities and indicated that food expenditure was close to one-half of total expenditure of the urban poor and that clothing and housing accounted for about 20 percent;[2] fuel, power, and transport accounted for a considerably smaller proportion, although these categories were more significant in the larger cities. In 1988/89, a small income and expenditure survey was carried out among the low-income groups in the traditional housing areas in Lilongwe and Blantyre. The survey showed that food expenditure constituted about 45 percent of total household spending in both cities in 1988/89, that fuel and transportation expenditures seemed to have increased in importance since the 1979–80 survey, and that the share of clothing expenditure had declined. It is unclear, however, to what extent these developments reflect changes in the number and composition of low-income households rather than adjustments in overall expenditure patterns of these households. Neither is it clear to what extent this reflects changes in spending habits or relative prices.

---

[2]A low-income household is defined in this survey as one with average monthly expenditures below MK 100 during the survey period; the World Bank (1990a) study adopted a much narrower definition of poverty.

ESAF Program and Implications for the Poor

The macroeconomic framework of the ESAF program for the fiscal years 1988/89–1990/91 focused on a sustained reduction in the budget deficit and on monetary restraint through a slowdown in aggregate credit expansion. Structural policies included import liberalization, parastatal and financial sector reforms, and pricing policies aimed at improving economic efficiency and productivity.

Financial Policies and Price Developments

The most pervasive influence of the ESAF program on prices and incomes stemmed from the tighter financial policies implemented over the period. The government's overall budget deficit, excluding grants, was reduced from 12 percent of GDP in 1986/87 to just over 6 percent on average in 1989/90 and 1990/91. This reduction was due mainly to restraint in recurrent expenditures, including wages and salaries. The share of recurrent social services expenditures (principally education and health) in total recurrent spending edged up over the program period from 20 percent in 1987/88 to 22 percent in 1990/91; recurrent social services spending remained on average almost 4.5 percent of GDP during 1987/88–1990/91. Tax reform was responsible in part for a reduction in the revenue-to-GDP ratio, with tax reductions having a stronger impact than base-broadening; the impact on the poor of the introduction of a value-added tax was eased by zero rating of unprocessed food. Tighter financial policies led to a marked decline in broad money growth from a 12-month rate of 30 percent in March 1988 to 12 percent in March 1991, and a switch from negative to positive real rates of interest.

Against this background, the annual average inflation rate, as measured by the composite consumer price index, declined from 31 percent in 1988 to 12 percent in 1990.[3] The price deceleration was considerably more pronounced in some categories than in others; for food, which has a larger weight in the low-income indices, the rate of price increase declined a little faster than the overall average, dropping from 37 percent in April 1988 to 9 percent in April 1991.

Apart from the broader impact of financial policies on price performance as indicated above, the specific fiscal measures adopted appear to have had only a moderate direct effect on the poorest segments of the population. Individual tax measures had a modest direct impact on

---

[3]The declines in the Blantyre and the Lilongwe low-income indices were from 33 percent to 10 percent, and from 34 percent to 12 percent, respectively.

consumer prices, as the focus of tax changes tended to be on imported or luxury goods not weighing significantly in the consumption of the poor. The effect of the increase in social expenditures on the poor seems to have been positive, but the extent of the impact is not certain. Fiscal and monetary policies have therefore had their favorable impact mainly through broader macroeconomic responses, reflected most notably in the pronounced slowdown in inflation.

Pricing Policies

As most prices had already been deregulated before the ESAF program commenced, the program focused on the periodic review and adjustment of prices of the few goods on which controls remained. Prices of the two main consumer items involved—petroleum and sugar—were kept unchanged during the first two years of the program. However, in keeping with their commitment to provide for an appropriate domestic pass-through of changes in world petroleum prices, and to ensure that cost developments were adequately mirrored in domestic prices, the authorities increased the domestic price of petroleum by 5 percent in April 1990 and 12 percent in October 1990. The domestic price of sugar was increased by 7 percent in April 1990, and by a further 19 percent in January 1991, reflecting concerns about the sustained increase in sugar prices in the southern African region, the high rate of domestic consumption, and the decline in Malawi's sugar export volume. The artificially low domestic price of sugar generated not only supply shortages, but also informal trade with neighboring countries; the higher prices were therefore aimed at enhancing production incentives and export potential.

With fuel and power combined accounting for 2–5 percent of the various low-income urban CPI baskets, the price increases in April and October 1990 for petroleum products implied only a modest direct impact on the low-income CPI. For smallholders and estate workers, the effect most likely was even less. Similarly, with the weight of 4–5 percent for sugar in the urban low-income basket, the increases in the price of sugar in April 1990 and January 1991 also had a relatively small effect.

The ESAF program also focused on establishing appropriate producer prices to help ensure adequate financial incentives for agricultural development and diversification among smallholders. These administered producer prices, reviewed each year in consultation with the World Bank, were announced at the beginning of the crop year and applied to purchases from smallholders by the major agricultural parastatal, the Agricultural Development and Marketing Corporation

(ADMARC). The main commodities were maize, tobacco, groundnuts, and cotton. As noted earlier, maize is grown by almost all smallholders, mostly for their own consumption, accounting on average for about three-fourths of their total cultivated area. Private sector traders were free to offer higher prices for maize, and ADMARC prices for this crop typically constituted a lower limit. Private trading activity did not make up a particularly important share of total trade in maize, partly reflecting the general tendency of producers to prefer the convenience of ADMARC marketing outlets. The administered price of maize was almost doubled in 1988–89, and was increased by a further 40 percent in 1990, mainly to help stimulate production after a period of adverse growing conditions, particularly drought. These increases in the administered price of maize, together with higher production, clearly had a positive effect on the real earnings of net maize producers, but a negative effect on net maize consumers. On balance, the poorest sectors of the population, who were more dependent on labor and food markets because of the low productivity of smaller plots, likely experienced a decline in real incomes, given the higher food prices that resulted from producer price incentives.

To improve productivity in the smallholder sector and help overcome their limited access to credit, a smallholder fertilizer program was started in 1983 involving a subsidy on imported fertilizer, the high cost of which was due to the sharp rise in world fertilizer prices and the large transportation costs that stemmed from the use of longer-haul road routes. Most of the fertilizer used by smallholders was for maize. Against this background, budgetary outlays for the fertilizer subsidy rose, reaching MK 27 million, or 2 percent of total budget expenditures in 1990/91, which implied an economic subsidy level of about 30 percent.

Although fertilizer prices charged to smallholders continued to rise despite this subsidy, the marked increase in producer prices over the period, particularly for maize, helped restore the incentive to use fertilizer and thus sustain productivity. The government remained committed to phasing out the fertilizer subsidy to minimize distortions in production. The elimination of the subsidy was expected to be compensated in broad terms by lower transportation costs resulting from improvements in the traditional supply routes, expanded access to rural credit, and gains in productivity related to the adoption of high-yielding maize varieties.

Wages

An important element of the government's strategy for improving living conditions of the poor in Malawi over the program period was the approximate doubling of minimum wages, effective May 1989, after several years of no change. The most significant impact of these increases occurred in the tobacco and tea estates, where large numbers of low-paid seasonal workers are employed. Still, the increase in the minimum wage is reported to have had some adverse impact, although not clearly measurable, on the level of employment in the tobacco and tea estates.

Interest and Exchange Rate Policies

The program supported by the ESAF provided for greater flexibility in interest rates. Even though nominal interest rates still tended to change rather infrequently, real rates of interest turned positive, reflecting the decline in the inflation rate. However, most smallholder estate workers and the urban poor did not have access to credit and were therefore not directly affected by changes in the cost of finance. The broader macroeconomic response to tighter financial policies— particularly the slower pace of inflation—had a more significant impact on the poor than monetary policy.

In an effort to bring down inflation, the government adopted a policy of nominal exchange rate stability for the Malawi kwacha in the context of nonaccommodating financial policies. Discrete adjustments to the exchange rate were made to strengthen external competitiveness. As with interest rates, the impact of exchange rate policy on the poor has been more closely related to the lower inflation associated with a stable exchange rate. This said, certain inputs—particularly fertilizer—relied heavily on imported supplies, where costs were affected directly by exchange rate developments (see above).

Import Liberalization

The import liberalization program, completed in January 1991, abolished the requirement of prior approval of foreign exchange allocations for imports. The liberalization program was carried out in stages, at first covering raw materials and intermediate goods and, in the final phases, consumer goods. The initial impact on consumer prices came through the domestic supply response related to the increased availability of imported inputs. Liberalization with respect to consumer goods could later be expected to generate greater import competition for such goods, thus lowering prices.

The deceleration in price inflation was particularly pronounced for commodities with a high import content in production (such as clothing, footwear, and transportation), whereas price increases for food—

Table 10.4. Malawi: Estimates of Real Earnings
(1986/87 = 100)

	1987/88	1988/89	1989/90
Poor smallholders			
Nominal wage[1]	102.9	117.7	158.8
Consumer prices[2]	127.5	162.3	187.5
Real wage	81.1	71.4	84.1
(Change in percent)	(–18.9)	(–11.9)	(17.8)
Poor estate workers			
Nominal wage[3]	100.0	131.5	226.0
Consumer prices[2]	127.5	162.3	187.5
Real wage	78.9	78.6	120.0
(Change in percent)	(–21.1)	(–0.3)	(52.6)
Urban poor, Lilongwe			
Nominal wage[4]	100.0	124.3	197.2
Consumer prices[5]	126.5	161.4	183.0
Real wage	79.6	75.1	107.0
(Change in percent)	(–20.4)	(–5.6)	(42.4)
Urban poor, Blantyre			
Nominal wage[4]	100.0	124.3	197.2
Consumer prices[6]	127.8	162.7	182.2
Real wage	78.8	74.6	107.4
(Change in percent)	(–21.2)	(–5.2)	(43.9)

Sources: Data provided by the Malawian authorities; and IMF staff calculations.

[1]Weighted average of ADMARC producer prices (with 1988/89 ADMARC sales used as the weights) and income from off-farm activities. The latter is assumed to have moved in line with the rural minimum wage.

[2]Based on food in the overall CPI.

[3]Minimum wage, rural areas.

[4]Minimum wage, cities.

[5]Lilongwe low-income CPI.

[6]Blantyre low-income CPI.

for which production was to a larger extent domestically based and which had a large weight in the consumption basket of the poor—decelerated less. Thus, while import liberalization led to an overall deceleration in inflation in the short run, it may have benefited low-income households less than other groups.

Estimates of Real Income Developments for the Poor

Because of limited data availability, only very rough estimates, concentrating only on first-round price effects and disregarding any quantity effects, were made of developments in real earnings for 1987–89 for the three poor groups identified above (Table 10.4).

For *poor smallholders,* the largest poor group, nominal earnings are assumed to have moved in line with a weighted average of ADMARC producer prices and the rural minimum wage (75 percent and 25 percent, respectively). The subindex for food in the overall CPI is taken to indicate trends in consumer prices, reflecting the predominance of spending on food in total expenditures of the poor.[4] Based on these income and consumer price assumptions, real earnings declined in 1987/88 and 1988/89 but increased in 1989/90 to a level 4 percent higher than that of 1987/88. Considering that ADMARC prices, particularly for maize, acted largely as floor prices, the real earnings of smallholders may have increased even more over the period. However, to the extent that these households produce less maize than they consume, the maize price increases would imply a real earnings decline for this group.

For *poor estate workers,* the nominal wage is assumed to have developed in line with the minimum wage for rural workers, whereas consumer prices are assumed to have moved in tandem with overall food prices, as was assumed for smallholders. The calculations indicate a drop in the real wage for estate workers in 1987/88 and 1988/89, followed by a sharp increase in 1989/90, so that in 1989/90 the real wage was about 50 percent above the 1987/88 level. However, the calculations probably overstate the variations in the real wage, especially as estate workers are paid partly in kind, and this part of overall remuneration may have been adjusted to offset movements in the formal minimum wage. To this extent, the real wage declines in 1987/88 and 1988/89 and the increase in 1989/90 might have been more moderate than suggested by the simple calculations. It should also be noted that employment was probably adversely affected to some extent by the overall rise in wages, although no quantification of this factor is available.

Real wage developments for the *urban poor* have been calculated on the assumption that the nominal wage has moved in line with the urban minimum wage in both Lilongwe and Blantyre. Consumer prices have been assumed to increase at the same rate as the respective low-income price indices. On these assumptions, the urban poor experienced sharp drops in their real wage in 1987/88 and 1988/89, which were more than compensated by a large increase in 1989/90, leaving the real wage in 1989/90 about 35 percent higher than in 1987/88. The caveats mentioned above with respect to the appropriateness of the minimum wage as an income indicator and the adverse effect on employment of the wage increase again need to be kept in mind. Note

---

[4]The results are not significantly changed if the overall CPI for low-income groups is used.

also that the urban poor who were engaged in informal sector activities and the urban poor who are unemployed were outside the formal protection of the minimum wage arrangements and may have been adversely affected by the strong increase in maize prices. However, there are no available data to assess the importance of this effect.

While keeping in mind the limitations of the estimates presented, particularly as regards the narrow range of data on wages, some general conclusions may be drawn. First, each of the three poor groups experienced declines in their real wages in 1988/89, the first year of the ESAF program, mainly because of continued high consumer price inflation. In 1989/90, the success in reducing inflation contributed to an increase in real wages. This increase, however, may have been much higher for the poor estate workers and the urban poor than for the poor smallholders, since the former were the main beneficiaries of the increase in minimum wages.[5] Real earnings for poor smallholders—the majority of the poor—appear not to have risen, although to the extent to which actual prices for their marketed output exceeded prices set by ADMARC, it is possible that their real earnings did develop more favorably.

Conclusions

This chapter has investigated the scope for assessing the impact of economic policies on the poor in Malawi during 1988–91. A simple methodology was applied that recognized the limitations of the available data. The approach was intended to illustrate the first-round (i.e., price) effects of the ESAF-supported adjustment program on the real earnings of the poor.

Even with this simple approach, we found that the requisite data were scarce and, in key respects, relevant information was not available. The definition of the poor needed to be rather ad hoc, based (for smallholders) on nutritional intake that can be derived from a given size of the household plot. Moreover, we found that information on income and expenditure patterns has severe limitations, particularly for the rural poor. Specifically, official household surveys covered only the main cities (which is typical of developing countries), where only a few of the poor are located. The scattered information available could

---

[5]It should be noted that these results hinge on the assumption that changes in the minimum wage are representative of changes in real wages for poor estate workers and the urban poor.

not be easily combined to establish clear patterns of income and expenditure, without recourse to rather crude assumptions. In light of these problems, a simplified numerical analysis was adopted. Notwithstanding the shortcomings with respect to data, the analysis indicated that a simple methodology can usefully gauge important short-run consequences of economic policies on poverty. This analysis can, in turn, be taken into account when formulating economic policies to mitigate adverse effects on the poorer groups.

The analysis found that poverty in Malawi is a predominantly rural phenomenon, with poor smallholders constituting the majority. The elements of the ESAF program that most clearly affected the real incomes of the poor relate to first-round price effects of agricultural pricing policies and overall anti-inflationary measures. Developments in minimum wages have also been important. Simple ad hoc calculations suggest that all poor groups experienced a decline in real wages in 1988/89, when the ESAF program began. In 1989/90, all poor groups appear to have improved their real income position, and, in particular, real wages of the urban poor and estate workers seemed to have increased strongly. More generally, it must be emphasized that Malawi's ESAF program did not incorporate measures directed specifically at the poor, given the pervasiveness of poverty and the fact that some agricultural policy changes, with World Bank support, were being implemented simultaneously to reduce poverty for poor smallholders (in particular, by increasing tobacco prices). Rather, the ESAF program focused on improving standards of living through more broadly based macroeconomic stabilization and structural changes.

References

Peters, Pauline E., and M. Guillermo Herrera, 1989, *Cash Cropping, Food Security and Nutrition: The Effects of Agricultural Commercialization among Smallholders in Malawi* (Cambridge, Massachusetts: Harvard Institute for International Development).

Pryor, Frederic L., 1988, *Income Distribution and Economic Development in Malawi: Some Historical Statistics,* World Bank Discussion Paper No. 36 (Washington: World Bank).

Roe, Gillian, and Wycliffe Chilowa, 1989, *A Profile of Low-Income Urban Households in Malawi* (Zomba: University of Malawi Centre for Social Research).

World Bank, 1990a, *Malawi—Growth Through Poverty Reduction,* Country Economic Report No. 8140-KAI (Washington: World Bank).

———, 1990b, *Social Indicators of Development* (Washington: World Bank).

11

Mozambique: Economic Rehabilitation and the Poor

Paulo S. Lopes and Emilio Sacerdoti

By any income standard or measure of living conditions, Mozambique is one of the poorest countries in the world. Despite its rich natural resources, inadequate production planning and acute social conflicts that had come to the open in the mid-1970s led the country into an alarming situation where the survival of the majority of the population depended on foreign aid. Starting in 1987, economic reforms were launched that have contributed to arresting the contractionary trends that had hindered the economy since the early 1980s.

This paper seeks to provide an overview of the impact on the poor of the policy measures included in the 1986–90 economic recovery program. The analysis, which focuses on the changes in relative prices and wages, indicates that between 1987 and 1990, minimum- and low-wage earners improved their purchasing power, notwithstanding large increases in official prices and an initial period in 1987 during which real wages eroded. In areas with adequate security, food production increased substantially, improving the situation of small farmers. Those parts of the population displaced or severely affected by the civil war had to continue to rely on emergency food aid, despite the increase in agricultural production. Poverty remains widespread among urban and rural households, and overall food security is inadequate. To improve food security for urban households, an income supplement scheme was introduced in 1990.

Note: This chapter is an abridged version of IMF Working Paper 91/101 (Washington: International Monetary Fund, 1991).

The authors are grateful to Ke-young Chu for his useful suggestions in preparing this paper.

Characteristics of the Poor

Defining a poverty benchmark for Mozambique is difficult. The great majority of the population have very low living and consumption standards. Even nutrition criteria fail to provide an adequate reference because hunger and malnutrition are widespread and recurrent. In these circumstances, the focus turns to the poorest segments of the population. According to Green, at least 60 percent of the population met the criterion of absolute poverty,[1] and the few social indicators available confirm the degree of misery that such high rates of poverty would imply.

In Mozambique's context of generalized food scarcity, access to additional food sources may be crucial. Even when food ration allotments were fully available, these accounted for not more than 60 percent of standard caloric needs. Although having access to a productive *machamba* (small farm plot) helped households escape serious malnutrition, the rural areas were not better off than the urban areas particularly because the lack of inputs was aggravated by the lack of security, which made even subsistence farming extremely difficult. In addition, the distribution of aid and other imported food staples remained irregular in the countryside. As a result, the incidence of absolute poverty was, according to Green's estimates, 68 percent in the rural areas (including displaced farmers), compared with between 32 percent and 52 percent in the urban areas. If, therefore, the "poorest of the poor" are to be designated, they might well be the displaced or war-affected rural dwellers who were more often victims of starvation and of war-related injuries than the urban poor.

Composition of Household Income and Expenditure

There is little diversity of income sources in Mozambique: 85 percent of the workforce is employed in the traditional agricultural sector, with few employment opportunities existing elsewhere. As much as 90 percent of the cultivated area is exploited by the family sector. Crop diversity is limited, given farm size, seed availability, and technical know-how, making producers very dependent on the prices of a few crops. In addition, the lack of security has rendered farming extremely risky, and many peasants have been forced to abandon their lands.

---

[1]Green defined absolute poverty as monthly per capita household income being so low that at least half is absorbed by the cost of the basic monthly food ration. Income survey data are available only for an estimated 10 percent of the poor (in urban areas) who earn wages in the formal sector (see R. Green, 1989, Estudio SDA: Social Dimensions of Adjustment [the Green Report], unpublished).

The remaining 15 percent of Mozambique's employed labor force is distributed evenly between the industry and services sectors, where, on average, standards of living are slightly higher and absolute poverty is less prevalent. Income from informal sector activities often complements official income, but the earnings potential is limited (typically up to 30 percent of the minimum wage).

The external sector has played an important role in mitigating poverty, as remittances from emigrant workers (mainly from miners in South Africa) in foreign currency and in merchandise are important sources of revenue for some families. During 1988–90, remittances from abroad recorded in the balance of payments averaged about $71 million a year, or about 66 percent of commodity exports. Unrecorded remittances were probably also very significant.

The regional incidence of poverty has different implications in terms of household revenue and expenditure patterns. In urban areas, wage earners dwell along with small merchants, providers of services, and unqualified laborers who operate for the most part in the informal sector. In rural areas, farmers' and traders' earnings and levels of self-provisioning (for own consumption) depend to a great extent on crop volumes and prices. Even the wage-earning agricultural workers employed in private and state farms and in cooperatives manage to produce for their own household consumption or for market exchange. However, in the determination of income and expenditure profiles for the absolute poor, only the two extreme rural (self-provisioning) and urban (salaried) cases will be considered. As will be shown later, each group has been affected differently by the economic rehabilitation program.

The distribution of income sources for self-employed rural households in 1980 was, according to some hypotheses formulated by Green, as follows: self-provisioning, 70–75 percent; agricultural sales, 10–15 percent; remittances, 10 percent; other, 5 percent. In the context of the economic deterioration that occurred during 1982–86, relief aid replaced a considerable part of self-provisioning. In addition, the totals for agricultural sales and for remittances declined, although they might still have accounted for an equal or greater share of rural household income (which in 1988 in real terms was 25–35 percent below the 1980 level). Income from informal sector activities may also have increased its share at the time.

Sources of income for urban wage earner households living in absolute poverty are not easily identifiable. Green estimated that if two members of a household (typically eight people) had minimum-wage jobs, then such a household would be above the absolute poverty level. If only one minimum or low wage was earned (which is not the case in 90 percent of the absolutely poor households), it would account for not more than 50–70 percent of an absolute poverty cutoff household income of Mt 32,000 per month ($62). Under these circumstances, income from informal sector activities and direct access to farm products from small family farm plots become very important. Estimates for the implicit income equivalent of that access or for informal sector income are not available.

The Economic Rehabilitation Program and Its Consequences

The period 1982–86 was characterized by economic collapse (minus 7 percent real growth a year), which was due in great part to the intensification of armed insurgency and to natural causes (droughts and floods), and also to a policy of centralization, which aggravated structural economic imbalances. Growth resumed (4–5 percent a year) following the launching of the Economic Rehabilitation Program (ERP) in 1987, supported by the IMF's structural adjustment loans and World Bank's rehabilitation loans.

The principal objectives of the ERP were (1) to restore a minimum level of income and consumption, particularly in the rural areas; (2) to curtail domestic financial imbalances and strengthen the external payments position; and (3) to establish the conditions for sustainable economic growth once security conditions permitted. The growth target for the period 1987–89 was set at 4 percent on average. Central to the program were major adjustments to the exchange rate, together with a full pass-through to domestic prices, price liberalization, and strengthening of the government budget by limiting current expenditure to a level below that of revenue growth. Price subsidies were to be reduced through increases in the consumer prices of the staple commodities, which were subject to a rationing system.

Following the stepwise devaluations in 1987 and 1988, fixed prices were increased sharply, including prices of subsidized commodities. In 1986, the latter included maize, maize flour, rice, sugar, edible oils, and soap. By the end of 1989, limited subsidies were maintained only for maize, as the prices of the other commodities were brought to the import parity level or, for domestically produced commodities, to the domestic cost level.

Concurrently, the cost of these subsidies to the budget increased from Mt 500 million in 1986 (1 percent of current expenditure) to Mt 5.1 billion in 1987 (1.2 percent of GDP) in light of the very large depreciation of the exchange rate, but declined to Mt 3.5 billion in 1988 and

1989 (1.5 percent of current expenditure and 0.4 percent of GDP). Other fiscal measures of the program included a comprehensive tax reform, which widened the coverage of the turnover tax and increased the consumption tax rate; streamlined personal income taxation; and accelerated corporate tax payments. School and hospital fees were also increased. In addition, in 1987 the civil service staff was reduced by 10 percent.

Consequences of Policy Measures

The rehabilitation program affected poverty through the official price increases, which in 1987 exceeded the rise in the minimum wage; the reduction in the size of the civil service; and the increase in indirect taxes and user fees. Each of these aspects will be addressed in turn.

Pricing Measures

In early 1987 official prices almost tripled, while prices in the parallel market remained broadly stable. During the following years, official prices were again adjusted several times.

The consumer price index, constructed on the basis of giving a 75 percent weight to official prices, and 25 percent to parallel market prices, rose by 163 percent in 1987, 50 percent in 1988, 42 percent in 1989, and 49 percent in 1990. A selected commodity index derived exclusively from the staples in the ration allotment basket rose almost 16-fold during 1986–89, and had a considerably different time pattern from the CPI, as the prices of rationed goods were increased much more sharply in 1988 than in 1987. The price of fuelwood, the single most important nonfood item in the budgets of poor households, and prices in parallel markets increased relatively little under the ERP. The relative stability of parallel market prices up to 1989 indicates that those prices already reflected the much-depreciated parallel market exchange rate and that scarcity premiums did not increase.

On the earnings side, minimum wages were raised by an amount designed to protect the purchasing power of a worker in a typical household. On the basis of the official CPI, real wages appear to have declined by as much as 15 percent during 1987. However, average real income levels for wage earners also appear to have been restored in the two subsequent years, while the supply of consumer goods increased. The urban population with no official wage income and only informal sector income might have been more seriously affected than wage earners.

Indices deflated with the quarterly CPI (which use December 1986 as a base) show that real wages had declined sharply by about 50 percent by June 1987, but that a recovery started in September 1987 with a 50 percent rise in nominal wages. With two additional increases in nominal wages in March and October 1988, by the end of 1988 real wages based on the CPI had returned to the level at the end of 1986 and by 1989 exceeded it somewhat. In 1990, as the CPI increase (49 percent on an end-of-period basis) exceeded the wage increases of 16–23 percent, real wages declined even after correcting for the exceptional thirteenth monthly wage paid to civil servants and many other employees in December.

The expenditure-weighted index provides a less favorable picture, in that real wages in 1989 were only 12–13 percent above average 1986 levels for agricultural workers and for technicians and administrative personnel. The relative income position of nonagricultural workers seems to have been the most affected, since the growth in their nominal wages was less than that of the other categories and, in 1989, their real wage was still 9 percent below the 1986 level. According to the expenditure index, the decline in real wages did not take place until 1988. This was due to the sharp increase in the prices of the basic food staples that constituted the bulk of the ration allotment basket.

The depreciation of the metical had an ambiguous impact on family income from remittances. In 1987, the parallel market foreign exchange premium fell from Mt 1,600 to Mt 1,200 per $1, which may have completely offset the gains from the higher official rate.[2] However, on the plus side, there was a rise in recorded remittances following 1987 that may have been related to the depreciation. Moreover, if the remittances were being used all along to buy products priced in foreign currencies (in special stores or in the black market), it is probable that the parallel market appreciation of the metical did not greatly affect households receiving remittances. In 1988 and 1989, the parallel market exchange rate again depreciated significantly, augmenting the purchasing power of remittances.

Rural producers probably fared better than the urban households. Family sector commercialized crop production expanded considerably in 1987–90, and producer prices were increased in 1987 by an amount larger than the increase in the CPI.

To estimate the real income of agricultural producers, a basic producer price index was developed from a list of 13 commodities, and a weighted average of the individual commodity producer prices was

---

[2]A part (60 percent) of the paychecks of emigrant miners in South Africa is remitted directly at the official rate through the central bank of Mozambique. The miners can dispose freely of the remaining part or remit it to be exchanged at the more favorable parallel market rate.

also computed, with weights determined according to the relative market value of the commercialized family sector production of each commodity during 1986. For 1986–89, the basic producer price index showed that prices rose more than 11-fold, compared with an 8-fold increase in the CPI. Since market production expanded, it would appear that the agricultural producers who were marketing a part of their production gained. An important element of overall welfare is also the availability of consumer goods in the countryside, which appears to have improved in 1988 and 1989. A general increase in commercialized farm output after 1987 indicates that producers responded positively to the newly introduced market incentives.

Fiscal Policy Measures

The increases in indirect taxes and consumption taxes under the ERP had a very modest price impact in comparison with the administered changes in official prices, and thus can probably be neglected. User fees for hospital consultations and for school enrollment were raised significantly in 1987 and 1988. School fees and charges were estimated to amount to 5 percent of the minimum wage.[3]

In 1987, to reduce the fiscal imbalance, 21,000 civil servants were laid off—approximately 10 percent of the total. The subsequent increase in urban unemployment was exacerbated by the repatriation of mine workers from South Africa (up to 350,000) and by the influx of displaced persons from the areas most affected by the lack of security. Some of these laid-off workers must have been absorbed through the expansion in economic activity and the resumption of economic growth following the implementation of the ERP. In 1988, the government conducted a rapid status survey of households in two major urban areas, Maputo and Tete, and subsequently took steps to complement the existing food rationing system by allocating land for cultivation and basic inputs in strategic, safe areas, as well as by expanding pilot programs that provide meals in primary schools and factories.

The basic social programs on health and education continued to be expanded, mainly through foreign aid. Continued war-related damages limited the impact of this effort. Existing social programs were maintained to benefit orphans, old-age pensioners, and disabled persons, as were feeding programs for primary school children. Income supplementation schemes were introduced in 1990, which became

---

[3]Green (1989).

fully effective in 1991, with the aim of limiting urban poverty, and covered large urban families with no more than one minimum wage.

Food Security and Urban Rationing System

The food security situation differed in rural and urban areas. In rural areas, as a result of the war and of recurrent droughts, more than 4 million people had been displaced or severely affected by the mid-1980s. Under these circumstances the government had to turn to international assistance to avert widespread starvation. The first international appeal for emergency assistance to Mozambique was launched in April 1987. The food aid received was used to help meet the population's nutritional needs—in rural areas free distribution to the more seriously destitute, displaced, and severely affected families and for urban dwellers and rural wage earners through subsidization of basic food staples.

In the following years, the emergency appeal widened its focus to cover inputs needed for rehabilitation in the areas of agriculture, water supply, health, and education. In 1990, the scope of the ERP was expanded to encompass all structural rehabilitation activities within a strategy for reconstruction and poverty alleviation. The emergency appeal concentrated on meeting basic human needs, especially in rural areas. The emergency programs focused particularly on the provision of food and other essential inputs to the populations displaced or severely affected by the war. Regrettably, the lack of security, poor accessibility of some areas, and logistic difficulties also constrained the emergency programs. Such logistic constraints exacerbated a situation already hampered by the insufficiency of food aid pledged relative to estimated requirements. As a result, in many areas, food rations often could not be distributed or were well below the levels required.

Relief aid was distributed at the local level by a special government relief department, while the actual distribution to households was handled by community leaders. Because of the deteriorating security situation, the number of households and communities requiring emergency assistance increased substantially in the period 1984–89, and relief operations had to be expanded. Food distributed amounted to 180,000 tons in 1988, compared with 57,000 tons in 1985; distribution in 1989 was estimated at about 170,000 tons.

In the two main cities of Maputo and Beira, food aid was marketed to a significant extent through the urban rationing system (Novo Sistema de Abastecimento, NSA). This system was designed initially to provide registered households the means to purchase at subsidized prices a fixed ration of food staples and some other necessities, which

would cover approximately 60 percent of the daily caloric requirement. However, the amount of food staples commercialized in urban
parallel markets increased. In addition, many urban residents managed
to obtain food directly from farms in the suburban countryside. In
Maputo, food is also imported from neighboring Swaziland. Overall, it
is estimated that the food security situation in urban areas is substantially better than in the countryside. In line with the objectives of the
ERP, by 1990, only the subsidy on yellow maize remained, while the
prices of the other products were raised to levels equivalent to import
parity.

Public Expenditures and the Poor, 1990–92

Within the framework of the 1990–92 economic and social rehabilitation program, the government decided to strengthen the poverty
reduction effort through better focusing of major public expenditure
programs and improvement of the safety nets to protect vulnerable
households. In addition, measures were implemented to generate
employment opportunities for the poor, including revision of the
investment program to promote labor-intensive projects, projects with
basic training components, small enterprises in the private sector, and
informal sector activities.

To alleviate poverty and stimulate growth, three priority areas of
expenditure were identified: the promotion of smallholder agricultural production; the improvement of health and education services; and
the strengthening of basic infrastructure.

Measures to assist small family farms recognized that the key to
reducing poverty in the rural sector was to increase agricultural production through adequate assistance to small farmers. To that effect, in
1990 the authorities formulated the Priority District Programs, which
aim at revitalizing production and improving living standards in the
regions with relatively more favorable security conditions through the
provision of extension services, adequate food, and inputs, along with
improved road and water supplies.

The provision of education and health services was severely hampered by the war, which resulted in the destruction of local schools and
a large part of the rural health network. Moreover, the economic crisis
led to a reduction in health expenditure as a share of the government's
recurrent budget. In the health care area, the government planned to
rebuild or rehabilitate health infrastructure and strengthen prevention
services throughout the country. In education, due to the effects of the
war, very limited educational services were provided outside the major

cities and provincial capitals, and schools in the main cities were over-crowded. Against this background, the 1990–92 investment program assigned priority to the provision of education in rural areas, together with improvement in the quality of teaching.

For the rural poor affected by the war, the emergency program was the main vehicle of assistance. To the extent that the improved security situation permitted refugees to return to their homes and farms, additional support was needed for returnees to start economic activities in the agricultural sector.

The safety net for poor households was expanded through a food security subsidy introduced in Maputo and other provincial capitals. Eligibility was limited to (1) households with not more than one salary earner and with over five members; (2) households with no salary or other substantial source of income; and (3) persons over 50 living alone and with no significant source of income. To limit coverage to urban households, a residency test is required. For the first category the monthly subsidy amounts to Mt 3,000 a member of a household exceeding five members. It has been estimated by the authorities that at least 120,000 households would be covered by the program, corresponding to 25 percent of urban Mozambican households. The cost of the program is estimated at Mt 18 billion a year (1.3 percent of 1990 GDP). The effective starting date of the program was slowed by the need to introduce appropriate mechanisms to control eligibility.

Conclusions

Poverty is widespread in Mozambique, affecting a large portion of both the rural and urban populations. After a sharp decline in production in 1981–86 during the war, the economic rehabilitation program was introduced in 1987, which aimed at reviving economic activity and reducing financial imbalances through containment of current budgetary expenditure, significant adjustment of the exchange rate, and introduction of tax reforms and major price reforms designed to restore incentives.

During a period of major price adjustments, the purchasing power of the lower-income groups was, overall, protected through wage increases. But at certain times, such as during 1987 and 1988, significant erosions occurred in the purchasing power of wages. Poverty remained widespread in the countryside because of the war, but was alleviated by a wide-ranging emergency program of distribution of food and other necessities. However, this program could not reach all the population severely affected by the war because of the lack of security and of transportation equipment. Also, insufficient amounts of food aid kept the distributed rations below the amounts required. In addition to the poverty relief measures, the government endeavored to stimulate rural production through the provision of inputs, improved access to markets, and better price incentives. The effect of these policies has been favorable, and significant increases were registered in agricultural production during 1987–90.

In the urban areas, the main instrument for ensuring food security is a rationing system that aims at providing food corresponding to approximately two-thirds of the caloric requirements. Price subsidies were largely eliminated in 1987–89, with subsidies remaining only on yellow maize, an inferior commodity. This scheme, however, is inadequate to provide security for large families or households that have no significant income. For this reason, an income supplement scheme for urban households was developed in 1990 and implemented in 1991.

The available evidence—based on the purchasing power of minimum wage levels, on producer prices, and on the actual availability of goods—suggests that the ERP, by stimulating food production in areas where adequate security exists, improved prospects for the poor. While poverty remained widespread, and available social indicators showed that little progress was registered in this area during 1986–89, purchasing power gains were attained by urban wage earners and rural producers. In addition, under the ERP, GDP per capita resumed its growth during the 1987–90 period.

12

Poland: The Social Impact of Transition

Gerd Schwartz

Poland was one of the first economies to undertake the transition from plan to market. This chapter looks at the safety net that existed at the outset, describes how it was reformed during the transition, and analyzes how the poor and needy fared during this process.

Social Safety Net at Outset of Transition

Poland's pretransition social protection arrangements centered around an extensive social insurance system, which, inter alia, provided for old-age, disability, and survivors pensions; health care; work injury benefits; sick pay; family allowances; and maternity benefits. In addition, there existed a limited system of local social assistance to support the poor. While, on the surface, this does not look unlike the arrangements found in many market economies, the differences were in fact striking.

A basic feature of Poland's pretransition social protection arrangements stems from the central role of labor in socialist societies: participation in the labor market was viewed as almost obligatory, also because access to many social benefits depended on being in the labor force. While employment and social protection policies aimed at providing a job guarantee to every citizen, the distinction between wages and cash benefits was blurred, with wages largely set to achieve distributional objectives. There was considerable hidden unemployment that disguised the need for unemployment benefits, job counseling, retraining, or social assistance.

Note: Reprinted from *Poland: The Path to a Market Economy,* IMF Occasional Paper No. 113 (Washington: International Monetary Fund, October 1994), pp. 80–88.

A basic feature of Poland's pretransition social protection arrangements stems from the fact that poverty was essentially viewed as a distinguishing feature of capitalism. Explicit basic income and emergency support policies were made largely superfluous by a combination of fixed prices, extensive subsidies for a large number of basic consumer goods, and substantial cash transfers in the form of family allowances and other benefits. In addition, many benefits were administered and provided directly by state-owned enterprises (SOEs). These included free vacations at designated resorts, housing, child care, access to consumer goods, and other in-kind benefits.

Who Were the Poor at the Outset of Transition?

Poland's income distribution before the outset of transition was similar to other socialist economies. It can be characterized by seven stylized facts (Milanovic, 1992a): (1) income inequalities were less pronounced than in market economies even though there existed problems of differential access to benefits; (2) rural incomes exceeded urban incomes (in Poland by about 16 percent); (3) property income was insignificant; (4) in-kind benefits were more important than in market economies while wage income was less important; (5) self-employment income, including in-kind consumption, was relatively more important than in many Western economies, reflecting a large agricultural sector; (6) similar to Western economies, cash transfers accounted for about one-fifth of gross income, but, unlike in Western economies, these cash transfers were distributed almost equally on a per capita basis; and (7) direct taxes played almost no role in redistribution.

The various existing studies on poverty in pretransition Poland all tackle the standard problems of defining a poverty line, measuring the number of people that fall below this poverty line, assessing by how much they fall below the line, and estimating how long they remain in poverty. Still, measuring the extent of poverty in pretransition Poland is complicated by the fact that the definition of living standards is somewhat abstract in economies with chronic shortages of goods and services, as having a higher income does not necessarily imply having a higher living standard (Graham, 1993). While there is no doubt that income in pretransition Poland was much more equally distributed than in market economies, the available data do not include various privileges enjoyed primarily by the *nomenklatura* and enterprise-specific in-kind benefits, such as subsidized vacations at company facilities, food, housing, and better access to scarce or subsidized goods.

Given these important limitations, the available evidence shows a rather consistent pattern of the degree to which different population groups were affected by poverty in pretransition Poland.[1] This is not surprising as all studies use data from the annual Household Budget Survey (HBS). Hence, differences in the results reflect differences in defining poverty lines and equivalence scales for various household types, and methods of calculation. The studies by Milanovic (1992c and 1993) and Panek and Szulc (1991) are typical in this respect. Their research suggests that, during 1988–89, the poverty rate was highest among pensioners and lowest among mixed farmer and worker households (Table 12.1).[2] All studies also agree that the probability of being poor was higher for single-parent households than for two-parent households, increased with the number of children, and decreased with the level of educational attainment. Contrary to some other studies, Milanovic (1992b) finds that in the 1980s there was a strong increase in the number of poor in urban areas: urban poverty increased from 7.8 percent during 1978–79 to 21.5 percent during 1987–88, largely as a result of a decline in real wages in the industrial sector during the 1980s.[3] At the same time, rural poverty remained rather constant, amounting to 13.3 percent in 1978–79 and 13.7 percent in 1987–88, probably due to favorable terms of trade in the agricultural sector. All studies show a slight increase in the overall extent of poverty even before the onset of the transition.

Social Protection During Transition

With the onset of transition, existing social protection arrangements quickly became unsustainable and needed to be reoriented in several aspects: to lend support to the transformation; to be aligned with the

---

[1]Also see Atkinson and Micklewright (1992) for a detailed comparison of the different studies.

[2]Until 1991, the Polish HBS sample contained four major occupational groups: households of manual and nonmanual workers employed in SOEs or cooperatives (workers), households of farmers, households with farmers and workers, households of pensioners. Households of the self-employed, private sector employees, military, and police were excluded from the sample. This was an omission that became increasingly serious as the private sector expanded. However, since 1992 all groups are represented. See Gorecki and others (1992) and Kordos (undated) for further details.

[3]Since the basic data are the same, this finding is essentially due to definitional differences: while Milanovic defines "rural" as farmers plus mixed farmer and worker households and "urban" as workers plus pensioners, other studies use more detailed data on town size.

Table 12.1. Poland: Poverty Headcount Indices by Source of Household Income

	1988	1989	1990	1991	1992
Milanovic (1992c and 1993)					
All households	15.2	17.3	31.5	34.3	. . .
Workers	14.8	15.8	36.1	38.1	. . .
Farmers	14.4	17.2	31.0	39.4	. . .
Mixed farmers and workers	8.0	7.9	16.1	21.2	. . .
Pensioners	25.9	36.2	38.6	33.0	. . .
Children	. . .	17.5	51.2	. . .	. . .
Panek and Szulc (1991)					
All households	15.3	16.7	. . .	. . .	. . .
Workers	6.4	16.1	. . .	. . .	. . .
Farmers	19.4	29.9	. . .	. . .	. . .
Mixed farmers and workers	6.1	8.6	. . .	. . .	. . .
Pensioners	33.1	33.1	. . .	. . .	. . .
Rural population	20.4	23.3	. . .	. . .	. . .
Nonrural population	9.7	9.7	. . .	. . .	. . .
UNICEF (1993)					
All households	. . .	21.8	40.3	39.3	41.4
Urban households	. . .	19.8	37.0	33.0	33.6
Rural households	. . .	24.4	43.1	48.4	52.4
Children	. . .	28.0	53.4	54.7	57.6
Adults	. . .	18.9	34.0	32.2	34.1
Pensioners	. . .	32.7	40.6	29.1	33.2
Ochocki (1993)					
a. Total "objective" poverty	. . .	. . .	19.4	24.8	38.7
b. Total "subjective" poverty	. . .	. . .	32.6	. . .	35.5
Rural population	. . .	. . .	38.5	. . .	47.4
Nonrural households[1]	. . .	. . .	29.3	. . .	30.0
One-person households	. . .	. . .	69.2	. . .	63.4
Three-person households	. . .	. . .	18.7	. . .	28.6
Six- and more person households	. . .	. . .	27.9	. . .	36.9
"Subjective" poverty, 1990–91			11.6		
Workers			11.9		
Farmers			11.0		
Mixed farmers and workers			5.1		
Pensioners			13.2		
Rural households			13.4		
Nonrural households[1]			12.4		

Sources: Cited studies; and IMF staff estimates.
[1]Unweighted average of various nonrural categories.

requirements of a market-based environment, and to prepare for changes in the demographic structure.

As a first step, several elements that were central to the old system of social protection, such as job guarantees, fixed prices, generalized subsidies, and various in-kind benefits, needed either to be curtailed or abolished. The extensive system of food subsidies, for example, had already de facto been abolished in 1989.

During the transition, the main elements of Poland's system of social protection were unemployment benefits, pensions, social assistance, family allowances, sickness benefits, and, more generally, health care. At the same time as direct consumer subsidies were dramatically reduced, there was a strong expansion of the system of cash benefits. Within the cash benefit system, the brunt of the transformation-induced increases in social expenditures was borne by social insurance arrangements (mainly pensions and unemployment compensation) rather than social assistance schemes targeted to the poor or other more temporary arrangements. This was largely due to the ease of access to social security and a more attractive benefit structure. Unemployment benefits and pensions can be used as examples of the many recent changes and current problems of the system of cash benefits.[4]

Unemployment Benefits

As regards unemployment benefits, the Employment Law of December 1989 fully recognized unemployment and stipulated that unemployment compensation was no longer a discretionary benefit. The initial provisions were fairly generous: in general, the level of benefits was linked to the claimant's last wage, and there was no duration limit. This invited abuse, particularly in larger cities where administration is more difficult and alternative employment opportunities are easier to come by. Often, people who were about to be laid off were given substantial wage increases to enable them to draw higher unemployment benefits. Unemployment benefits initially had the character of general income support rather than targeted assistance, particularly since many beneficiaries continued to work in the shadow economy. Also, being registered as unemployed was a way to retain access to various social insurance benefits, particularly free health care, and to continue to accumulate pension rights (Ksiezopolski, 1991). Hence, even people who intended to withdraw from the labor market generally decided to remain registered as unemployed.

Unemployment benefits underwent several reforms during 1990–93. Most important, a general 12-month duration limit was introduced in December 1991, and a generally flat-rate benefit structure at 36 percent of the average wage that prevailed in the economy during the previous

---

[4]See Maret and Schwartz (1993) or the World Bank (1993) for detailed reviews.

quarter was introduced in February 1992. The level of unemployment benefits appears roughly in line with minimum subsistence, but more so for smaller households than for larger ones. Still, problems remain. The system does not provide an explicit minimum subsistence guarantee, and there are concerns regarding the adequacy of the indexation mechanism. Also, to the extent that the duration limit is binding, much of the burden of caring for the long-term unemployed and those withdrawing from the labor market subsequently falls upon basic income support and emergency assistance schemes, which implies a major devolution of responsibilities from the national level to the local authorities. Finally, the value of active labor market measures by the government would tend to be reduced to the extent that labor mobility remains constrained by the absence of a housing market and the existence of a general housing shortage.

The Pension System

As regards the pension system, there has been an impressive number of changes during 1990–93, but fundamental reform has yet to take place. The major changes tried to address the six main problems of Poland's pension system:[5]

- *liberal eligibility criteria* for early retirement and disability pensions and generous stipulations regarding the right to receive pensions while continuing to be employed;
- a *high average replacement rate,* largely a result of the formula for calculating the pension base;
- *inadequate mechanisms* for cost of living adjustments (COLAs);
- persistent *structural abnormalities,* including occupation-specific privileges and incorporation of noninsurable risks into the social security system;
- *insufficient pension system financing,* also due to evasion and the buildup of arrears to the social security system; and
- *weak administration,* resulting from inefficient management, insufficient modern equipment, and inadequate regulations.

In general, it was easier to address the obvious excesses that invited abuse than to address fundamental issues.

As a result, a main unresolved problem of the Polish pension system is the reform of eligibility criteria for early retirement and disability

---

[5]See Maret and Schwartz (1994), and Schwartz (1994) for detailed reviews of pension system reform in Poland.

pensions. During 1990–93 the number of pensioners increased rapidly while the number of contributors dwindled. During the four-year period from December 1989 to December 1993, the total number of pensioners grew by 28 percent, from 6.9 million to 8.8 million (Figure 12.1). Much of this increase already occurred in the early stages of the transition: between December 1989 and December 1991 alone, the total number of pensioners increased by 21 percent to 8.4 million. There was a particularly pronounced increase in the number of old-age pensioners, including early retirement pensioners, which, for the main pension fund (FUS), increased by over 36 percent during the December 1989–December 1993 period. At the same time, the number of contributors dropped from 14.8 million in December 1989 to 12.5 million in December 1993. Excluding the pension scheme for farmers, which traditionally has covered over 90 percent of its expenditures by transfers from the state budget, the ratio of contributors per pensioner (dependency ratio) dropped from 2.7 at the end of 1989 to below 1.9 at the end of 1993 (Figure 12.2).

The drop in the dependency ratio has been accompanied by a drop in the average pension age, largely due to a sharp increase in early retirement. While in 1990 the average retirement age for FUS pensioners was 57 for women and 58 for men (Hambor, 1992), the overall average was estimated to have dropped to below 55 years by mid-1993. The pronounced shift toward early retirement can be attributed to four main factors: (1) early retirement, which is widely perceived as an alternative to unemployment and offers more attractive benefits than unemployment; (2) liberal eligibility criteria that, initially, did not penalize pensioners who continue to work; (3) limited supervision and enforcement capacities that make it difficult to keep track of working pensioners; and (4) anticipation of restrictive pension reforms that would adversely affect those who were to retire later.

However, it is not only the steep increase in the number of old-age pensioners that created problems for the Polish pension system but also the high level of disability pensioners. In December 1989, there were only 1.1 old-age pensioners per disability pensioner, implying that almost 50 percent of all labor market participants who had left the labor force had done so for health-related reasons before reaching regular retirement age. To some extent, the large number of disability pensioners is a legacy of socialism. Liberal eligibility criteria for disability pensions reduced some of the pressures of having to provide a job guarantee for every citizen, and thereby alleviated the extent of excessive employment. Accordingly, disability was basically defined in terms of "damage to health" rather than "inability to work."

Figure 12.1 Main Pension Fund (FUS): Contributors and Pensions
(In thousands)

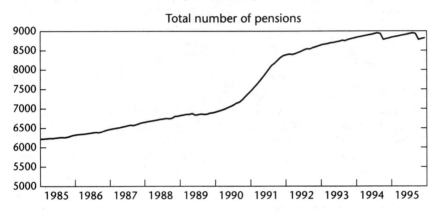

Total number of pensions

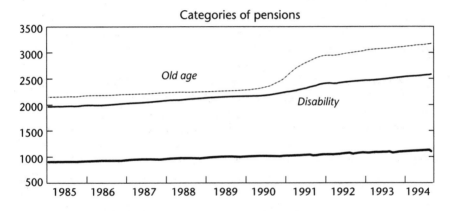

Categories of pensions

Total contributors

Figure 12.2 Main Pension Fund (FUS): Dependency Ratios[1]

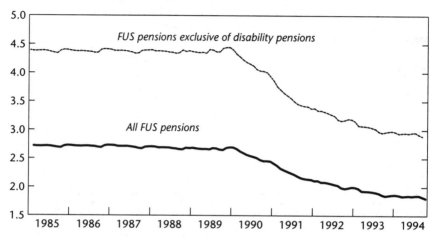

Sources: Polish authorities; and IMF staff estimates.
[1]Number of labor force participants to number of retirees.

A second unresolved problem concerns the statutory replacement rate, that is, the average ratio of an individual pension to the work income it replaces. In Poland, the rate is relatively high, particularly considering the low dependency ratio. Related to this is the issue of cost-of-living adjustments. Until 1990, all COLAs occurred ad hoc and were constrained by the need to prevent a financial collapse of the pension system. Frequently, delays in indexation were used to generate actual replacement rates that were significantly below statutory levels. While there is no optimal level for statutory replacement rates, the arbitrary way in which the system was maintained would appear undesirable. In general, two main issues arise in connection with COLAs: the selection of the indexation mechanism, and the selection of the index itself. In 1993, pensions were indexed to average wages in the previous quarter, and the indexation mechanism was invoked when average wages in the previous quarter increased by at least 10 percent over the average wage that was used for the last COLA. While the choice of the index that was in effect in 1993 allowed pensioners to share in general productivity increases (at least to the extent that these are reflected in wages), the mechanism was somewhat tardy, and only limited, but did not prevent temporary erosions of the real value of pensions. In particular, the minimum pension, that is, 35 percent of the average wage in the economy that was used in the last COLA, did not provide an effective minimum subsistence guarantee.

Other Social Expenditures

Various other changes in social expenditures during 1990–93 largely reflected the need to contain government expenditures and were interim solutions that eventually needed further reform. Two examples may suffice. One example is the freezing in early 1992 of family allowances at a level of Zl 167,000 per beneficiary, a measure that helped to control expenditures without addressing the actual problem of finding ways to improve the targeting of these allowances. Another example is the free distribution of drugs to pensioners and health service staff that was discontinued in late 1991 (UNICEF, 1993). Whereas improving the cost-effectiveness of the health care system is important, improving the targeting of benefits would seem to be a more desirable way of containing costs than blanket reductions or withdrawals of benefits.

The Poor During Transition

What the Data Show

How did the transition affect the character and extent of poverty during 1990–93? Two main factors seem particularly relevant. First, the significant decline in output, particularly during 1990–91, affected the average level of well-being; second, new opportunities that were brought about by the transition-induced changes in the income distribution increased relative income disparities.

While it is difficult to measure the exact quantitative extent of these effects, there is general agreement on two things: first, the extent of poverty increased significantly during 1989–93; second, much of the observed increase in poverty is transition-induced. Also, there is fairly broad agreement that the increase in poverty cannot be attributed to a dramatic worsening of the income distribution, or to a contraction of social transfers, or to a retreat of the state (UNICEF, 1993). In general, the extensive safety nets in place prior to the transition have been maintained, and even extended to include unemployment compensation and social assistance benefits, which is not to say, however, that these mechanisms have been effective or efficient. Again, the general agreement on central aspects of poverty during the transition is not surprising because much of the available quantitative evidence is based on the same data source, the annual HBS.

Milanovic (1992c and 1993) finds that poverty increased significantly in 1990, the first year of the transition, from 17 percent of the population (6.6 million) in 1989 to 31.5 percent (11.9 million) in 1990 (Table 12.1). The increase was most pronounced among wage earners (workers), particularly those employed in the state sector. The extent of poverty among pensioners increased only slightly during the first year of transition but still continued to exceed any other group. These changes in poverty are mirrored by changes in income: with overall real per capita income dropping by 31 percent in 1990, farmers experienced a drop of 40 percent, and pensioners a drop of 19 percent. While the drop in the income of farmers was steep, poverty among farmers in 1990 remained below the levels found among workers and pensioners. Children appear to have been particularly severely affected during the first year of the transition: over 50 percent of all children are estimated to have lived in poverty in 1990, whereas in 1989 it was, at most, 28 percent (UNICEF, 1993).

Moreover, the poverty gap, that is, the total income needed to bring all poor households to the estimated poverty threshold level, increased by 40 percent in real terms, even though it declined by 23 percent in per capita terms (Milanovic, 1993). This may suggest that many people are just below the poverty threshold, and that estimates on the extent of poverty are quite sensitive to the definition of the poverty line. If this is correct, it would help to explain the significantly different estimates of the extent of poverty: in 1990, for example, these ranged from 19 percent of the population (Ochocki, 1993) to over 40 percent (UNICEF, 1993). Regardless of the exact extent of poverty, the principal gainers in the first year of transition were private sector entrepreneurs, some workers who shifted from the public to the private sector, and possibly property owners (Milanovic, 1992b).

During 1991–92, the extent of poverty largely stabilized at the increased 1990 level (Table 12.1). Still, the pattern of poverty underwent a marked change: while in 1990 the increase in poverty was most severe among urban households, particularly state-sector workers, in 1991 the social costs began to shift more strongly toward farmers and mixed farmer and worker households (Milanovic, 1993). Accordingly, the incidence of poverty was most severe among households that were (1) headed by pensioners, single parents, young workers, or persons with a low level of educational attainment, (2) large, with five or more members, and (3) located in small towns (below 20,000 inhabitants). While some other studies, such as UNICEF (1993), show that the transition affected urban and rural poverty to a similar extent during 1990, it is generally agreed that urban poverty did not increase during 1991–92 as rural poverty continued to increase (Table 12.1). Another interesting result is that poverty rates among pensioners remained fairly stable (albeit at a relatively high level), possibly indicating that the pension system was used as a social safety net device during the transition. Also, during 1991–93, the incidence of poverty became particularly prevalent among the unemployed: poverty among the unemployed increased to a level that was almost 50 percent higher than among the overall population.

Are the Data Correct?

Did the welfare of the population really decrease during the transition? There are at least five main problems with the available evidence. First, the discussion generally ignores the counterfactual of the transformation: at least in the long run, if not already in the short and medium term, the extent of poverty would have been likely to be even more severe in the absence of the reforms that were undertaken.

Second, the annual HBS data may not always provide an adequate reflection of reality. For one, the HBS has on occasion generated dramatic changes in poverty even before the onset of transition. For example, Panek and Szulc (1991) estimated an increase in poverty from 14 percent to 30 percent of the population during 1982–84, which is not unlike the increase from 17 percent to 34 percent of the population that was estimated by Milanovic (1993) during 1989–91. While 1982–84 were also years of crisis, and at least some increase in the extent of poverty may have been expected, the reduction in poverty to 15 percent of the population during 1984–88, as estimated by Panek and Szulc (1991), is quite surprising. These strong variations in the extent of poverty cast doubt on the reliability of the HBS data and reveal the weakness of poverty-line-based head-count analysis in this context.

Also, as already mentioned, until 1991 the HBS did not cover the self-employed, workers in the private sector, and the military and police—groups that are generally considered to be among the better off. Excluding these groups would tend to overestimate the extent of poverty and underestimate changes in the income distribution, which may help to explain the surprising stability of the Gini coefficients shown in Table 12.2. In addition, some recent estimates have suggested that about 20 percent of economic activity goes unreported. Hence, it would not seem unreasonable to assume that an equal share of income is unreported. In fact, for the fourth quarter of 1989, the Central Statistical Office (GUS) estimated that incomes reported for the annual HBS were 21 percent below the incomes reported by enterprises (Gorecki and others, 1992). If anything, this gap can be expected to have increased during 1990–93, particularly considering the growth in

Table 12.2. Poland: General Indicators of Population Well-Being

	1989	1990	1991	1992
	(Average per capita consumption)			
Calorie intake (calories a day)	2,891	. . .	2,767	2,744
Milk consumption (liters a year)	125.8	121.3	119.0	114.4
Meat and fish consumption (kilograms a year)	64.3	68.9	72.1	69.5
Bread and cereal consumption (kilograms a year)	120.5	118.4	121.1	120.6
	(In percent)			
Total consumption spent on food	49.2	51.8	45.8	43.5
Population receiving social assistance				
Receiving assistance regularly	0.2	0.2	0.3	0.3
Receiving assistance occasionally	2.6	5.7	4.5	4.6
Rate of children with low birth weight	7.6	8.1	8.0	7.9
Infant mortality rate	1.6	1.6	1.5	1.4
Under age 5 mortality rate	1.9	1.9	1.7	1.7
Preprimary education enrollment rate	48.7	47.1	43.9	42.6
	(Other as indicated)			
Life expectancy at birth (years)				
Men	66.8	66.5	66.1	66.7
Women	75.5	75.5	75.3	75.7
Income inequality (Gini coefficient)	24.9	19.1	23.2	24.0

Sources: UNICEF (1993); and IMF staff estimates.

private sector employment. In this context, it is interesting to ask why the available evidence suggests that pensioners suffered least during the transition. A possible answer would be that pensioners are probably least able to underreport income as their main source of income comes directly from the state.

Third, the high-inflation environment that existed at the outset of transition is likely to have created severe measurement distortions. Average consumer price inflation amounted to about 250 percent in 1989 and 585 percent in 1990. Given the extent of price liberalization during 1989–90, the high inflation rates largely reflected step-adjustments and significantly exceeded the underlying rate of inflation. These inflation-induced distortions may help to explain some of the strong intertemporal variations in the extent of poverty: Panek and Szulc (1991), for example, estimated a drop in poverty from 23 percent of the population in the second quarter of 1989 to 11 percent in the third quarter.

Fourth, it has sometimes been suggested (Lipton and Sachs, 1990) that Polish pretransition statistics had a bias toward presenting a rosier picture of the reality, and that once this bias is eliminated, as happened during the transition, the new situation necessarily appears worse.

Fifth, even if it could be assumed that HBS data provide an adequate reflection of reality, estimates of poverty are entirely determined by the definition of equivalence scales and the poverty line for different population groups. This is a rather subjective science, as shown by the range of poverty estimates for Poland, where, for example, depending on the study, either 19 percent or 40 percent of the population lived in poverty in 1990.

Future Issues for Discussion

Given these data limitations, it would be desirable to supplement the HBS-based research. This may be accomplished in at least three ways. First, one could carry out more detailed analyses with the existing data. This could include measuring the duration of poverty and estimating the size of interhousehold transfers (or private-family safety nets). Second, explicitly subjective estimates could be employed, that is, asking household members about the income level necessary to maintain the household at its subjectively perceived poverty line, and then comparing the actual income with the subjective poverty line. Third, one could use nonmonetary indicators, particularly indicators of deprivation (e.g., nutrition, calorie intake, food consumption, and so forth), but also information concerning dwelling conditions, possession of household durables, and others.

Research along these lines has just begun. As regards the first option, recent research has shown that the duration of poverty may actually not be long for many of the poor. Ochocki (1993) has estimated, based on the Survey of Living Conditions of the Population (SLP) carried out periodically by the Central Statistical Office since 1984, that only 12 percent of the population considered themselves poor both in 1990 and 1991, although about twice as many people were considered poor in either 1990 or 1991 (Table 12.1). Still, the available evidence is not clear: from among households surveyed in both years, close to 60 percent of those who were poor in 1990 remained so in 1991, whereas evidence for 1991–92 suggests that this increased to about 80 percent, indicating that poverty shows a tendency toward becoming persistent.

Similarly, recent research has shown that private interhousehold transfers increase in response to household earning losses, and that family networks can complement governments as a means of income redistribution. Simulation exercises by Cox, Jimenez, and Okrasa (1993) on the basis of the 1986 HBS indicate that these private-family safety nets are an important part of Polish income, filling about one-sixth of the income gap left by lost earnings, and that these are well targeted to low-income households. The response was highest for households with one income earner (replacing 30 percent of the income lost) and lowest for households with more than one income earner (replacing 5.5 percent of the income lost). Thus, in many cases, increases in private interhousehold transfers could have substantially narrowed or even bridged the poverty gap.

As regards the second option, the use of subjective poverty estimates has yielded results that are not unlike the headcount indices derived from the annual HBS. Ochocki (1993) has estimated, again based on the SLP, that about one-third of all households could be considered "subjectively" poor in 1990 and 1992 (Table 12.1). These subjective poverty estimates also suggest that some of the recent research claiming that over 40 percent of the population lived in poverty during 1990–92 may overestimate the extent of poverty. Again, a high estimate of the number of poor people is the result of using a relatively high poverty line, such as the Polish "social minimum," which is generally agreed to exceed minimum subsistence significantly (World Bank, 1993; and Graham, 1993).

As regards the third option, there are a number of largely nonmonetary indicators available. Indicators of deprivation are of particular interest for estimating the extent of poverty. In general, the available indicators do not suggest that basic needs have been threatened by the transition (Table 12.2). Probably most interestingly, the sharp curtailing of transfers to households (excluding pensions) from 8.4 percent of GDP in 1989 to 3.9 percent in 1990, and particularly the discontinuation of food subsidies, which, before the transition, accounted for nearly 30 percent of the total value of food consumption (Graham, 1993), appear to have had little effect on the average nutritional status. While milk consumption, which before the transition had a producer price that was six times above the consumer price, dropped by 9 percent during 1989–92, meat consumption, which was rationed before the transition, increased by 8 percent during the same time period. Although the energy content of the average Polish diet fell by 2 percent during 1989–91, total calorie intake remains more than adequate. It is also interesting to note that, while maintaining their calorie intake, people spent significantly less of their total consumption on food in 1992 than in 1989 (Table 12.2).

A number of other indicators have sometimes been used to estimate the extent of poverty in Poland. Usually, these indicators are not very comprehensive but may provide useful supportive evidence. For example, between 1990 and 1992, 18 percent of all kindergartens were closed, which would tend to support the argument that children are particularly affected by the transition. However, under socialism, having an abundance of child care facilities was an important element for achieving the dual policy goal of high labor force participation with full employment, and the current level of child care facilities is probably more commensurate with the requirements of a market economy.

Often, though, these alternative or complementary indicators do not achieve what they set out to demonstrate. For example, it has been argued that the fact that "at the end of 1992 rent was not being paid regularly for 43 percent of the housing units owned by cooperatives, municipalities, and employers, and that payment delays were of three months or more in about 11 percent of the cases" reflects inability to pay, which in turn is a sign of growing poverty (UNICEF, 1993). However, nonpayment is not automatically equal to inability to pay, particularly since the absence of a credible threat of eviction creates a strong element of moral hazard. In addition, while much of the housing stock is eventually to be privatized, property rights remain unclear, a situation that may also have contributed to an erosion of payment discipline.

Conclusions

Poland's social protection mechanisms became fiscally unsustainable once transition got under way. The authorities' efforts to reform the social protection system coincided with a strong increase in poverty rates in the initial stages of reform. Yet, the available data provide conflicting evidence on the adverse impact of the transition on the population's well-being, which has complicated policymaking. Nevertheless, the Polish authorities generally succeeded in replacing the old social protection system, which relied heavily on job guarantees, generalized subsidies, and in-kind benefits with a modern system of social protection.

References

Atkinson, Anthony B., and John Micklewright, 1992, *Economic Transformation in Eastern Europe and the Distribution of Income* (Cambridge, England: Cambridge University Press).

Cox, Donald, Emmanuel Jimenez, and Wlodek Okrasa, 1993, "Family Safety Nets During Economic Transition: A Case Study of Poland," paper presented at a conference on Privatization and Socioeconomic Policy in Poland (unpublished; Krakow).

Gorecki, Brunon, and others, 1992, "Country Paper—Poland 1992" (unpublished).

Graham, Carol, 1993, "The Political Economy of Safety Nets During Market Transitions: The Case of Poland," Research Paper Series No. 3, Research Project on Income Distribution During the Transition (Washington: World Bank).

Hambor, John, 1992, "Issues in Eastern European Social Security Reform," Research Paper No. 9201 (Washington: U.S. Treasury Department).

Kordos, Jan, "Poverty Measurement in Poland" (unpublished; Warsaw: Central Statistical Office).

Ksiezopolski, Miroslaw, 1991, "Labour Market in Transition and the Growth of Poverty in Poland," *Labour and Society,* Vol. 16, No. 2, pp. 175–92.

Lipton, David, and Jeffrey Sachs, 1990, "Creating a Market Economy: The Case of Poland," *Brooking Papers on Economic Activity: 1* (Washington: Brookings Institution), pp. 75–148.

Maret, Xavier, and Gerd Schwartz, 1993, "Poland: The Social Safety Net During the Transition," IMF Working Paper 93/42 (Washington: International Monetary Fund).

———, 1994, "Poland: Social Protection and the Pension System During the Transition," *International Social Security Review,* Vol. 47, No. 2, pp. 51–69.

Milanovic, Branko, 1992a, "Income Distribution in Late Socialism: Poland, Hungary, Czechoslovakia, Yugoslavia, and Bulgaria Compared," Research Project on Income Distribution During the Transition, Research Paper Series, No. 1 (Washington: World Bank).

———, 1992b, "Social Costs of Transition to Capitalism: Poland 1990–91," Research Paper Series, No. 2 (Washington: World Bank, June).

———, 1992c, "Poverty in Poland, 1978–88," *Review of Income and Wealth,* Vol. 38 (September), pp. 329–40.

———, 1993, "Social Costs of Transition to Capitalism: Poland 1990–91," Policy Research Paper No. WPS 1165 (Washington: World Bank).

Ochocki, Andrzej, 1993, "Information on Poverty in Poland" (unpublished; Warsaw: Central Statistical Office).

Panek, Tomasz, and Adam Szulc, 1991, "Income Distribution and Poverty Theory and a Case Study of Poland in the Eighties" (unpublished; Warsaw: Central Statistical Office Research Centre for Statistical and Economic Analysis and Polish Academy of Sciences).

Schwartz, Gerd, 1994, "Public Finances," in *Poland: The Path to a Market Economy,* IMF Occasional Paper No. 113, ed. by L. Ebrill, and others (Washington: International Monetary Fund).

United Nations Children's Fund (UNICEF), 1993, *Central and Eastern Europe in Transition: Public Policy and Social Conditions,* Regional Monitoring Report No. 1 (Florence, Italy: UNICEF, November).

World Bank, 1993, *Poland: Income Support and the Social Safety Net During the Transition* (Washington: World Bank, January).

13

Social Protection During Russia's Economic Transformation

Sanjeev Gupta and Robert Hagemann

The transition to a market economy in Russia has reduced most people's real incomes, especially the incomes of the poor. The sharp decline in output and the manifold increases in prices have taken their heaviest toll on the more vulnerable segments of the population—the elderly or disabled, unemployed workers, workers receiving delayed or partial wages, and families with many children (Table 13.1). Cash income for many of these groups is below the estimated subsistence level.

As a result, poverty in Russia is increasing. In 1991, some 17 million persons, or 11.7 percent of the population, had incomes below the subsistence level; by 1992 that number had increased to 44 million, or about 30 percent of the population. Recent studies by Russia's statistical agency suggest that the gap between the highest and lowest income brackets has widened significantly in the past two years, whereas social indicators (e.g., health and education) have declined markedly.

Despite indications that poverty may have declined slightly in 1994, only broadly based, sustained growth can permanently reduce poverty in Russia over the longer term. In the meantime, the key issues are how to shield the vulnerable from the impact of price liberalization and reduced employment opportunities, and how to strengthen existing social protection schemes to protect their living standards. In fact, the IMF-supported economic program being pursued in Russia includes measures aimed at strengthening the existing system of social protection.

Note: Reprinted from *Finance & Development*, Vol. 31 (December 1994), pp. 14–17.

Table 13.1. Coming Through the Transition: Economic and Social Indicators

	1992	1993 Estimate
Real GDP (percentage change)	−19.0	−13.0
Consumer price index (percentage change)	1,353.0	932.0
Employment and wages		
Average employment (in millions of persons)	72.3	71.5
Registered unemployment (in millions of persons)	0.6	0.7
Average nominal wage (thousands of rubles a month)	6.0	58.5
Average real wage (percentage change)	−38.0	1.0
Minimum wage/average wage (in percent)	11.9	11.3
Major cash benefits		
Average benefit/average wage (in percent)		
Pensions	31.3	36.3
Unemployment benefits	18.0	11.6
Child allowances	5.3	4.3
Number of beneficiaries/number of employed (in percent)		
Pensions	47.2	49.4
Unemployment benefits	0.2	1.0
Child allowances	62.2	62.6

Source: Russian authorities.

The Safety Net

Russia has an elaborate system of primary social protection, which includes subsidies on some food and other consumption items (e.g., public transportation), pensions, newly established unemployment benefits, sickness and maternity benefits, child allowances, and social assistance programs (Box 13.1). Pensions and unemployment insurance are permanent social security instruments and can play important social protection roles during the transition period. Secondary instruments of social protection are social assistance programs that assist individuals who receive insufficient or no benefits from the primary programs.

These social protection schemes are financed and administered by a variety of extrabudgetary funds, as well as directly by the central and local governments (Table 13.2). In 1993, Russia spent some 8 percent of GDP on social protection, excluding outlays on education and health. Roughly two-thirds of spending on social protection was for pensions, while most of the remainder was for the other primary social programs (Figure 13.1).

Box 13.1. Social Protection in Russia

Pensions. One out of every four Russians is a pensioner (35 million people). For many, pensions are the primary, and in many cases the sole, source of cash income. The ratio of the average pension to the average wage, the so-called replacement ratio, was 36 percent in 1993, an improvement over the mid-1992 ratio of about 31 percent. There are, however, roughly 10 million pensioners who receive a minimum or very low pension that is less than the estimated minimum subsistence income for pensioners.

Unemployment benefits. The number of registered unemployed in Russia since the beginning of the reform process has been relatively modest. There were some 1.2 million registered unemployed in May 1994—a registered unemployment rate of about 1.6 percent. Of these, only 1 million drew unemployment benefits, however, and another 3 million unemployed had either exhausted their unemployment benefits or had chosen not to register. Close to an estimated 8 million individuals were on short working days, partially paid or on unpaid leave in the first quarter of 1994. Consequently, only about 9 percent of the total unemployed and underemployed received cash unemployment benefits. The average unemployment benefit in relation to the average wage was meager at about 12 percent in 1993—about one-third of the average benefit received by pensioners—and substantially lower than the minimum subsistence income for a working person.

Other social-insurance type benefits. These include birth, maternity, and sickness benefits to meet various contingencies of short-term income loss of those who are employed.

Child allowances. A traditional means of providing financial assistance in Russia, as elsewhere in the former Soviet Union, is through child allowances.

Inadequacies of the System

Russia's current system of social protection suffers from a number of shortcomings. The challenge is to make the existing system cost-effective while ensuring adequate protection for those who need it most. Some of the major shortcomings of the system are discussed here.

Unequal and Low Benefits

During Russia's economic transformation, only the real incomes of those considered to be most at risk can be shielded, and, within this group, the burden of adjustment has to be borne equitably. During recent years, pensioners have on average fared somewhat better than

There are some 39 million children in Russia below the age of 18. Until the end of 1993, there were 14 types of child allowances, but these were consolidated into three types in 1994. Child allowance is linked to the minimum wage and varies with the age of the child. The amount of the average child allowance has been rather small—about 4 percent of the average wage in 1993. Federal and local budgets, together with the social insurance fund, share the cost of child allowances. Faced with the need to contain the fiscal deficit, and lacking a well-defined, cost-sharing mechansim, state and local governments have tended to underfinance child allowances.

Social assistance programs. A number of social assistance programs, run by the Ministry of Social Protection in collaboration with local authorities, target the disadvantaged, including, especially, disabled persons. An extrabudgetary fund, the Fund for Social Protection of the Population (FSPP), is also engaged, among other things, in selling humanitarian aid received from abroad. Because of a lack of regular sources of revenue, however, the FSPP engages extensively in income-producing activities, ostensibly helpful to the poor, such as investment in the production of goods consumed heavily by the poor.

Food subsidies. In Russia, three food items—bread, milk, and meat—are subsidized, mostly at the local level. Local governments can regulate the prices of these commodities, and what they spend on subsidies depends in part on their financial position, and in part on the transfers they receive from the federal budget. As a result, the data most probably do not fully capture the amount spent on food subsidies and do not include any implicit subsidies borne by producers because of price regulation.

the unemployed. The low level of unemployment benefits is due partly to the fact that unemployment compensation is determined with a declining statutory replacement rate, which measures the relationship between unemployment benefits and a worker's last wage, and no price indexation. This factor, together with the social stigma attached to being unemployed, results in many unemployed not registering for benefits. Moreover, the cost of becoming unemployed is especially high because of the extensive provision of social benefits within enterprises. Because unattractive unemployment benefits create incentives for state-owned companies to hoard labor, the system clashes with reforms designed to promote economic restructuring and to improve economic efficiency.

About 30 percent of pensioners receive a minimum pension below the estimated minimum subsistence income. Hence, many of these

Table 13.2. Administering Social Protection in Russia, 1994

Program	Agency	Funding Source
Pension	Pension Fund (PF)	Payroll tax of 29 percent for most workers
Food subsidies	Local governments	Local budget, central government transfers
Unemployment benefits	Employment Fund (EF)	Payroll tax of 2 percent for most workers
Child allowances	Local governments, enterprises	Central and local government budgets and SIF
Birth, maternity, sickness benefits	Social Insurance Fund (SIF)	Payroll tax of 5.4 percent for most workers
Social assistance programs	Local and central governments	Local and central government budgets and an extrabudgetary fund

Source: Russian authorities.

pensioners (16 percent) try to make ends meet by continuing to work. However, a large proportion of pensioners with higher benefits also work. In many cases, these pensioners continued to work at the same job after reaching the statutory retirement age. In a tight fiscal situation, this practice has introduced an inequity in the social protection system—between those receiving below-subsistence pensions and those with two income sources. Paradoxically, while some vulnerable groups receive inadequate protection, others may receive relatively generous benefits. For instance, the social insurance fund provides sickness benefits that are generous by international standards, and subsidizes workers' stays in health spas and resorts by covering their operational costs and providing discounted vouchers.

The average amount of child allowance is also too low to have an appreciable impact on the well-being of a poor family. There is evidence that many children are in fact not receiving the payment because of fiscal difficulties at both local and federal levels. If, as a result of tight fiscal conditions, the average benefit is set too low, inequities result, because less needy families continue to receive payments.

Fragmented Benefit Administration

The average benefit level has also been affected adversely by the fragmentation of administration between the local and federal gov-

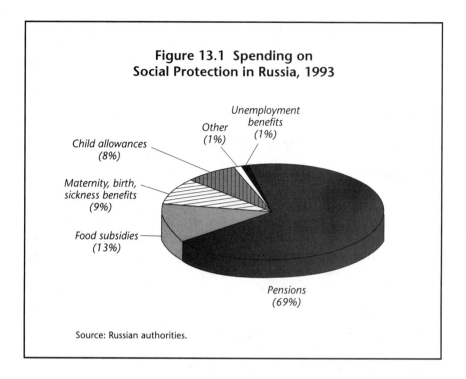

**Figure 13.1 Spending on
Social Protection in Russia, 1993**

*Unemployment
benefits
(1%)*

*Other
(1%)*

*Child allowances
(8%)*

*Maternity, birth,
sickness benefits
(9%)*

*Food subsidies
(13%)*

*Pensions
(69%)*

Source: Russian authorities.

ernments. For instance, the central employment fund receives 10 percent of payroll tax receipts, and the other 90 percent is received at the local level. The center's share is hardly sufficient to meet the needs of localities whose level of unemployment increases and, hence, whose revenue base contracts. At present, there are no intergovernmental mechanisms for equalizing funding among the different local governments.

Poor Coverage

Currently, those unemployed who are not registered receive hardly any income support, as reflected in exceedingly low take-up rates of retraining and public works programs. Thus, a large number of unemployed are not covered by the existing system of social protection, although some of them work in the informal sector and earn enough for a minimum standard of living.

At the local level, various programs are geared to serving the disabled, who need to be sustained during the difficult period of transition, but few mechanisms, if any, exist at the local level to reduce the gap between family income and the minimum necessary to attain an adequate standard of living. Such mechanisms are necessary to track the working poor and those individuals who do not receive enough from the primary social protection network.

Weak Financial Base

Statutory payroll tax rates in Russia are relatively high. However, the "effective rates"—the rates actually paid by the working population— are lower than the statutory rates by 20–35 percent, reflecting amounts lost due to nonpayment and/or underpayment of taxes by businesses, legal exemptions, and, more recently, delays in receipt of payments or arrears. Low effective rates also reflect the lower rates applied to some sectors (agriculture) and enterprises (those employing the handicapped), and the self-employed, designed ostensibly to reflect differential risks. Lower-than-expected revenue collection, in turn, has severely limited the ability to close the gap between minimum benefits and minimum subsistence levels.

Wasteful Expenditures

Two of the extrabudgetary funds—Employment Fund and Fund for Social Protection of the Population—provide wage and other subsidies to enterprises with the principal objective of maintaining employment. There seems to be little rationale for providing subsidies for employment that are also financed by workers' social insurance contributions meant to cover unemployment.

Making the System Effective

The social safety net in Russia can, and should, be made more effective. This can be done within the tight fiscal constraints present during the transition to a market economy. In the short term, the existing social protection instruments can be adapted to establish a more effective social safety net. During the transition, however, Russia faces potential conflicts between short-term and long-term reform agendas. Over time, it is critical that social insurance schemes—especially pensions and unemployment compensation—be made as effective as possible, based on sound economic and actuarial principles.

In the short term, a number of principles that recognize the financial and institutional constraints in Russia today should underpin more effective safety nets:

- Eligibility requirements should aim to provide effective protection to potentially all members of vulnerable groups; this requires careful targeting.
- Benefits should be set at levels that balance social adequacy with available resources.
- Protection schemes should recognize short-run administrative constraints.
- The design of social benefits should be compatible with fostering the development of the private sector and competition.

One of the critical principles for an effective safety net is that minimum benefits should at least equal the minimum subsistence levels and be fully protected against inflation. The minimum pension remains below the minimum subsistence income for pensioners, and should be raised. The decision in Russia in the latter part of 1993 to switch from full price indexation of all pension benefits to a flat, indexed payment to all pensioners reflects the need to protect the purchasing power of less well-off retirees to a greater extent than their counterparts with more income.

For the system of unemployment insurance to operate as a catalyst for the macroeconomic and structural adjustment needed in Russia, however, the average benefit must clearly be increased from levels observed to date. A higher average benefit could induce more unemployed people to register and assist the process of industrial restructuring. Beyond unemployment compensation, and especially for those workers who have exhausted the allowed benefits, additional resources for retraining and public works are needed to complement other forms of assistance.

If direct identification of larger poor families is not possible, improved targeting of child allowances could be achieved by limiting allowances to second and additional children. This will also save resources that could be used to finance other benefits or to increase the value of child allowances. Further improvements in the minimum and, in some cases, average benefits currently provided in the Russian social protection system can be financed without recourse to new forms of financing.

A number of steps will be required to increase revenue and make expenditures more cost-effective. About one-half of additional resources can be found by rationalizing the benefits structure. For example, pensions for working pensioners receiving more than the minimum pension could be reduced. The retirement age for both women and men—low by international standards at 55 and 60, respectively—could be raised gradually. The cost of sickness benefits could be borne by employers for the first few days, and subsidies for vouchers for admission into sanatoriums could be eliminated. Wasteful practices, such as wage subsidies paid by the Employment Fund to enterprises, could be eliminated.

On the revenue side, compliance with the payroll tax could be strengthened through more widespread and frequent audits and by levying a positive real interest rate on overdue contribution payments. Also, payroll tax exemptions could be reduced or totally eliminated. Both the pension and employment funds could generate additional resources by putting their surpluses in accounts that pay market interest rates. The resulting strengthened social safety net can be expected to play an extremely catalytic role in accelerating the transition to a market economy.

14

Reforming Ukraine's Social Safety Nets: Short-Term and Medium-Term Options

Sanjeev Gupta, Elliott Harris, and Alexandros Mourmouras

Ukraine has experienced severe economic dislocations since its independence in 1991, following the breakup of the Baltics, Russia, and other countries of the former Soviet Union. High inflation and large declines in real wages and output have imposed severe economic and social hardship on the population, particularly on the vulnerable groups (Table 14.1). Beginning in October 1994, the authorities intensified their economic reform efforts, resulting in a slowdown of the decline in real GDP and a reduction in monthly rates of inflation. In 1995, the consolidated budget deficit fell to 5.0 percent of GDP, from 8.2 percent of GDP in 1994. The authorities' economic reform program for 1996 aims at a further reduction of the fiscal deficit, to 3.5 percent of GDP, and includes, inter alia, measures to accelerate the privatization of enterprises and to increase the cost recovery ratios for housing and communal services.

Ukraine inherited a well-developed system of social protection, comprising pensions, allowances for families with children, unemployment and disability benefits, subsidies for housing and communal services, and compensation to victims of the Chernobyl nuclear accident. It spent 17.4 percent of GDP on these programs in 1995; in 1996, these outlays are projected to rise to 18.0 percent of GDP (Table 14.2). Most social programs are financed through the taxation of wages. But tax

Note: Reprinted from *Ukraine: Accelerating the Transition to Market,* ed. by Peter K. Cornelius and Patrick Lenain (Washington: International Monetary Fund, 1997), pp. 97–131.

With the assistance of Robert Gillingham and Tom Hoopengardner. The authors would like to thank Ke-young Chu and Albert Jaeger for many comments and discussions on the issues raised in this paper.

Table 14.1. Economic and Social Indicators

	1993	1994	1995	1996 Projection
Real GDP (percentage change)	–17	–24	–13	–2
Average monthly inflation (December to December)	47.1	14.4	9.0	2.5
Employment and wages				
	(In percent of population)			
Average employment rate	46.0	44.5	42.7	42.7
	(In percent of labor force)			
Average registered unemployment	0.3	0.3	0.3	0.5
	(In millions, at year-end)			
Pensioners	14.9	14.0	14.0	14.0
Pensioners/contributors	0.62	0.61	0.64	0.64
	(In thousands of karbovanets a month)			
Average nominal wage	155.1	1,375.1	7,347.8	13,377
Average real wage	100.0	76.1	91.0	96.0
Minimum wage	13.6	60	60	1,500
Minimum income[1]	23.9	214.3	1,368.0	. . .
Average pension	66.0	498.0	2,374.0	4,122.8
Minimum pension	25.4	389	1,930	3,544
Average unemployment benefit	21.6	253.7	1,098.2	4,488.0
	(In percent)			
Major cash benefits				
Average pension/average wage	43	36	32	31
Average unemployment benefit/ average wage	13.9	19.8	15.3	33.6
Average child allowance/average wage	9.2	6.4	6.1	5.0
Average housing compensation/ average wage	—	—	16.2	20.0

Sources: Data provided by the Ukrainian authorities; and IMF staff estimates.
[1]Consists of minimum salary (itself a multiple of the minimum wage) plus the bread supplement.

rates amounting to 52 percent—a very high level by international standards—have raised the cost of labor.[1]

The problem with the Ukrainian social protection system is that its structure is quite diffuse. Benefits are currently extended to almost half of the population, while the burden of wage taxation is borne by some

---

[1]A 37 percent tax is levied on the wage fund of enterprises, supplemented by a 1 percent contribution from employees. The revenue collected is shared between the Pension Fund (88 percent) and the Social Insurance Fund (the residual 12 percent). Another 2 percent tax on the wage fund is collected for the Employment Fund. A principal reason behind the relatively high wage taxation in Ukraine is the need to finance benefits for those affected by the Chernobyl catastrophe—an additional tax of 12 percent of the wage fund is levied for this purpose.

Table 14.2. Costs of Social Protection Programs

	1994	1995				1996 Projected			
		Preliminary estimate	Payroll taxes	Budget	Other	Total	Payroll	Budget	Other
	(In trillions of karbovanets)								
Social protection expenditure	186.1	894.2	589.1	300.9	4.2	1,333.3	1,015.6	295.7	22.0
Pensions[1]	92.0	426.0	424.1	1.9	—	776.6	729.4	30.5	16.7
Child, maternity, and sickness allowances	13.5	69.3	54.4	11.2	3.6	104.3	90.0	14.3	—
Unemployment-related benefits	6.5	16.4	15.8	—	0.6	31.3	26.0	—	5.3
Chernobyl-related benefits	24.0	94.7	94.7	—	—	170.1	170.1	—	—
Housing Subsidy Program	—	2.9	—	2.9	—	86.9	—	86.9	—
Consumer subsidies	50.1	284.9	—	284.9	—	164.0	—	164.0	—
Memorandum items									
General government balance[2]	-93.0	-259.2	n.a.	n.a.	n.a.	-261.4	n.a.	n.a.	n.a.
Revenue of state and local budgets	504.0	2,049.7	n.a.	n.a.	n.a.	3,332.0	n.a.	n.a.	n.a.
Expenditure of state and local budgets	608.7	2,308.2	n.a.	n.a.	n.a.	3,593.4	n.a.	n.a.	n.a.
Extrabudgetary funds balance	11.7	-0.7	n.a.	n.a.	n.a.	n.a.	n.a.	n.a.	n.a.
Wage bill	312.0	1,763.5	n.a.	n.a.	n.a.	3,184.9	n.a.	n.a.	n.a.
	(As percent of GDP)								
Social protection expenditure	16.4	17.4	11.5	5.9	0.1	18.0	13.7	4.6	0.3
Pensions[1]	8.1	8.3	8.3	—	—	10.5	9.8	0.4	0.2
Child, maternity, and sickness allowances	1.2	1.3	1.1	—	0.1	1.4	1.2	—	—
Unemployment-related benefits	0.6	0.3	0.3	—	—	0.4	0.4	—	0.1
Chernobyl-related benefits	2.1	1.8	1.8	—	—	2.3	2.3	—	—
Housing Subsidy Program	—	0.1	0.1	—	—	1.2	—	1.2	—
Consumer subsidies	4.4	5.5	—	5.5	—	2.2	—	2.2	—
Memorandum items									
General government balance[2]	-8.2	-5.0	n.a.	n.a.	n.a.	-3.5	n.a.	n.a.	n.a.
Rvenue of state and local budgets	44.3	39.9	n.a.	n.a.	n.a.	44.9	n.a.	n.a.	n.a.
Expenditure of state and local budgets	53.5	44.9	n.a.	n.a.	n.a.	48.4	n.a.	n.a.	n.a.
Extrabudgetary funds balance	1.0	n.a.	n.a.	n.a.	n.a.	n.a.	n.a.	n.a.	n.a.
Wage bill	27.4	34.3	n.a.	n.a.	n.a.	42.9	n.a.	n.a.	n.a.

Sources: Data provided by the Ukrainian authorities; and IMF staff estimates.

Note: n.a. = not applicable.

[1]Includes transfers from Chernobyl Fund for payment of pensions to persons affected by the disaster.

[2]Includes the balance of extrabudgetary funds, other than the Pension Fund and the Chernobyl Fund, and the Employment Fund from 1996 (1.0 percent of GDP in 1994, and less than 0.1 percent of GDP in 1995).

20 million active workers. There is a plethora of overlapping benefits, combined with privileges for certain population groups for the use of public services, which greatly complicates the assessment of benefit incidence. At this stage of transition in Ukraine, it is important to focus assistance on the population groups most at risk. A rationalization and improved targeting of the existing social protection system would help achieve this objective and support the ongoing economic reforms, since a system that pays benefits to the bulk of the population would undermine the reform process by exacerbating macroeconomic imbalances.

Targeting benefits to the truly needy is a challenge for the authorities because of the growth of the informal sector. A recent household income and expenditure survey indicates that reported incomes account for only half of reported expenditures. This suggests that the use of official incomes for determining benefit eligibility may lead to mistargeting. The growth of informal and private sector activity also has ramifications for the design and financing of social benefits: it has further narrowed the base for wage taxation, since much of the informal and private sector activity escapes the tax net.

Against this background, this chapter presents a series of short- and medium-term options for enhancing the cost-effectiveness and social adequacy of Ukraine's social protection system, in terms of both reducing the cost of delivering a given benefit and increasing the benefits that can be provided at a given cost. These reforms would increase the effectiveness of Ukraine's social protection system while delivering budgetary savings of about 3.5 percent of GDP.

Housing Subsidy Program

Ukrainian households paid very little for housing and communal services until the fall of 1994. The untargeted subsidies used to finance these services distorted domestic prices, prevented the emergence of a private housing market, and exerted a pressure on both the budget and the external balance. In 1993–94, mounting budget deficits and external payments arrears to energy suppliers (the Russian Federation and Turkmenistan) prompted the government to begin shifting the burden of financing housing services and utilities to households. Tariffs have been allowed to rise gradually, with the ultimate goal of achieving full cost recovery.

The reduction in generalized subsidies, while indispensable for supporting broad fiscal and macroeconomic stabilization objectives, creates an immediate need for a safety net for the most vulnerable, notably households with low incomes. In order to address concerns for these households, Ukraine introduced a housing subsidy program in May 1995. This program has sought to limit households' expenditures on housing and communal services to not more than 15 percent of recorded family income.[2] In determining eligibility, total reported income of all family members over 16 years of age in the preceding three months is taken into account. Households are eligible for compensation for expenditures on a specified list of communal services based on certain norms. The utilities initially included in the program were apartment maintenance, water, hot water, heat, and sewage. The scheme has gradually been extended to include liquid gas and coal (July 1995) and electricity (October 1995).

Since direct measurement of consumption of communal services (mostly energy-related) by households in Ukraine is not technically feasible at present owing to the lack of meters, individual assessments have to be made on the basis of norms. These norms relate the size of a household to the allowable expenses for granting targeted subsidies. Subsidy calculations are now based on a norm of 21 square meters per person, plus 10.5 square meters of common space—generous compared with an actual average amount of per capita space of 16 square meters in Ukraine. Since the budget cannot afford to make payments on the high norm of 21 square meters, subsidies are based on actual expenses up to the norm and receipts must be furnished in order to make payments.[3]

While the scheme is open to all Ukrainian households, the income criterion is expected to limit the coverage rate to about 25 percent of the

---

[2]The Ukrainian housing subsidy program is discussed extensively in Roger J. Vaughan, 1995, *A History and Overview of Ukraine's Housing Subsidy Program* (Kiev: PADCO Inc., November).

[3]Assuming a single threshold and no lag in information on incomes, a household with n members that occupy an apartment of z square meters and that has reported income Y_t, would receive a monthly subsidy S_t in month t given by

$$S_t(Y_t, n, z) = C_t(n, z) - \tau Y_t. \tag{1}$$

In equation (1), τ is the income threshold rate set by law, while C_t is the household's cost of housing and communal services. There are different ways of estimating the costs of housing and communal services for the targeted subsidy. One possibility is to rely on the actual charge, C_a, for apartments no larger than a per capita space "norm," where the norm is defined on the basis of health (or sanitary) considerations. The assumption is that there is a fixed relationship between space and consumption of other communal services. For households that live in housing units larger than the norm, the assessed cost would not exceed the sanitary norm. For example, the norm may include the estimated cost for a fixed amount of space, $\bar{z}$, plus a per capita space allocation α. The cost may be written as

$$
\begin{aligned}
C_t(n, z) &= \min[C_a, C_n(n, z)] \\
&= \min[p_z z n, p_z(\bar{z} + \alpha n)].
\end{aligned} \tag{2}
$$

Table 14.3. Coverage Rates and Housing Subsidy Program Expenditures

	1995	1996 Jan.–Feb. Preliminary	1996 Projection
Coverage rate (in percent)[1]	8	13.7	20
	(In thousands of households)		
Monthly flow	176	488	171.6
Average monthly stock	605	2,058	2,626
End-of-period stock	1,407	2,383	3,467
Expenditure			
In trillions of karbovanets	2.9	3.8	86.9
In percent of GDP	0.1	0.4	1.2
Memorandum items			
Number of households (in thousands)	17,406	17,406	17,406
Threshold income rate (in percent)	15	15	15
Average monthly subsidy			
In thousands of karbovanets	599	931	2,680
In percent of average wage	8.2	7.7	20.0

Sources: Ukrainian authorities; USAID/PADCO Inc., Kiev; and IMF staff estimates.
[1]Fraction of Ukrainian households covered by the Housing Subsidy Program by year-end.

households (Table 14.3). So far, actual coverage has been substantially less than expected. By the end of February 1996, 13.9 percent of Ukraine's 17 million households were receiving subsidies. This represented 83.8 percent of all households who had submitted applications. The 1995 budget allocated Krb 17 trillion to the Housing Subsidy Program, which was later revised to Krb 70 trillion. In the event, the actual cost of the program was very small (Krb 2.9 trillion or 0.1 percent of GDP). The 1996 budget envisaged a reduction in outlays for housing and communal services to 3.4 percent of GDP from 5.5 percent of GDP in 1995, with outlays on the Housing Subsidy Program increasing to 1.2 percent of GDP. Accordingly, the net budgetary savings from the targeting of generalized subsidies for housing and communal services are expected to be 1.0 percent of GDP in 1996. Available data suggest that so far the program has been effective in targeting the poor.[4]

---

[4]In two Kiev-area samples, reported average household income in January 1996 for subsidy recipients was 47 percent, and the average subsidy about 20 percent of the average wage. Family income and subsidies seem to rise with family size; however, per capita subsidies decline with income, reflecting a measure of progressivity in the program. The distribution of families receiving support is heavily skewed

Despite the program's success in targeting the poor, several problems, as enumerated below, will make the achievement of its objectives difficult.

(1) The income threshold has remained at 15 percent even as the list of services covered by the Housing Subsidy Program was expanded in 1995.

(2) The sanitary (health) norm benefits households living in housing units larger than the actual average. Most families in Ukraine live in homes smaller than the sanitary norm and subsidies increase with the amount of space occupied by a household *up to* the norm.

(3) Several categories of persons and their families receive substantial discounts, ranging from 25 percent to 100 percent from ordinary tariffs for housing, communal services, and fuel.[5] The working group of the Council of Ministers in charge of limiting existing preferences estimated that 10.8 million (including 3.6 million war participants and invalids), or about 63 percent of all Ukrainian households, are not paying the full energy tariffs.[6] Additional subsidies are being provided to some categories of persons and their families through a lower threshold for the Housing Subsidy Program of 8 or 10 percent in 3 *oblasts*, decided by the *oblast* itself on the basis of its financial position.

(4) The Housing Subsidy Program's low coverage rate in 1995, and the associated low budgetary costs, are attributed in part to cumbersome administrative procedures. The monthly flow of applications and the task of recalculating subsidies for existing beneficiaries every six months are already straining the present administrative capacity. The system of eligibility determination still requires that calculations be redone for every housing unit when tariffs are adjusted. Because there

---

toward one- and two-member families. Single pensioners are the largest and poorest group receiving support under the program. In the sample, over 42 percent of all recipients are single pensioners with an average income of a little over Krb 3,320,000 ($17.50) a month, or 28 percent of the national average wage.

[5]These privileges are derived from about 50 legislative acts, some of them passed under the former Soviet Union. Persons who performed "great service for the Motherland" and/or are war invalids (groups 1, 2, and 3) receive free housing services, or both. Combat participants pay only 25 percent, and war veterans who served on the home front in World War II pay only 50 percent. Families affected by the Chernobyl accident (categories I and II) pay 50 percent. The norm for gas consumption allowed for families consisting of only disabled persons is twice the ordinary norm. Politically oppressed individuals also receive discounts. In addition to the tariff discounts for housing and communal services given to pensioners and disabled persons, discounts are given to those in certain occupations, such as police officers, the military and their families, judges, and firefighters.

[6]Free passenger transport is also extended to 28 categories of persons (17 million persons, of which 16 million are pensioners, children, or disabled).

are no computers, manual operations have delayed the processing of applications. To complicate matters, many households do not receive the revised utility bills immediately after a tariff increase, thereby delaying their application for the benefit.

(5) The current tariffs for housing services include only maintenance expenses, not rent. Since charges paid by consumers do not cover depreciation, the housing stock is deteriorating.

(6) Unemployed persons not registered with the Employment Service are not covered by the Housing Subsidy Program. The only exceptions made are for mothers taking care of young children or persons taking care of the disabled. Although a large proportion of those who have "vanished" from official employment rolls have found gainful employment elsewhere in the system, they are not covered by the Housing Subsidy Program.

(7) Restrictions on labor mobility, such as *Propiska*,[7] may be limiting access to the Housing Subsidy Program.[8] The institution of *Propiska* could be hindering the Housing Subsidy Program from targeting the truly needy, because benefit eligibility is based on the officially listed place of residence. With the shortage in housing and increased labor mobility, an increasing number of individuals living with relatives and friends are being deemed ineligible for Housing Subsidy Program benefits.

(8) Although the data suggest that the program is reaching single pensioners and other vulnerable groups, means testing is not without its problems in the presence of misreported incomes.

(9) Official family income for the previous three months is used in the calculation of initial subsidies. Tariffs for housing and communal services, wages, and pensions have typically been adjusted at the same time, tending to bias household incomes downward, leading to a larger number of households becoming eligible for subsidies.

Short-Term Reform Options

There are a number of short-term reform options, including the following:

---

[7]A *Propiska* is a permit that designates a person's place of residence. *Propiskas* are recorded directly in passports and labor books and are prerequisites for the provision of state housing and most other allowances, benefits, and privileges.

[8]The changes introduced on January 10, 1996 allow families with persons on administrative leave from enterprises to participate in the program, provided they certify to the Housing Subsidy Office that the unemployed person's monthly income does not exceed 50 percent of the minimum untaxable income. The law provides for recertification of the family and extension of benefits after the initial three-month period. This option is not open to the unregistered unemployed.

(1) Consider raising the threshold income rate by a modest amount. This would reflect the increasing number of services covered under the Housing Subsidy Program and the expanding share of unreported incomes.

(2) Gradually eliminate all pricing preferences. It is estimated that in 1996, the elimination of all preferences would provide budgetary savings of about 0.7 percent of GDP.

(3) Replace the sanitary norm with a social norm. This would encourage efficient allocation of available housing by creating incentives for smaller households to downsize. Such a system would also be simpler to administer, because families would not need to supply the housing subsidy offices with evidence of their payments. The social norm could be set at a level close to the average amount of space available in Ukraine. Subsidies would be calculated on the basis of the normative space for each family size; poorer families living in relatively smaller, overcrowded apartments would receive an income transfer.

(4) Eliminate subsidy recertification for certain types of households, such as nonworking pensioners, disabled persons, and families with single parents and no other income earners. This would help ease the administrative load while ensuring that the vulnerable groups continue to receive benefits after the initial income test. The benefit amounts for these groups could be recalculated automatically as tariff or pension payments change.

(5) Reduce lags in information on household incomes as much as possible. Subsidy calculations should reflect current incomes to the extent possible. Optimally, if the current three-month information lag for family income is maintained, wages should be increased three months prior to the scheduled tariff increases to avoid distorting eligibility calculations.

Medium-Term Reform Options

Medium-term reform options include the following:

(1) Include all economic costs in the calculation of tariffs and cost recovery rates. The user cost of housing services should be used to calculate the true costs to the households. A first step could be to gradually include housing depreciation in maintenance fees.

(2) Replace the *Propiska* with a national identity card. With increased labor and family mobility, replacing the *Propiska* with an identity card would facilitate the authorities' verification of citizens' status and residence for the purpose of establishing Housing Subsidy Program eligibility.

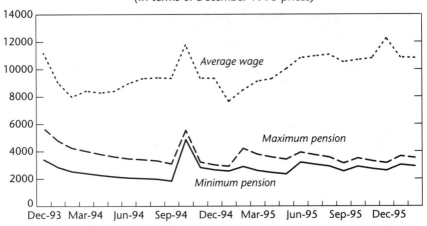

Figure 14.1 Ukraine: Real Wages and Pensions
(In terms of December 1995 prices)

Sources: Ukrainian authorities; and IMF staff estimates.

(3) Given the Housing Subsidy Program's temporary, short-term nature, the authorities should consider phasing it out over the medium term. After the *Propiska* system is eliminated and means testing improved, the authorities should consider consolidating child allowances, social pensions, and the means-tested supplemental pension benefits with the Housing Subsidy Program, with the objective of establishing a broad-based poverty benefit.

Pensions

In January 1995, 14 million people—more than a quarter of the entire population— received benefits from the Pension Fund. Whereas the number of pensioners declined by some 900,000 between 1993 and 1995, the number of contributors declined even more, raising the ratio of pensioners to contributors marginally, from 0.62 to 0.64 (see Table 14.1). About 12 percent (1.7 million) of retirees continue to work.

Ad hoc adjustments of pensions in the face of high inflation and difficult budgetary conditions have led to a significant compression of pension benefits, both in relation to the average wage and across contributors with different earnings histories (Figures 14.1 and 14.2). Thus, the replacement rate—the average pension as a share of the average wage—

Figure 14.2 Ukraine: Average Replacement Rates
(As percent of average wage)

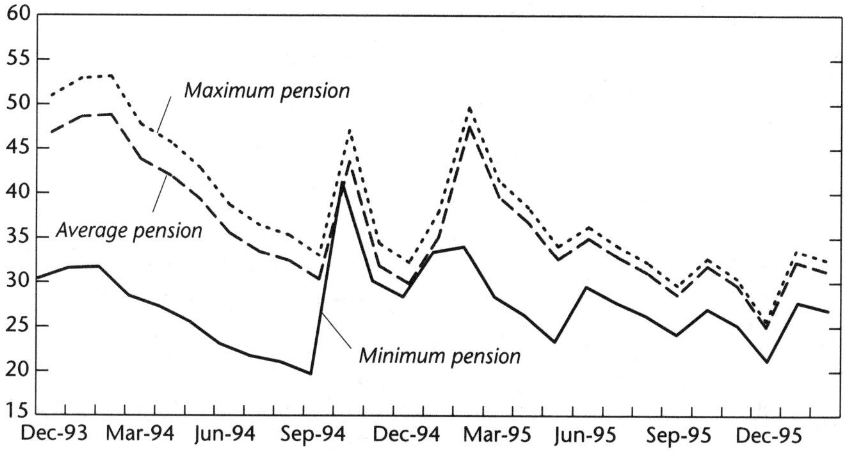

Source: Ukrainian authorities; and IMF staff estimates.

declined from 43 percent in 1993 to 32 percent in 1995. Over time, wage histories have played a declining role in setting pensions as more and more pensioners have bumped up against the maximum pension; and the importance of the compensation payments in the total pension has increased (see Figure 14.3 and Appendix Tables 14.8 and 14.9).

The growing compression between minimum and maximum pensions was achieved by retaining a ratio of 3 to 1 between the maximum and minimum basic pensions and by instituting a variety of compensation payments to adjust pensions for inflation and protect the most vulnerable citizens. In December 1993, the maximum pension was some 66 percent higher than the minimum pension, and the average replacement rate was 43 percent. By the end of 1995, the maximum pension was 21 percent higher than the minimum pension, and the average replacement rate was 25 percent. The 92 percent increase in the minimum pension announced in January 1996, and the accompanying restructuring of inflation and low-income compensation, maintained the relationship between the maximum and minimum pensions, but increased the average replacement rate to slightly over 30 percent.

The policy of ad hoc pension adjustment combined with the pension compression has allowed the Pension Fund to continue to pay pensions on time without creating a severe imbalance in its finances. In 1995, the Pension Fund spent Krb 381 trillion (8.4 percent of GDP)

Figure 14.3 Ukraine: Pension Components
(As percent of average wage)

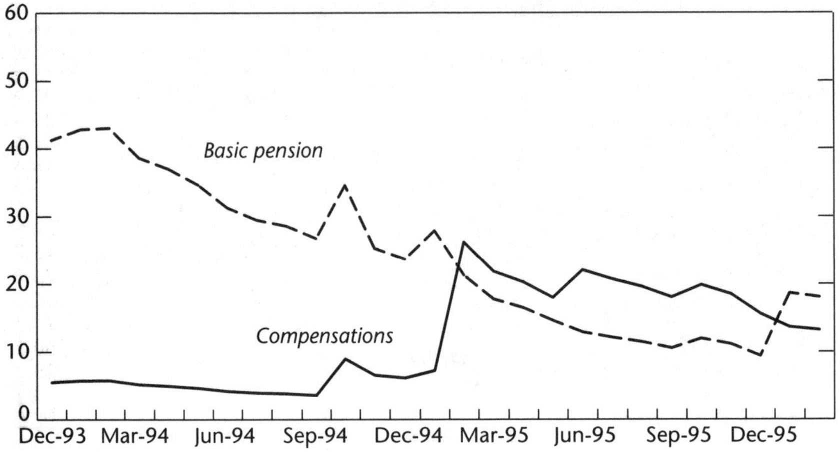

Source: Ukrainian authorities; and IMF staff estimates.

on pension benefits; Krb 20.9 trillion (0.5 percent of GDP) on child allowances; and Krb 30.2 trillion on administration, bank and postal operations, and other expenses (Table 14.4). It received Krb 415.4 trillion (9.1 percent of GDP) in insurance contributions, Krb 13.1 trillion (0.3 percent of GDP) from state and local budgets, and Krb 8.7 trillion (0.2 percent of GDP) from the Chernobyl Fund. It ran a small surplus of Krb 6.0 trillion, or 0.13 percent of GDP. The Pension Fund's budget was projected to be in balance in 1996 with revenues and expenditures distributed in roughly the same fashion as in 1995.

In the recent past, the performance of the Pension Fund has been affected by the following:

(1) Certain aspects of the eligibility and benefit structure. The retirement age—60 for men and 55 for women—is low by international standards, and about 12 percent of pension recipients worked in occupations in which they became eligible for retirement at an even earlier age. Furthermore, at any time about 12 percent of pensioners are working but still receiving full pensions, in addition to a full wage and employer-provided benefits, and their pensions are recalculated every two years on the basis of their most recent wages. Finally, pension benefits are also accrued for years of service in such endeavors as higher education or caring for a young child, even though no pension contributions are made.

Table 14.4. Pension Fund

(In trillions of karbovanets)

	1994	1995 Preliminary	1996 Projected
Revenues	99.9	437.2	790.9
Insurance contributions	93.4	415.4	729.4
Transfers from budget[1]	3.1	13.1	44.8
Transfers from Chernobyl Fund	2.5	8.7	16.0
Other revenues	0.4	n.a.	0.7
Expenditures	89.2	431.1	790.9
Pensions	70.5	313.3	412.2
Child maintenance	2.3	20.9	25.3
Children under 1.5 years of age	1.0	9.7	11.0
Children between 1.5 and 3 years of age	1.3	11.2	14.3
Inflation compensation	11.3	64.4	260.1
Assistance to low-income pensioners	1.0	2.8	26.2
Administration	0.6	4.1	4.8
Bank and post operations	3.0	24.8	25.4
Lump-sum aid to low-income pensioners	0.7	0.5	n.a.
Other	0.0	0.3	36.9
Balance	10.6	6.0	0.0
As percent of GDP	0.9	0.1	0.0
Memorandum items			
Covered employment (in millions of persons)	23.0	22.0	22.0
Number of pensioners	14.0	14.0	14.0
Ratio of workers to pensioners	1.64	0.64	0.64
Average wage (in thousands of karbovanets)	1,375.1	7,347.8	13,270.4
Average pension (in thousands of karbovanets)	498.0	2,374.0	4,109.1
Average pension as a share of the average wage	36.2	32.3	31.0
Wage fund	349.5	1,629.0	2,413.1

Sources: Ukrainian authorities; and IMF staff estimates.

[1]Includes Krb 31.7 trillion in 1996 for payment benefits at the beginning of the year in anticipation of revenue collection.

(2) Provisions in current pension legislation for higher pensions for several categories of pensioners, especially in mining and metallurgy, including disabled workers and military veterans. This raises the lifetime compensation of these workers in relation to other pensioners.

(3) The revenue uncertainty arising from a declining share of wages subject to payroll contributions. Despite the authorities' efforts to keep benefits manageable, the pension system faces a major problem in maintaining an adequate revenue stream in the near term, with rising open and "hidden" unemployment. Moreover, the share of wages subject to payroll contributions has declined markedly, as employers increasingly shift compensation into categories of remuneration not subject to the pension contributions—these include income in-kind; per diem expenses for business trips; relocation costs; the provision of

free apartments, communal services, fuel; and wages used to purchase shares in the enterprise. Were it not for the rapid growth of the share of wages in GDP, which partially offset the decline in the share of wages subject to pension contributions, the revenue situation of the Pension Fund would be far more precarious. Finally, the Pension Fund has increasingly suffered from contribution arrears, which rose to Krb 79 trillion (1.7 percent of GDP) at the end of December 1995, up from Krb 7.3 trillion a year earlier. This problem has been especially acute in mining and agriculture, but even budget organizations have accumulated significant arrears (7 percent of the total).

Short-Term Reform Options

Benefit Policies

The following measures would make the pension system more equitable, besides improving its cost-effectiveness:

(1) Reduce pensions for working pensioners. Since the replacement rate is low, it is unlikely that pensioners who earn reasonable salaries would forgo their earned income if their pensions were reduced. Pensioners who must work simply to make ends meet, however, should not face the same reduction in benefits. Only those pensioners earning employment income beyond a threshold should face a reduction in their pensions.

(2) Abolish the higher pensions for several categories of able-bodied civilian pensioners under the current pension law (mostly in mining and metallurgy) and establish a uniform maximum pension for these workers. This would reduce or eliminate the transfer implicit in providing these workers with higher lifetime compensation.

(3) Raise the official retirement age. The pension age could be raised by five years in annual increments of six months, and eventually a uniform retirement age for men and women could be established. This increase would bring the Ukrainian system more in line with those in other economies. The fact that so many pensioners continue to work indicates that they are both able and willing to participate in the labor market.

Revenue Policies

The authorities have recently taken measures to protect the revenue base of the pension system by harmonizing the contribution rates;[9]

---

[9]Contribution rates for specific sectors (e.g., the self-employed) were brought closer to the standard rate.

broadening the wage base;[10] and ensuring that accrued contributions are effectively paid. Additional measures to improve compliance and widen the tax base should be adopted to strengthen the Pension Fund's revenue base. They include:

- Widening the tax base. The authorities have already taken steps to ensure that appropriate pension contributions are made by enterprises that use a bank for paying wages. Similar safeguards should be applied to establishments that are able to trade in cash and for which a bank authorization is not required to pay wages. The Pension Fund should also more effectively capture pension contributions on income in kind.
- Eliminating the nontaxed threshold for material assistance. Under current law, the first Krb 20.4 million of material assistance per worker a year is not subject to pension contributions.

Medium-Term Reform Issues

The policy alternatives described above could substantially ease the financial pressure on the Pension Fund in the near term. If these policies are adopted, and when the macroeconomic situation in Ukraine improves, attention must be paid to the structure of the pension system in the medium and long term. A number of issues should be considered in this evolution.

Benefit Issues

Pensions should be based on years of contribution, rather than years of service. This provision has little effect at this time, when most pensioners are at or near the benefit ceiling, but will inappropriately distribute benefits if and when the compression of pension benefits eases.

The elimination of privileged early pensions should be considered. Although the financial responsibility for them has shifted to enterprises, the mandated existence of these early pensions reduces labor market flexibility, and pension contributions are reduced to the extent workers actually retire early. Furthermore, the enterprises do not now completely reimburse the Pension Fund for the full cost of early pensions and cannot be relied upon to do so in the future.

The initial pension is currently set on the basis of the wage experience in either the past two years or other 60-month period. This procedure ignores the bulk of a worker's contributions to the system. As

---

[10]Wages used to buy shares in enterprises were added to the base for calculating contributions.

data on individual contribution histories are accumulated, the initial pension should be based on the worker's entire contribution history, with early years suitably adjusted based on a price or wage index.

As real wages rise, allowing for more generous benefits, the role of compensations should be reduced, the spread among pensions should be increased, and the position of pensioners within that spread should be based on their contribution histories. In the long term, fully funded components might be added to the basic pension system; however, the medium-term transition costs would be substantial.

Revenue Issues

If the policies described above are implemented, and as fiscal pressure eases, a reduction in the payroll tax—currently among the highest in the world—should be considered. This would have to be carefully balanced against the need to increase benefits to restore the link between benefits and contributions and to ensure that vulnerable pensioners are protected. But a reduction in the payroll tax could be an important component of a program of structural reforms that would enhance economic growth.

There is also a need to reflect on the appropriate scope of the Pension Fund's responsibilities. Under the current system, the Pension Fund shares the responsibility for determining benefits, collecting, and distributing benefits with the Ministries of Social Protection and Communications. It also acts as an agent for the state and local governments and the Chernobyl Fund in paying military pensions, child allowances, social pensions, and Chernobyl-related benefits. Consideration should be given to assigning to the Pension Fund the ultimate responsibility for the collection of pension contributions and the distribution of the benefits. Responsibility for the other programs could be reassigned to the Ministry of Social Protection (child allowances and social pensions) and to the Ministry of Defense (military pensions). This would avoid the duplication of effort and make it more difficult to redirect pension resources to other uses, as happens now when the Pension Fund is incompletely reimbursed for benefits that it distributes for other agencies.

Child, Sickness, Maternity, and Other Allowances

An important element of the social protection system in Ukraine is the financial support provided to families with children. In addition to the lump-sum childbirth grants, maternity leave benefits, and parental leave provisions, a series of other benefits are targeted to children: there are 12 different child allowances and child care support payments, as well as allowances for specific categories of children, including the handicapped (see Appendix Table 14.10).

There is no limit to the number of allowances for which one family can be eligible. However, the tightness of the means test, together with the low level of the allowances, has narrowed the coverage of the child allowance to only an estimated 27 percent of children, and somewhat less than a third of the 668,000 families with three or more children. The means test is thus quite effective in limiting eligibility, but may have the perverse effect of excluding a large number of truly needy families.

Benefits are paid only to working parents and to nonworking parents registered as unemployed. The system thus excludes those who are not employed in the formal sector or not registered as unemployed, and may penalize parents who stay at home to raise a family. This effect is undesirable in the present context of declining employment opportunities and the contraction in the availability of child care facilities, and there is a growing likelihood that these people will fall through the safety net.

Child allowances have typically been adjusted according to the availability of general budgetary resources, and the budgetary constraints have led to their erosion relative to wages and other social benefits. At the same time, cumbersome administrative procedures may lower the take-up rate. Moreover, the child allowances are paid from resources of the local budgets, which are not always able to ensure the timely reimbursement of payments made on their behalf by the enterprises and the Pension Fund, leading to arrears. In 1995, Krb 28 trillion (0.6 percent of GDP) was spent on child allowances. For 1996, total expenditures under the child allowance program are projected at 0.7 percent of GDP.

Ukrainian workers in the formal sector are eligible for a series of short-term cash benefits for maternity and for temporary disability owing to sickness, which are paid through enterprises but administered and financed by the Social Insurance Fund. The Social Insurance Fund provides wage replacement during parental leave for the care of a sick child under 14 years of age, a lump-sum childbirth grant, and funeral assistance; it also provides medical rehabilitation services at sanatoriums throughout the country, as well as recreation and vacation facilities for children and families.

Since the Social Insurance Fund pays the replacement wage in case of sickness, there are incentives for employers and workers to misuse sick leave to avoid the use of administrative or unpaid leave. Moreover,

Table 14.5. Social Insurance Fund
(In billions of karbovanets)

	1995 Preliminary	1996 Projection
Revenues	58,078	90,032
Mandatory contributions of insurance premiums	54,433	90,032
Other revenues	3,645	
Expenditures	55,355	90,032
Temporary disability allowance	25,515	44,889
Maternity allowance	5,130	7,475
Lump-sum childbirth grant	896	920
Funeral assistance	286	390
Medical service at sanatoria and rehabilitation centers	21,357	34,517
Other expenses	2,171	1,840
Balance (as a percent of GDP)	0.06	—

Sources: Ukrainian authorities; and IMF staff estimates.

the provision of medical rehabilitation and recreation services is inefficient—vouchers are often provided to workers at an average cost recovery rate of about 10–12 percent. The system increasingly provides highly specialized medical rehabilitation mandated by the supervising physician but paid entirely by the Social Insurance Fund, without any cost participation from the Ministry of Health.

The Social Insurance Fund registered a very small surplus in 1995, and its finances were projected to be in balance in 1996 (Table 14.5). While the Social Insurance Fund has paid all the cash benefits on time, financial balance has been achieved through the marked decline in the provision of medical rehabilitation and recreational services. Typically, allowances provided by the Social Insurance Fund have been adjusted according to the availability of budgetary resources—the available resources have had to be shared among the numerous allowances, preventing a substantial increase in any one allowance. Close to 90 percent of the Social Insurance Fund's total expenditure is for temporary disability allowances and for medical rehabilitation and recreational services (45–50 percent and just under 40 percent, respectively).

Finally, eligibility for these benefits is too closely linked to employment in the formal sector, with enterprises playing a pivotal role in their delivery—a holdover from the previous economic system. This system may no longer be appropriate in an environment characterized by declining employment in state enterprises and increasing private sector and self-employment activity.

Short-Term Reform Options

Child Allowances

The main objectives of the reform of the child allowances system must be to strengthen the adequacy of the allowances and to ensure that the system does not exclude the truly needy. In this regard, there are two choices: reallocate resources within the given budget envelope to direct additional funds to child allowances or raise the level of some of the child allowances by combining overlapping benefits and rationalizing the benefit structure.

The reform options presented below are guided by the second consideration:

- Eliminate allowances for older children. Limiting the benefit to children under the age of 12 would result in a 40 percent decline in the number of eligible children and generate savings that could be used to increase the allowance for children under the age of 12 by as much as 58 percent.
- Combine the child allowances and the child care support payments. This option would facilitate an increase of some 40 percent in the child allowance and would enhance administrative simplicity. Centralization of the administration of child allowances at the Ministry of Social Protection would be helpful.
- Consolidate the four different allowances for families with three or more children into one flat allowance at the lowest level presently in effect. The resulting savings could be used to increase the benefit for over 70 percent of present recipients by as much as 25 percent.

Further, to address the possibility that the tight eligibility requirements and the limitations of coverage to those employed in the formal sector and formally registered as unemployed might prevent truly needy families from receiving protection under the system, it would be worthwhile to:

- Eliminate the distinction between working and nonworking parents in determining eligibility, thus removing the current disincentive to parents who decide to stay at home to raise a family; and
- Extend benefits to children of unregistered unemployed.

Sickness, Maternity, and Other Allowances

The short-term revenue position of the Social Insurance Fund could be significantly enhanced by the adoption of the revenue reform policies proposed for the Pension Fund. Furthermore, certain aspects of the benefits structure could be reformed to reduce the incentives to abuse the present provisions as well as improve efficiency.

With regard to the temporary disability benefits, it would be worthwhile to:

- Shift the cost of the first two weeks of sick leave to enterprises (up to an annual limit of four weeks per worker), after which the Social Insurance Fund would assume responsibility for the payment. This would reduce the employer's incentive to save on the wage bill by shifting the cost of the worker to the Social Insurance Fund and would encourage the employer to monitor workers' sick leave more closely.
- Introduce a flat wage-replacement rate of 80 percent. The sick leave benefit could replace wages at a uniform 80 percent for all employees, instead of the present system of differentiated rates ranging from 60–100 percent. This would reduce the employee's incentive to take unjustified sick leave.
- Extend maternity and childbirth benefits to unemployed, unregistered women. Consistent with the policy options for the child allowances, to prevent these women from slipping through the social safety net, the implementation of a flat-rate maternity and childbirth benefit not linked to a formal wage should be considered. This would be provided by the Ministry of Social Protection to all unemployed women, regardless of their registration status.

The savings generated by the benefit and revenue options could be used either to increase the share of the wage tax allocated to financing pensions, or to reduce the wage tax by up to 1.5 percentage points.

The system of medical rehabilitation and recreation should also be reformed along the following lines. There should be a proper determination of the economic cost of providing vouchers. This should be based on appropriately estimated occupancy rates for sanatoriums, recreation and other facilities and differentiated to reflect seasonal and regional demand patterns, as well as on a gradual increase in the price paid by workers for the vouchers. In addition, the practice of extending the vouchers free to unaccompanied children should be eliminated, as it obscures the economic cost of the program.

Considerations for the Medium Term

Over the medium term, protection should be extended to all vulnerable families with children, which is difficult to achieve under the present system. One possibility would be to integrate child allowances with the Housing Subsidy Program with the objective of establishing a broad-based poverty benefit, as noted earlier.

Further, the pivotal role of the enterprises and trade unions in the provision of social benefits is no longer appropriate. The social protection system must be gradually weaned from its dependency on the enterprise structure and trade unions, and the responsibility for social benefits should be centralized in the Ministry of Social Protection.

Unemployment Benefits

The role of the state Employment Service in Ukraine's labor market is limited. As indicated above, Ukraine's GDP has declined about 40 percent since 1992, yet officially measured unemployment has never risen above 0.5 percent. Nevertheless, Ukraine devotes considerable resources—0.5 percent of the wage bill, or about 0.2 percent of GDP in 1995—to the Employment Service. Wages paid to employees of the Employment Service and the Employment Fund have exceeded benefits paid to the unemployed in every year. In 1995, the 685 employment offices registered a total of 176,000 unemployed—about one person per working day per office. The Employment Fund had a small surplus (0.1 percent of GDP) in 1995 and is projected to be in balance in 1996 with revenues and expenditures projected at Krb 31.3 trillion (Table 14.6).

Enterprises in Ukraine, perhaps dissuaded by the prospect of paying 3 months' severance pay, are not explicitly firing workers; instead, they are put on unpaid leave, sick leave, or involuntary part-time work, thereby creating hidden unemployment. In 1995, by official estimates, enterprises and organizations gave long-term unpaid leave at some time during the year to 18 percent of workers, and about 900,000 people worked an incomplete day. Official calculations show that hidden unemployment at the end of 1995 was equivalent to 2.4 percent of the labor force. The apprehension has been that hidden unemployment would suddenly convert to open unemployment. However, the experience shows that the Employment Service has always overprojected unemployment, an approach that has led to overbudgeting, a surplus, and the inefficient use of that surplus.

Furthermore, unemployment benefits are low in relation to the average wage. Workers who lose their jobs are presently entitled to 3 months' severance pay, payable by employers.[11] Following 3 months'

---

[11]In fact, if they work at a financially troubled enterprise, workers may not receive any severance pay at all.

Table 14.6. Employment Fund

	1995 Preliminary	1996 Projection
	(In trillions of karbovanets)	
Revenue	16.4	31.3
Insurance contributions	15.8	26.0
Other[1]	0.6	5.3
Expenditures	9.5	31.3
Programs	2.5	20.4
Unemployment benefits	1.0	13.7
Vocational training and retraining	1.1	6.1
Job creation	0.4	0.6
Operational	6.4	8.9
Wage payments to Employment Fund and Employment Service employees	3.2	4.5
Premises and facilities	3.2	4.4
Other	0.6	2.0
Balance	6.9	—
As percent of GDP	0.1	—
	(As percent of total expenditure)	
Expenditure	100.0	100.0
Program spending	26.3	65.2
Unemployment benefits	10.5	43.8
Vocational training and retraining	11.6	19.5
Job creation	4.2	1.9
Operational expenses	67.4	28.4
Other	6.3	6.4
Memorandum items		
Unemployment benefit (in millions of karbovanets a month)[2]		
End-December	2.3	6.6
Monthly average	1.098	4.488
Replacement rate (in percent)[2]		
End-December	18.4	46.0
Monthly average	15.3	34.9
Registered unemployment		
End-December	126,000	262,174
Monthly average	94,883	199,761
Claiming unemployment benefits		
End-December	74,353	215,010
Monthly average	55,729	163,825
Effective tax rate (in percent)	0.9	0.8
Wage bill (in trillions of karbovanets)	1,764	3,185
Covered employment (in millions of persons)	22	22

Source: Ukrainian authorities; and IMF staff estimates.
[1]For 1996, "other" revenue has been adjusted to bring the account into balance for the year.
[2]Excludes severance pay.

severance pay and a 10-day application period, the registered unemployed are eligible for 3 months' unemployment benefits at a rate equal to 75 percent of their last wage, and 50 percent of their last wage thereafter. Unemployment benefits are normally limited to 12 months: 6 months in the first year of registered unemployment, another 3 months in the second year, and a final 3 months in the third year.[12] Enterprises pressure workers to quit instead of firing them, so that the enterprises do not have to make severance payments. Because unemployment benefits for job quitters are less generous than for workers who are fired (50 percent rather than 75 percent of the last wage), workers who are pressured to quit lose both severance pay and part of the unemployment benefits to which they would be entitled if they had been fired. Unemployment benefits are not indexed, so they erode rapidly in a period of high inflation. As a result of these factors, the ratio of the average unemployment benefit to the average wage at end-1995 was only 18.4 percent. Furthermore, unemployed workers who are sent for training receive a training stipend that may be less than the unemployment benefit would have been.

Credit programs currently being run by the Employment Fund constitute an inappropriate use of mandatory payroll contributions. A declining share of the Employment Fund's resources are devoted to the "creation of new jobs and work places" through low-interest loans to enterprises and zero-interest loans to the unemployed for business start-ups. In 1994, these programs absorbed 24 percent of total spending, with most of the funds used for subsidized credit to state enterprises.[13] In 1996, only 2 percent of total spending by the Employment Fund was budgeted for this purpose.

The fraction of employment spending devoted to loans for business start-ups for unemployed workers is rather small (0.6 percent of planned spending), but in 1996 this program was to be extended. At present, start-up loans for small businesses are interest-free, inviting misallocation and corruption.

The Employment Fund is permitted by statute to support public works programs, and for 1996 about 10 percent of total Employment Fund spending was budgeted for this purpose. Unemployed workers

---

[12]However, unemployed workers within 2 years of pension age are eligible for a total of 18 months of benefits.

[13]Between 1992 and 1994, 650 loans were granted to enterprises that, according to the Employment Fund, created 35,500 job opportunities, mostly at state enterprises and collectives. In late 1994, the Central Bank of Ukraine ruled that the Employment Service could not make such loans because it was not a registered bank. Since then, new subsidized loans to enterprises have been stopped, and only agreements reached before the end of 1994 are being fulfilled.

who accept public works assignments are eligible for unemployment benefits as well as a wage, and the two combined can exceed the wage of a normally employed worker. This creates an incentive not to leave public works employment. The present structure creates perverse incentives, whereby public works programs compete with other sources of labor demand.

The following short-term reform options are recommended:

(1) Adopt the revenue proposals discussed above for the Pension Fund to discourage erosion of the tax base.

(2) Shift the burden of severance payments from enterprises to the Employment Fund. A proposal has been approved by the Cabinet of Ministers that would make enterprises responsible for severance pay equivalent to only one month's wages. The next two months, payable at the average regional wage, would become the obligation of the Employment Fund. Following the expiration of severance pay, the registered unemployed would be eligible for three months of unemployment benefits at 75 percent of the last wage and seven months at 50 percent of the last wage.

(3) Increase the replacement ratio. The ratio of average unemployment benefit to average wage should be increased. The 1996 budget assumes an increase in this ratio to 46 percent by the end of 1996. This would likely require significant changes in the benefit formula.

(4) Develop a contingency plan for unemployment benefits. With the obligation of two months' severance pay shifted to the Employment Fund instead of the enterprises, it becomes especially important to have a contingency plan in case the number of beneficiaries is greater than expected. One possibility would be for the Cabinet of Ministers to approve a decree that would automatically increase the employment tax rate by 0.25 percentage points if the number of beneficiaries increases beyond 130,000 before the end of 1996. This would avoid the problem of overbudgeting yet at the same time provide for an almost immediate increase in revenues if necessary. In any case, the employment tax rate should be reconsidered at the end of 1996 as part of the 1997 budget exercise.

(5) Reform "job-creation" credit programs. Low-interest loans to enterprises for job creation should not be resumed. In principle, some directed credit to the unemployed for business start-ups is acceptable. However, these should be kept modest, and the interest rate should be higher than the rate of inflation and reflect the credit risk. The credit should flow through commercial banks—if possible, private ones— that bear the risk.

(6) Strengthen public works programs. Public works programs may have a temporary, short-term effect on unemployment, and they may

be a reasonable "last resort" for the long-term structurally unemployed and for women who are likely to experience great difficulty in finding placement. The wage paid for public works should be harmonized with the unemployment benefit so that people in public works jobs are better off than if they did not work at all, but not as well off as they would be in normal jobs. This gives them an incentive to leave public works employment as soon as they can.

Chernobyl-Related Benefits

The Chernobyl Fund has an important role in Ukraine's social protection system, helping to absorb the human and environmental costs of the Chernobyl accident of April 1986. The Chernobyl Fund provides benefits to the victims of the accident, including resettlement outside the contamination zone, specialized medical treatment and rehabilitation, and supplements to the wages of workers in the zone (see Table 14.7 and Appendix Table 14.11). In 1995, the Chernobyl Fund ran a very small surplus, equivalent to 0.15 percent of GDP; it was projected to be in balance in 1996.

The financing of the Chernobyl Fund imposes a substantial additional tax burden on wage incomes in the formal sector, but several groups and sectors are exempt from this tax. Since few contributors benefit from these expenditures, this raises equity concerns, in addition to intensifying the disincentive to wage employment inherent in any wage tax.

A substantial share of overall expenditures is devoted to capital investment—housing, urban infrastructure, schools, and hospitals. However, while capital expenditures have generally exceeded the budgeted amounts, the actual implementation of projects has often fallen well short of the stated objectives, particularly in the social sphere. This situation raises questions as to the efficiency and scope of the investment program. Also, many projects, especially in areas not directly affected by the catastrophe, would typically be financed by the budget—it is not clear whether the Chernobyl Fund should be involved at all in these areas.

There is anecdotal evidence that the criteria for benefit eligibility may be unevenly applied, and that not all those actually affected by the accident have been registered. There may also be some laxity in the application of certification standards, as evidenced by the fact that the number of registered victims in most categories continues to rise. These problems may reflect difficulties with the regular and timely provision to the Ministries of Health, Social Protection, and Finance of

Table 14.7. Chernobyl Fund

	1995 Preliminary	1996 Projection
	(In billions of karbovanets)	
Revenues	103,434	170,125
Contributions	103,434	170,125
Expenditures[1]	94,907	170,125
Capital[2]	20,967	31,730
Voluntary resettlement from contaminated zone	3,751	8,000
Jobs in contaminated zone	6,644	13,269
Administration of the cleanup program	6,199	9,524
Social protection of the affected population	57,346	107,602
Of which		
Compensations and benefits	34,922	
Reimbursement of expenses to other agencies and levels of government[3]	34,535	...
Transfers to administration of contaminated zone[4]	11	...
Social protection	13,685	...
Transfers to Social Insurance Fund, for short-term disability payments	15	...
Administration of contaminated zone (rehabilitation)	74	...
Children's rehabilitation	6,915	...
Adults' rehabilitation	5,707	...
Social protection fund for the disabled	695	...
Pension supplements	8,740	...
Balance	8,527	0.0
As percent of GDP	0.15	...
	(As percent of total expenditure)	
Capital investment	22.1	18.7
Administration of the cleanup program	4.0	5.6
Social protection	60.4	63.2
Of which		
Compensation and benefits	36.8	...
Pension supplements	15.2	...

Source: Ukrainian authorities.

[1]Cash expenditures throughout current year, including outlays committed in previous years and executed in current year.

[2]Includes construction of housing facilities, medical facilities, and purchase of diagnostic equipment on behalf of the Ministry of Health for the treatment of Chernobyl victims.

[3]Reimbursement and compensations through financial bodies.

[4]Reflecting the "second wage."

comprehensive data on the number of registered victims or on the support actually provided.

It is also not clear that the Chernobyl Fund's administrative structure is suited to manage appropriately the considerable resources at the Chernobyl Fund's disposal or to deliver the services effectively, although there is no indication of excessive administrative overhead. There is evidence that some benefits are not delivered in an effective and timely manner to all eligible victims.[14]

Short-Term Reform Options

Short-term reforms should aim at rationalizing the financing of the Chernobyl Fund, and enhance the efficiency of its investment program and benefit delivery. On the revenue side, the base of the wage tax should be made consistent with that of the other social funds by removing the exemptions specific to the Chernobyl Fund. This would eliminate the relative distortions in the cost of wage labor between the exempt and the nonexempt groups and sectors; it would also widen the revenue base and could facilitate a reduction in the wage tax earmarked for the Chernobyl Fund.

The following options should be considered:

- Review the priorities and scope of the investment program. This should be done in close coordination with the activities of other ministries. However, the Chernobyl Fund's investment program should be designed with the sole objective of meeting the victims' needs and not be allowed to substitute for general budget resources in the execution of capital expenditure.
- Strengthen the targeting of benefits. This could be achieved through a review of the eligibility criteria, their uniform application across regions, and occasional random audits of recipients to identify possible cases of fraud.
- Ensure consistency and equity between Chernobyl-related benefits and other social protection benefits.

Medium-Term Issues

Ten years after the accident, a comprehensive review of the structure of Chernobyl benefits seems called for. This review would allow the elimination of the overlap or duplication of benefits, or unnecessary payments. For example, health benefits could be reviewed in the context of medical and pharmaceutical aid already being provided free of charge to Chernobyl victims. Similarly, wage premiums for hazardous

---

[14]For example, although the total number of registered victims has risen since 1993, the number of beneficiaries of the various support programs in rural areas has declined in most categories, and only 7 percent of eligible persons actually received priority housing from the state housing fund in 1995, down from 12 percent in 1993.

occupations currently paid by the Chernobyl Fund could be based on labor market conditions in the contaminated zone and paid by the employers.

It would also be appropriate to consider the introduction of a more broadly based tax to generate the Chernobyl Fund's revenues in order to reduce the present disincentive to employ labor. Possibilities could include a broad-based taxation of consumption, to be phased out after a few years.

Finally, it is also necessary to reflect on the time frame for the expiration of the Chernobyl Fund's mandate. Over time, and as the Chernobyl Fund fulfills its social objectives, the benefits to Chernobyl victims will be primarily health-related. It may then be appropriate to provide these benefits through the established health system, financed by general budget resources. This would allow the Chernobyl Fund to end its activity, thus reducing the tax burden on the economy.

Conclusions

Ukraine's social protection system has a critical role to play during the country's transition to a market economy. While creating conditions for sustaining the economic transformation, it should not exacerbate macroeconomic imbalances. This chapter's discussion of the present system's structure illustrated that it is too diffuse, with many overlapping benefits, privileges for certain groups, incomplete coverage, and inappropriate targeting mechanisms for shielding the vulnerable. The system in its present form is thus cost-ineffective and inadequately targeted.

Various reform options—identified in this chapter—are available to the Ukrainian authorities in the short term for enhancing the cost-effectiveness of the social protection system, as well as for strengthening its coverage and adequacy. This alone, however, is unlikely to be sufficient. Measures would also have to be implemented to ensure that the revenue base for financing the social protection system is not eroded. At the same time, it must be recognized that the relatively high statutory rates of payroll taxes in Ukraine have raised the cost of labor and are acting as a disincentive to formal employment. In this context, the implementation of certain policy options, also listed in the chapter would facilitate a modest lowering of payroll taxes in the short term. Altogether, the suggested measures could yield up to 3.5 percent of GDP in expenditure savings and additional revenue.

Over the medium term, the design of the social protection system should be recast to make it better suited to the needs of a market-oriented economy. In this regard, it would be important to reduce the excessive role of enterprises, as well as redefine the function of different agencies in the delivery of social benefits. It is equally important to find alternative sources for financing some benefits, such as those related to Chernobyl, which would also allow some reduction of payroll taxes.

Appendix

The following appendix tables provide detailed information on the system of pensions, child allowances, and compensation of the accident at Chernobyl in 1986.

Table 14.8. Number and Amount of Pensions by Size[1]

Minimum Pensions Paid	As of December 31, 1994				As of September 30, 1995			
	Number of pensioners	Share of total	Average size (In thousands of karbovanets)	Total amount (In billions of karbovanets)	Number of pensioners	Share of total	Average size (In thousands of karbovanets)	Total amount (In billions of karbovanets)
Total	14,016,823	100.0	784	10,898	13,995,994	100.0	1,181	16,523
<1	420,257	3.0	174	73	413,430	3.0	433	179
1	515,520	3.7	288	148	491,255	3.5	575	283
1–2	2,751,592	19.6	448	1,233	2,673,501	19.1	768	2,053
2–3	5,809,482	41.4	780	4,530	5,862,510	41.9	1,163	6,817
3–4	3,557,801	25.4	997	3,546	3,688,901	26.4	1,445	5,330
4–5	633,972	4.5	1,245	789	500,456	3.6	1,642	822
5–10	285,305	2.0	1,824	520	305,681	2.2	2,351	719
10–15	37,851	0.3	3,215	122	40,223	0.3	3,852	155
15–20	3,594	0.0	4,685	17	7,637	0.1	5,751	44
>20	1,449	0.0	6,533	9	12,400	0.1	9,871	122
>4	962,171	6.9	1,515	1,458	866,397	6.2	2,149	1,861

Source: Ukrainian authorities.
[1]The pension amounts exclude compensations.

Table 14.9. Size of Pensions with Additional Payments
(In thousands of karbovanets)

	Starting Date								Adjustment Factor						
	1993	1994		1995				1996	1994		1995				1996
	Dec. 1	Oct. 1	Dec. 1	Jan. 1	Feb. 1	Jun. 1	Oct. 1	Jan. 1	Oct. 1	Dec. 1	Jan. 1	Feb. 1	Jun. 1	Oct. 1	Jan. 1
Average monthly pension	371	824	989	1,157	2,047	2,487	3,065	3,839	2.22	1.20	1.17	1.77	1.21	1.23	1.25
Basic pension	327	654	785	918	918	918	1,152	2,216	2.00	1.20	1.17	1.00	1.00	1.25	1.92
Additional payments	44	170	204	239	239	239	290	—	…	…	…	…	…	…	…
Compensation payments	—	—	—	—	890	1,330	1,623	1,623	…	…	…	…	…	…	…
Minimum monthly pension	241	780	940	1,100	1,466	2,100	2,599	3,300	3.24	1.21	1.17	1.33	1.43	1.24	1.27
Basic pension	120	240	288	337	337	337	411	790	…	…	…	…	…	…	…
Additional payments	44	170	204	239	239	239	290	—	…	…	…	…	…	…	…
Compensation payments	—	—	—	—	890	1,330	1,623	1,623	…	…	…	…	…	…	…
Special purpose payment	77	370	448	525	—	195	275	887	…	…	…	…	…	…	…
Maximum monthly pension	404	890	1,068	1,250	2,140	2,580	3,146	3,993	2.20	1.20	1.17	1.71	1.21	1.22	1.27
Basic pension	360	720	864	1,011	1,011	1,011	1,233	2,370	…	…	…	…	…	…	…
Additional payments	44	170	204	239	239	239	290	—	…	…	…	…	…	…	…
Compensation payments	—	—	—	—	890	1,330	1,623	1,623	…	…	…	…	…	…	…
Maximum size of pension (four minimum pensions)	524	1,130	1,356	1,587	2,477	2,917	3,557	4,783	2.16	1.20	1.17	1.56	1.18	1.22	1.34
Social pension	181	660	796	932	1,100	1,267	1,584	2,092	3.65	1.21	1.17	1.18	1.15	1.25	1.32
Basic pension	60	120	144	169	169	169	206	395	…	…	…	…	…	…	…
Additional payments	44	170	204	239	239	239	290	—	…	…	…	…	…	…	…
Compensation payments	—	—	—	—	445	665	812	812	…	…	…	…	…	…	…
Special purpose payment	77	370	448	525	—	195	275	887	…	…	…	…	…	…	…

Source: Ukrainian authorities.

Table 14.10. System of Child Allowances, 1996

Allowance	Number of Allowances (In thousands)	Amount of Allowance (In thousands of karbovanets)	Annual Amount (In billions of karbovanets)	Paid at the Expense of:	Type of Payment	Means
Childbirth and maternity						
Lump-sum childbirth allowance	520.0	3,230	20,155	Social Insurance Fund[1]	At place of employment; or at residence	No
Additional lump-sum childbirth allowance[2]	500.0	1,620	9,720	Social Insurance Fund	At place of employment; or at residence	No
Maternity leave	...	1,500	...	Social Insurance Fund	At place of employment; or at residence	No
Child allowances						
Children up to age 3 of working parents	1,332.8	1,500	23,990	Local budget[3]	At place of employment or study	No
Children up to age 3 of nonworking parents	133.6	470	754	Local budget	At residence	No
Children from age 3–16 (age 18 for students)	3,439.5	600	24,764	Local budget	At place of employment or study; or residence	Yes
Invalid children[4]	19.2	1,330	306	Local budget	At place of employment or study; or residence	No
Temporary assistance to underage children for child support[5]	19.8	470	112	Local budget	At place of employment or study; or residence	No
Child care allowances				Local budget	At residence	No
Single mothers—special category[6]	2.6	950	30	Local budget	At residence	No

Single mothers—others	399.0	470	2,250	Local budget	At place of employment or study	No
Working families with three children	156.0	810	1,516	Local budget	At residence	Yes
Nonworking families with three children	12.0	950	137	Local budget	At place of employment or study	Yes
Working families with four or more children	45.0	1,620	875	Local budget	At residence	Yes
Nonworking families with four or more children	6.0	1,890	136	Local budget	At residence	Yes
Persons providing foster care	8.8	1,890	200	Local budget	At residence	No
Children of military personnel	1.1	810	11	Local budget	At residence	No
Custodial parent who does not receive child support[7]	4.4	240	13	Local budget	At residence	No
Total	6,600	...	84,969			

Source: Ukrainian authorities.

[1]If employed and paying the payroll tax at the time of pregnancy; otherwise, paid for by the local budget.

[2]Paid to women with natal complications whose maternity leave extends beyond 12 weeks.

[3]The allowance for children up to 1.5 years of age is paid out of the resources of the Pension Fund and is deducted from the pension contribution payments of the enterprise where the mother works.

[4]Payable to eligible individuals providing full-time care for invalid children.

[5]Support to children whose parents do not pay the required alimony.

[6]Including mothers who grew up as orphans, without parental care, or as wards of the state.

[7]Allowance to parent who receives none or only part of court-awarded alimony.

Table 14.11. Population Affected by the Chernobyl Accident, January 1, 1996

(In thousands)

	Total Number Affected[1]	Of Which:			
		Working		Pensioners	
		Total	Pensioners	Total	Nonworking
Category I	45.0	21.1	21.1	45.0	23.9
Category II	350.9	277.9	41.9	114.9	73.0
Of which					
Participants in cleanup operations	257.4	216.1	32.4	73.7	41.3
Affected by the accident	93.5	61.8	9.5	41.2	31.7
Category III	561.5	435.4	54.7	180.8	126.1
Of which					
Participants in cleanup operations	71.9	64.9	12.2	19.2	7.0
Affected by the accident	489.6	370.5	42.5	161.6	119.1
Category IV	1,242.3	874.3	131.1	499.1	368.0
Workers in the zone of obligatory resettlement in 1996	1.6	1.4	—	0.2	0.2
Child victims of accident	945.2	6.7	—	—	—
Total	3,146.5	1,616.8	248.8	840.0	591.2

Source: Ukrainian authorities.
[1]Sum of total working persons and nonworking pensioners (columns 2 and 5).

Additional Papers on Social Safety Nets Prepared by IMF Staff

Ahmad, Ehtisham, 1993, "Poverty, Demographic Characteristics, and Public Policy in CIS Countries," IMF Working Paper 93/9 (Washington: International Monetary Fund).

———, 1992, "Social Safety Nets," in *Fiscal Policies in Economies in Transition,* ed. by Vito Tanzi (Washington: International Monetary Fund).

———, and Nigel Chalk, 1993, "On Improving Public Expenditure Policies for the Poor—Major Informational Requirements," IMF Working Paper 93/43 (Washington: International Monetary Fund).

Ahmad, Ehtisham, and Ke-young Chu, 1993, "Russian Federation—Economic Reform and Policy Options for Social Protection," in *Transition to Market: Studies in Fiscal Reform,* ed. by Vito Tanzi (Washington: International Monetary Fund).

Ahmad, Ehtisham, and Richard Hemming, 1991, "Poverty and Social Security," in *Public Expenditure Handbook,* ed. by Ke-young Chu and Richard Hemming (Washington: International Monetary Fund).

Ahmad, Ehtisham, Sergio Lugaresi, Alex Mourmouras, and Jean-Luc Schneider, 1994, "Pensions, Price Shocks, and Macroeconomic Stability in Transition Economies: Illustrations from Belarus," IMF Working Paper 94/52 (Washington: International Monetary Fund).

"Camdessus Urges Steps to Help Alleviate Impact of Adjustment Measures on Poorest Groups," 1988, *IMF Survey,* August 15, pp. 258–60.

Chand, Sheetal K., and Parthasarathi Shome, 1995, "Poverty Alleviation in a Financial Programming Framework: An Integrated Approach," IMF Working Paper 95/29 (Washington: International Monetary Fund).

Chu, Ke-young, and Sanjeev Gupta, 1993, "Protecting the Poor: Social Safety Nets During Transition," *Finance & Development,* Vol. 30 (June), pp. 24–27.

Cornelius, Peter K., 1994, "Defining, Measuring, and Alleviating Poverty in an Economy in Transition: The Case of Lithuania," IMF Working Paper 94/116 (Washington: International Monetary Fund).

———, and Beatrice S. Weder, 1996, "Economic Transformation and Income Distribution: Some Evidence from the Baltic Countries," IMF Working Paper 96/14 (Washington: International Monetary Fund).

Expenditure Policy Division Staff, 1995, "Social Safety Nets for Economic Transition: Options and Recent Experience," IMF Paper on Policy Analysis and Assessment 95/3 (Washington: International Monetary Fund).

Heller, Peter S., and others, 1988, *The Implications of Fund-Supported Adjustment Programs for Poverty: Experiences in Selected Countries,* IMF Occasional Paper No. 58 (Washington: International Monetary Fund).

International Monetary Fund, 1990, "The Fund and Poverty Issues: A Progress Report," *Development Committee Report,* No. 26 (September 24, 1990) (Washington: World Bank).

Johnson, Omotunde, and Joanne Salop, 1980, "Stabilization Programs and Income Distribution," *Finance & Development,* Vol. 17 (December), pp. 28–31.

Kanbur, Ravi, 1987, "Measurement and Alleviation of Poverty: With an Application to the Effects of Macroeconomic Adjustment," *Staff Papers,* International Monetary Fund, Vol. 34 (March), pp. 60–85.

Koliadina, Natasha, 1996, "The Social Safety Net in Albania," IMF Working Paper 96/96 (Washington: International Monetary Fund).

Maret, Xavier, and Gerd Schwartz, 1993, "Poland: The Social Safety Net During the Transition," IMF Working Paper 93/42 (Washington: International Monetary Fund).

Namor, Eugenio, 1987, "Issues in the Targeting of Food Subsidies for the Poor: A Survey of the Literature," IMF Working Paper 87/75 (Washington: International Monetary Fund).

Nashashibi, Karim, and Sanjeev Gupta, 1990, "Poverty Concerns in Fund-Supported Programs," *Finance & Development,* Vol. 27 (September), pp. 12–14.

Paull, Gillian, 1991, "Poverty Alleviation and Social Safety Net Schemes for Economies in Transition," IMF Working Paper 91/14 (Washington: International Monetary Fund).

Sala-i-Martin, Xavier, 1996, "Transfers, Social Safety Nets, and Economic Growth," IMF Working Paper 96/40 (Washington: International Monetary Fund).

Van Rijckeghem, Caroline, 1994, "Albania: Income Distribution, Poverty, and Social Safety Nets in the Transition, 1991–93," IMF Working Paper 94/123 (Washington: International Monetary Fund).

World Bank and International Monetary Fund, 1989, "Strengthening Efforts to Reduce Poverty," *Development Committee Report,* No. 19 (Washington: World Bank).

———, 1990, "Strategies for the Effective Reduction of Poverty in the 1990s," *Development Committee Report,* No. 26 (September 24, 1990) (Washington: World Bank).

———, 1993, "Social Security Reforms and Social Safety Nets," *Development Committee Report,* No. 32 (Washington: World Bank).